FEDERALISM AND THE FRENCH CANADIANS

Pierre Elliott Trudeau

Federalism and the French Canadians

with an introduction by
John T. Saywell

Laurentian Library 48

Macmillan of Canada • *Toronto*

Originally published in French with the title *Le Fédéralisme et la société canadienne-française* by Editions HMH, Ltée, Montreal; © Editions HMH, Ltée 1967.

ISBN 0-7705-1560-6

First printing February 1968
Reprinted March 1968
           April 1968
           May 1968
           July 1968
           October 1968
           February 1970
           May 1972
First Laurentian Library edition 1977

Printed in Canada for The Macmillan Company of Canada Limited, 70 Bond Street, Toronto, Ontario M5B 1X3

Contents

Introduction

by John T. Saywell

To many people, Pierre Elliott Trudeau has seemed enigmatic and paradoxical: a man of substantial wealth, yet a democratic socialist; an advocate of extensive state power who denies that anyone knows better than he what is good for him; a French Canadian proud of his identity and culture, yet a biting critic of French-Canadian society, determined to destroy its mythology and illusions; a Jesuit-educated Catholic, but an outspoken anti-clerical; a staunch upholder of provincial autonomy holding the Justice portfolio in the federal government; and a bachelor presently catapulting Canadian legislation on such matters as abortion and divorce into the second half of the twentieth century.

Trudeau describes himself as a man who has always rowed against the current, whose thought had only one consistent principle – that of opposing prevailing ideas – and whose position could be summarized in two words – to counterbalance. But consistency is, in fact, the most remarkable quality of Mr. Trudeau's thoughts and actions over the past two decades. And his work belongs in that rare catalogue of Canadiana entitled 'political thought' less because of its enlightened comment on contemporary affairs than because it is based on philosophic premises about the nature of man, society, and the state, and the realization that statecraft is a constant search for that balance of liberty, progress, and order which best serves the needs of the individual and society at any given time. Without the philosophic base, this balance could have, under the pressure of events, degenerated into the same kind of pragmatic relativism that our political leaders of the past century have offered as an alternative to political thought.

In short, as the reader of these essays will discover, Mr. Trudeau's views on Canadian federalism or French-Canadian society have not basically changed. But the prevailing currents of thought have changed – in part because of Pierre Trudeau. And, while others have been left bewildered in the whirlpool or motionless in the backwater, he has rowed consistently toward his conception of constitutionalism in the federal system and a fundamentally reformed political, social, and economic order in Quebec.

Born in Montreal in 1921 and brought up in a bilingual and bicultural home, Trudeau was educated at the Collège Jean-de-Brébeuf and the University of Montreal. After being called to the Bar in 1943, he pursued post-graduate studies in economics, political science, and law at Harvard, Paris, and the London School of Economics. When he returned to Canada in 1949, he saw the country through the eyes of a skilled social scientist.

Quebec was firmly under the control of Maurice Duplessis, who had used the reform movement to bring the Union Nationale to power in 1936 and then had ruthlessly betrayed it. Defeated in 1939, he returned in 1944 determined to pursue that policy described by Pierre Vadeboncoeur as 'to resist assimilation from without, to resist emancipation from within'. To achieve the first, provincial autonomy and cultural survival were equated. A firm alliance between the government and the conservative elements in society – rural Quebec, the Church, big business, and right-wing nationalists – was successful in achieving the second. Politically, corruption was built into a system and freedom of speech and action was, as many discovered, reserved for the foolhardy, the courageous, or (to use a later phrase) for those who had nothing to lose.

Trudeau and other Davids formed a small band to bring down Goliath. Using the new weapons of social science research, they tried to bare the realities of a changed and rapidly changing Quebec and to expose the façade behind which Duplessis ran his tyrannical and reactionary régime. Some laboured in the universities, particularly at Laval, and published seemingly innocuous (but in the long run extremely valuable) articles in learned journals. Trudeau and five others founded the magazine *Cité Libre*. The first issue was a call to arms: 'déclencher la crise de conscience politique; faire table rase de toutes nos superstitions; renier nos lamentables logomachies'. Because the English press studiously reflected the corporate (if not the individual) views of its readers and the French press was apparently unable to see that 'emancipation' and 'assimilation' could be separated, and with the universities sullenly respectful of the unscrupulous power of *le chef*, *Cité Libre* stood almost alone. For years, as André Laurendeau ruefully confessed, *Cité Libre* said out loud what others dared only to whisper.

What *Cité Libre* said out loud, long before the much-publicized pamphlet of the abbés Dion and O'Neill and Laurendeau's famous editorial on *le roi nègre*, was that political life in Quebec was hopelessly corrupt. The July 1952 election, for example, sparked articles in *Cité Libre* by Trudeau and his colleagues – Gérard Pelletier, Marcel Rioux, Pierre Laporte, and Charles Lussier. In his 'Réflexions sur la politique au Canada français', Trudeau wrote: 'In our relations with the state we are fairly immoral: we corrupt civil servants, we use blackmail on M.P.s, we put pressure on the courts, we defraud the treasury, we obligingly look the other way when "it concerns our interests". And in electoral matters, our immorality becomes really scabrous.'

In 'Some Obstacles to Democracy in Quebec', he concluded that 'French Canadians fundamentally do not believe in democracy. . . . For such is the legacy of a history during which – as a minority – they hammered the process of parliamentary government into a defensive weapon of racial warfare, and – as Catholics – they believed that authority might well be left to descend from God in God's good time and in God's good way.' Nor could he see in 1952 that business, the Church, rural Quebec, or the middle class had any interest in democratizing Quebec and changing the *status quo*; whatever hope there was lay with the working class.

Four years later, Editions Cité Libre published *La Grève de l'amiante*, an account of the strike which, as Trudeau wrote, 'annonçait violemment l'avènement de temps nouveaux'. In his masterful background chapter Trudeau revealed how social and economic thought in Quebec had failed disastrously to keep pace with the realities of a society that had become urbanized and industrialized, and criticized those responsible – politicians and educators, nationalists and ecclesiastics. Time was short, he suggested in the epilogue: 'If, in the last analysis, we continually identify Catholicism with conservatism and patriotism with immobility, we will lose by default that which is at play between all cultures; and the notion of French Canadian, with that of Catholicism which is grafted to it, will finish by becoming something very small indeed. An entire generation is hesitating at the brink of commitment.'

During 1956 when Duplessis won his fourth consecutive election, Trudeau was instrumental in organizing the *Rassemblement*, which called for a new and broadened Left in Quebec. But when political squabbling destroyed the effectiveness of *Rassemblement*, he published 'Un Manifeste démocratique' in 1958. What was of critical importance, he argued, was less the direction of reform than the democratic revolution. ' "Democracy first!" should be the rallying cry of all reforming forces in the province. Some may be active in the chambers of commerce and others in the trade unions; some may still believe in the glories of free enterprise while others spread socialist doctrines. There is no harm in that – as long as they all agree to work out democracy first of all. After that it will be up to the sovereign people to opt freely for the choices they prefer.' The social revolution, he firmly believed, would follow.

This commitment to democracy before ideology led Trudeau to appeal to the readers of *Cité Libre* to support the Liberals in the provincial election of 1960, the party that attempted to provide a common front against the Union Nationale. With the Liberal victory, the democratic and social revolution seemed underway, and Trudeau urged his readers to give the Liberals their support while reminding the government of its superhuman commitment to reform.

But it was not only a movement for political and social reform that had been generated during the ferment of the 1950s. New currents of nationalism had also been released. The Liberal platform itself was strongly and positively nationalistic. Also, in 1960 *L'Action Socialiste* and the *Rassemblement pour l'indépendance nationale* joined the three-year-old *L'Alliance Laurentienne* as advocates of separatism, and in the spring of 1961 surveys in *La Presse*, *Le Devoir*, and *Le Magazine Maclean* suggested that separatist support in Quebec had reached alarming proportions. 1962 was the year of the *Maître chez nous* election. And 1963 witnessed a reign of terror in Montreal, Daniel Johnson's call for 'the alliance of two communities with equal rights to self-determination', Premier Lesage's declaration that Canada was 'in the hour of the last chance', and René Levesque's warning that 'there must be a new Canada within five years or Quebec will quit Confederation'.

Amid the tempest in Quebec, where few dared challenge the new nationalism or oppose separatism outright, one man rowed boldly against the current. In 'L'aliénation nationaliste' (*Cité Libre*, March 1961) he dismissed the nationalists as reactionary, and nationalism as irrelevant to the major concerns of Quebec: 'Ouvrons les frontières,' he urged, 'ce peuple meurt d'asphyxie!' A year later he published the long and carefully reasoned 'New Treason of the Intellectuals'. And that in turn was followed by 'The Separatist Counter-Revolutionaries', a masterpiece of political writing, impassioned yet restrained, an unforgettable orchestration of wit, scorn, indignation, and contempt. In 1965 he prepared the essay on 'Quebec and the Constitutional Problem' as a working paper for a brief to the Quebec Legislative Committee on the Constitution, in which he explained his objections to independence, associate statehood, 'particular status', and other variants of nationalistic panaceas.

Trudeau is no less concerned about the preservation and enrichment of French culture and values than the most determined Separatist, nor any less critical of English-Canadian opposition to the development of a genuine bilingualism and biculturalism in Canada. But in principle he is adamantly opposed to the organization of any political society – Quebec, Canada, or whatever – on an ethnic or 'national' base. Moreover, he is convinced not only that the divided jurisdiction of a federal state helps to protect the liberty of its citizens, but also that in fact the economic, social, and cultural goals of Quebec can best be achieved (and French-Canadian culture can best flourish) within a Canadian federal state. Since his views are so fully set out in this book, further comment is unnecessary. The English-Canadian reader must realize, however, that Trudeau's federal state is one where each level of government operates within its own jurisdiction, where the power to tax and spend is not used to justify legislative encroachment or initiative in other jurisdictions, where equalization and stabilization are accepted as equitable and necessary constituents of a highly regionalized federal state, and where federal-provincial consultation is maximized, even on matters exclusively within federal jurisdiction.

The same consistency that has marked his views of French-Canadian society is evident in his views of Canadian federalism. In the 1950s he was a staunch supporter of Duplessis's policy of provincial autonomy and a severe critic of the post-war centralization in Ottawa, even to the point of taking the unpopular stand of opposing federal aid to universities. In 1965, when the extension of provincial autonomy threatened to destroy legitimate federal power, he entered federal politics as a defender of constitutionalism and Canadian federalism.

This change in the form of Pierre Elliott Trudeau's engagement – from words to action – has already had its effects, and a careful reading of the essays on federalism is much more than an academic exercise. The substance of his position was accepted by the federal Quebec Liberal Federation in March 1966, much to the displeasure of those, like Claude Ryan of *Le Devoir*, for example, who insisted that Quebec was not a province like the others and that the others could never be a province like it. It was also a view very similar to Trudeau's that the federal government adopted as the basis of its new tax-sharing agreement with the provinces, negotiated – or rather imposed – in the fall of 1966. Both as assistant to the Prime Minister and later as Minister of Justice, Mr. Trudeau has been in a position to play a key role in the evolution of federal constitutional policy, and the constitutional conference in February 1968 may well reveal that his role has been decisive. Whether the Marchand-Trudeau-Sauvé-Pepin alliance can establish a viable federal presence in Quebec and whether their constitutionalism will be accepted in Quebec as a realistic alternative to some form of 'particular status', is in the process of being determined. The future of this country might hang on the result.

There are also many glimpses here of a Minister of Justice passionately dedicated to civil liberties and human rights and privacy, and anxious to see a Bill of Rights firmly embedded in the constitution beyond the reach of the state; of a man determined not only to see the law reflect the social realities of 1968 but also, as he told Peter Newman, 'to move the framework of society slightly ahead of the times, so there is no curtailment of intellectual or physical liberty'. Trudeau's state is one that exists for the individual; one that must find that precarious balance between order and liberty; one that, as he says, 'must take great care not to infringe upon the conscience of the individual. I believe that, in the last analysis, a human being in the privacy of his own mind has the exclusive authority to choose his own scale of values and to decide which forces will take precedence over others.' Those were the words of Trudeau, the engaged intellectual; Trudeau, the engaged politician, put it even more forthrightly: 'The state has no business in the bedrooms of the nation.'

Trudeau is an experiment in Canadian public life, a refreshing combination of intellectual capacity and common sense, forthrightness and diplomacy, and a man who combines a quiet independence of mind with a strong socially oriented sense of purpose. The experiment will measure the depth and breadth of our public life, and test its quality and maturity. The result will bear watching.

Preface to the French Edition

by Gérard Pelletier

'POLITICAL THEORY' must surely be one of the most abused expressions in contemporary speech. But, strangely enough, we should be glad that it is.

For only terms in current use can be abused. The meaning of 'empyreuma' is in no danger of being altered: the word is quite safely embalmed in the dictionary. But such words as 'ideal' and 'sincerity', which are trotted out a thousand times a second, eventually come to mean anything at all – which is to say, very little.

The same is true of 'political theory'.

Ever since the decline of traditional parliamentary eloquence, since the demise of great oratorical gestures, lengthy tirades, and attempts to sweep the electorate off its feet, there has been a meteoric rise in the value of political theory. Acquisition of some theory or other has become an essential part of one's equipment. No one involved in public affairs, from Members of Parliament down to journalists and even to academics, can afford to be without one. Are not more and more politicians publishing books? Even professors are no longer content to formulate abstract ideas: now they grapple with solutions to immediate problems, invading the politician's field to compete with him on his own ground.

Of course, not everyone will define political theory in the same way, nor take the same means of creating his own.

Many find an easy solution by accepting one or another of

the popular ideologies. It is not very difficult to declare oneself a capitalist or a socialist, a liberal or a conservative, or even a Marxist-Leninist. In intellectual equivalents of Woolworth's can be found complete sets of these great systems, simplified for daily use and boxed in attractive, convenient packages. It is even possible to combine pieces from different sets, thereby producing unexpected results, for example Marxist-Leninist nationalism, or progressive conservatism, or even rather reactionary forms of Marxism.

It is rare to find persons in whom an entire lifetime of study and meditation has resulted in a genuine theory of politics – that is, a complete and coherent system of responses based on a clear conception of men and society. It is even rarer to find a work in which the author has not been content merely to outline his ideas or to define his aims, but has tried to relate his thought to the human, historical, social, and economic realities of a given group of men in a given society.

I have no hesitation in saying that I consider Pierre Trudeau's work to be the most serious effort to formulate a political theory for Quebec and Canada that has been attempted in the past twenty-five years. Whether or not his conclusions, or even the general direction of his thought, are accepted, no one can deny the intellectual integrity that characterizes these essays, the exceptional erudition on which they are based, or the trenchant wit of his remarkable style.

The essays that follow were written over a number of years and not originally conceived as parts of a single book. This makes it all the more admirable that they complement each other so well, and are moulded by the internal logic of an unwavering line of thought into a solid, coherent whole.

A reader accustomed to the academic style usually associated with treatises on political science may be astonished to find that the author, while never falling into any kind of pamphleteering excess, occasionally writes with considerable passion, giving his reasoned analyses the rhythm and vehemence of polemic literature. But this book does not claim to establish eternal truths merely for themselves, in the abstract. Each of the articles was a contribution to an intellectual struggle that is now part of our collective past, although it is not yet resolved. Seen from this point of view, Pierre Trudeau's book has an amazing serenity of thought, a fundamental resistance to passing fads. Read, for example, his analysis of federal grants to universities. I have never come across a more vigorous plea for provincial autonomy. Yet it was written at a time when very few intellectuals managed to keep sane and moderate views on constitutional matters. The majority preferred being wrong against Mr. Duplessis to being right with him; which is to say that, lacking a coherent philosophy, they let themselves be governed by emotion.

On the other hand, how many of the same people who were centralizing federalists in the 1950s are now riding the separatist wave, as incapable of resisting the present trend as they were of resisting the opposite one just after the war?

I must warn the reader: some passages in this book are painful to read. Not that they are obscure, for the discussion is lively, clear, and never dull. But it does happen that in reading some of his pages we are caught out by our flagrant ignorance. At other times, our most secret prejudices, our weaknesses of thought, however well concealed, are suddenly violently illuminated by his uncompromising analyses. The experience is painful; it is also extremely beneficial.

In conclusion, if I may be allowed to express a wish, I should like to say that I hope the publication of this book will give a new impetus to the discussion of our collective political objectives that has been going on in our province for the past twenty years; and that it will help boost it into a better-defined and higher orbit.

Foreword

The only constant factor to be found in my thinking over the years has been opposition to accepted opinions. Had I applied this principle to the stock market, I might have made a fortune. I chose to apply it to politics, and it led me to power – a result I had not really desired, or even expected.

In high school, when the only politics I was taught was history, I had already made up my mind to swim against the tide. But what was then an ill-defined reflex against intellectual regimentation became a conscious choice as soon as I went to university.

In 1944, and particularly in 1948, society in Quebec fell under the domination of the Union Nationale. I fought this régime until its downfall in 1960. During the entire period, while nearly everyone connected with the Left was urging Ottawa to redress the situation in Quebec, I remained a fierce supporter of provincial autonomy.

By 1962, however, the Lesage government and public opinion in Quebec had magnified provincial autonomy into an absolute, and were attempting to reduce federal power to nothing; and so, to defend federalism, I entered politics in 1965.

I did so as a member of the federal Liberal Party, which I had often condemned while it was at the height of its power. Then the Party had lost its majority and was not to regain it for some time; but in spite of everything it advocated an open federal system, and that was what attracted me to it.

In joining the Liberals, I turned my back on the socialist party for which I had campaigned at a time when Quebec considered socialism to be treason and heresy; but I had no regrets because by then – in 1965 – most of its Quebec followers were in fact exchanging socialism for nationalism. They did this in the hope of finding a foothold in Quebec, but as a result they merely drew closer to the rising *bourgeoisie*. The latter was beginning to use Marxist terminology to justify its preaching of *national* socialism.

The fifteen years that followed the war saw the height of clerical power in Quebec. I was then 'anti-clericalist' and advocated, among other things, the separation of Church and State. This is how I came to advocate the establishment of a Ministry of Education at a time when those who were later to establish it did not even dare mention the word.

My reputation as a radical was, however, based mainly upon the fact that I defended the importance of the provincial state as an instrument for collective action and progress. That was what was considered radical, before 1960! Since then the idea has gone such a long way – unfortunately in the wrong direction – that I have had to start denouncing ethnocentric and *bourgeois* abuses.

The *Quebec* State was becoming the *French-Canadian* State, and was sacrificing true social and economic progress to policies designed merely to promote *bourgeois* prestige. Worse still, people began to believe that the *Quebec* State (which people in our province persist in writing with a small 's') could give French Canadians more than they collectively possessed. So, for example, professional associations put pressure on the State to allow their members to be the highest paid in the country: nothing less could possibly satisfy the honour of Quebec! In this way, doctors, nurses, policemen, university professors, teachers, engineers, technicians, civil servants, and everyone involved in some way with public service, managed to wrest from the Quebec government salaries that were among the highest in the land. As these salaries were paid from tax revenues, and as taxes were levied in a province that was economically *below* average, the result was that the State's role in the new Quebec consisted of transferring to the rising middle classes funds taken from the mass of workers. I could not agree with that.

From 1952 to 1960 I worked for labour unions, both as a

lawyer and as an economist. At that period they represented a movement for social liberation struggling against entrenched power. I began to feel uneasy about them when an excessive number of their leaders started to promote nationalism, thus joining forces with the secure, rising middle classes.

Still, in the years between 1952 and 1960, I was several times forbidden to teach in the universities, supposedly because of my anti-clerical and communist leanings. But I was invited to do so, with almost indecent haste, when power had passed to the other camp. In universities I found a rather sterile atmosphere: the terminology of the Left was now serving to conceal a single preoccupation: the separatist counter-revolution.

I could give further examples of what my friend Vianney Décarie, in a speech sponsoring my admission to the Royal Society, called my 'sign of contradiction'. But what would be the point? It would be more useful to explain where this 'sign' comes from.

I have never been able to accept any discipline except that which I imposed upon myself – and there was a time when I used to impose it often. For, in the art of living, as in that of loving, or of governing – it is all the same – I found it unacceptable that others should claim to know better than I what was good for me. Consequently, I found tyranny completely intolerable.

In Canada, and this includes Quebec, we have never known tyranny except in its figurative forms, for example the tyranny of public opinion. I am, however, far from considering that particular form the least terrible. For public opinion seeks to impose its domination over everything. Its aim is to reduce all action, all thought, and all feeling to a common denominator. It forbids independence and kills inventiveness; condemns those who ignore it and banishes those who oppose it. (Anyone who thinks I am exaggerating may count the number of times I have been called a 'traitor' in recent years by the nationalist pundits of Quebec.)

I early realized that ideological systems are the true enemies of freedom. On the political front, accepted opinions are not only inhibiting to the mind, they contain the very source of error. When a political ideology is universally accepted by the élite, when the people who 'define situations' embrace and venerate it, this means that it is high time free men were fighting it. For political freedom finds its essential strength in a sense of balance and proportion. As soon as any one tendency becomes too strong, it constitutes a menace.

The oldest problem of political philosophy, although it is not the only one, is to justify authority without destroying the independence of human beings in the process. How can an individual be reconciled with a society? The need for privacy with the need to live in groups? Love for freedom with need for order? . . . The most useful conclusion philosophy has come to is that one must keep an equal distance from both alternatives. Too much authority, or too little, and that is the end of freedom. For oppression also arises from lack of order, from the tyranny of the masses: it is then called the Reign of Terror.

In this sense it is possible to say that there are no absolute truths in politics. The best ideologies, having arisen at specific times to combat given abuses, become the worst if they survive the needs which gave them birth. Throughout history all great reformers were sooner or later betrayed by the excessive fidelity of their disciples. When a reform starts to be universally popular, it is more than likely that it has already become reactionary, and free men must then oppose it.

There is thus the danger that mass media – to the extent that they claim to reflect public opinion – constitute a vehicle for error, if not indeed an instrument of oppression. For my part, I have never been able to read newspapers without a sense of uneasiness, especially newspapers of opinion. They follow their customers and are therefore always lagging behind reality.

Since the function of political science is to seek and define the conditions of progress in advanced societies, this discipline naturally favours institutions that guarantee freedom without destroying order. This is the reason for their great interest in parliamentary and federal systems. The former, because they make the various organs of power independent of each other and give a prominent role to the opposition. The latter, because they divide the exercise of sovereignty between the various levels of government, and give none of them full powers over the citizen. Strangely enough, the classic analyses of these two systems are found in French thinkers: Montesquieu observing the British parliamentary system, and de Tocqueville describing American democracy. (In view of the fact that it was the Canadian constitution that united the qualities of these two systems for the first time in history, it is rather paradoxical that

French-Canadian 'thinkers' should have such difficulty in perceiving its merits.)

The theory of checks and balances, so acutely analysed by these two writers, has always had my full support. It translates into practical terms the concept of equilibrium that is inseparable from freedom in the realm of ideas. It incorporates a corrective for abuses and excesses into the very functioning of political institutions.

My political action, or my theory – insomuch as I can be said to have one – can be expressed very simply: create counterweights. As I have explained, it was because of the federal government's weakness that I allowed myself to be catapulted into it.

With these principles, and being a citizen of this country, I would have become a French Canadian by adoption had I not been one by birth. And had French Canadians needed someone to preach collective pride to them, no doubt I would have been first on the soap-box. But good God! that is all we've had, sermons on pride and divine missions! We possessed a wealth of immense syntheses and elaborate superstructures; we went overboard on constitutional or judicial reforms, the most obvious merit of which was their lack of contact with reality. Lenin said that such superstructures were *bourgeois* fads, and I can well understand why: they allow the middle class to play around with a great many concepts, to give the impression that nearly everything is to be reformed, and yet never be forced to change the slightest thing in actual fact.

In the introduction to *La Grève de l'amiante* (Editions Cité Libre, 1956), I demonstrated that our history has been riddled with these elaborate constructions, each one designed to make a great nation of us. During the thirties, it was the theory of corporatism. I do not think I am far wrong in saying that during this period nearly all French-Canadian thinkers, politicians, journalists, and editors advocated corporatism as a kind of extraordinary panacea; in any case, no one was far-sighted or courageous enough to say that it was all nonsense. The consequence was that we had to wait twenty years for the only reform that really counts: education. Net result? Of all Canada's ethnic groups, French Canadians have the second lowest standard in education, barely above that of the poor immigrants just arrived from Sicily.

Well, times have not changed much. Or if they have, it is for the worse. The fads are not the same, but official French-Canadian thinking has become even more monolithic and sterile, its supporters more intolerant: I do not think that using dynamite in a country that enjoys freedom of speech can be considered a sign of rational progress.

'Special status' (a completely illogical concept) has now taken the place that corporatism occupied a generation ago and is showing approximately the same characteristics. In the past, people neither wanted, nor were able, to abolish capitalism; but the dominating theories required them to pretend they did: hence all the talk about corporatism. Today, people neither want, nor are able, to *really* make Quebec independent, so they speak of 'special status'. We must have the expression, if nothing else. It is a way of assuring ourselves that the constitution will be fundamentally transformed, while telling the rest of the country that it will not.

A woollier concept would be hard to imagine: and it is unanimously supported simply because anyone can give it whatever meaning he wishes. In fact, there are as many interpretations of 'special status' as there are persons discussing it. The most striking example of this is the New Democratic Party which interprets it in two diametrically opposed ways, according to whether it is speaking to English or French Canadians. (On this point, Professor Ramsay Cook has done an essential job of clarifying the issues, in the *Globe and Mail*, August 5, 1967.)

We French Canadians are terribly lacking in tenacity. Rather than devote all our efforts to the real improvement of our intellectual, social, and economic condition, we let ourselves be carried away by legal superstructures without even inquiring whether they will work.

All the various kinds of 'special status' which have been discussed until now, whatever their content, lead to the following logical problem: how can a constitution be devised to give Quebec greater powers than other provinces, without reducing Quebec's power in Ottawa? How can citizens of other provinces be made to accept the fact that they would have less power over Quebec at the federal level than Quebec would have over them? How, for example, can Quebec assume powers in foreign affairs, which other provinces do not have, without accepting a reduction of its influence in the field of foreign affairs through the federal government? How can Quebec be made the national state of French Canadians, with really *special* powers, without abandoning at the same time demands for the parity of French and English in Ottawa and throughout the rest of the country?

These questions remain unanswered, because they are unanswerable. For to think about them is to realize that we must have the courage and lucidity to make a choice.

Either the federal government exercises approximately the same powers over Quebec as it does over other provinces; Quebeckers will then be entitled to be represented in Ottawa in exactly the same way as other Canadians. This option would obviously not prevent Quebeckers from adopting whatever special policies they wished *within their provincial jurisdiction*, for example through the Civil Code, social legislation, development of resources, or a completely revised *provincial* constitution. This option would also allow parity between the English and French languages in all federal institutions, and the same parity could eventually be negotiated with other provinces.

Or, the central government's power over Quebec is substantially reduced compared to what it is over other provinces. Quebec's constitutional position having thus become really special, its electorate would not be entitled to demand complete representation at the federal level; and, more specifically, it would have to accept that the French fact be limited, legally and politically, to the province of Quebec.

The second alternative is the 'special status' one. We can adopt it, or not. But those who think that they can have both options are deceiving themselves.

I have had the same ideas on our constitution for a long time, as these essays will demonstrate. But as soon as I started expressing them in Parliament – which was after all the purpose of my being elected – *Le Droit* accused me of having become a slave to the Pearson government!

'Progressive' circles in Quebec, on the other hand, had condemned me for joining an 'old party', maintaining that it was impossible to exert a significant influence within it. A year later I was accused of exerting too much influence, and the federal Members were warned against my ideas on the grounds that I did not speak 'on behalf of French Canadians'.

When I think of all the nonsense that has been spoken 'on behalf of French Canadians' in the past fifty years, I am not very worried by this accusation. In any case, I never claimed to speak 'on behalf' of anyone; if the Party does not agree with my opinions, it can repudiate me; if my constituents do not, they can elect someone else.

To 'ready-made' or second-hand ideas, I have always preferred my own. They form the substance of this book, and together constitute what Mr. Pelletier has very kindly called my theory of politics.

The first chapter has not been previously published; Chapters 5, 6, and 8 first appeared in English; the rest has been taken from *Cité Libre*. Date and place of publication appear at the end of each chapter. Very little has been changed in the original text: occasionally a few words to make the sense clearer, or, more infrequently, criticisms have been deleted because I did not wish to repeat them now that controversy has died away.

The title of this volume indicates the criteria used to select, from everything I had written, the articles and essays reprinted here. Taken as a whole, this work is not a hymn in honour of what my elders called 'our race' and what my juniors now call 'our nation'. But it is none the less dedicated to the progress of French Canadians.

August 1967   P.T.

FEDERALISM AND THE FRENCH CANADIANS

Part One

Quebec and the Constitutional Problem

Introduction

The mandate given to the 'Constitution Committee' of the Quebec Legislative Assembly on May 22, 1963, by a unanimous vote of the Assembly, reads as follows: 'To determine the objectives that should be pursued by French Canada in the revision of the Canadian constitution, and the best means of attaining them.'

I understand the great importance of Canada's ethnic problem, and I can also see that the Legislature of a province that is the home of 83 per cent of all Canadians whose mother tongue is French (according to the 1961 census) should take this fact into account when considering constitutional questions.

Having said this, however, I should like to make a few comments on the mandate of the Constitution Committee.

(a) From a constitutional point of view, the Quebec Legislature has no authority to speak on behalf of 'French Canada'. French Canada includes 850,000 Canadians whose mother tongue is French, who live outside Quebec, and over whom the Legislature has no jurisdiction. On the other hand, Quebec includes a million people whose mother tongue is not French and from whom the Legislature cannot constitutionally dissociate itself. I do understand, however, that because of historical circumstances Quebec has had to, and must still, assume responsibility for the French language and culture; and that in any case it will always have to protect and give particular consideration to the values held by the majority of its citizens.

(b) From a philosophical point of view, the aim of a political society is not the glorification of a 'national fact' (in its ethnic sense). A state that defined its function essentially in terms of ethnic attributes would inevitably become chauvinistic and intolerant. The state, whether provincial, federal, or perhaps later supra-national, must seek the general welfare of all its citizens regardless of sex, colour, race, religious beliefs, or ethnic origin.

(c) From a practical point of view, most labour organizations in Quebec, despite their very large majorities of French Canadians, do nevertheless contain important ethnic minorities. These organizations are obliged by their own constitutions as well as by law to represent all their members without distinction of sex, belief, colour, or national origin. If the mandate of the Constitution Committee is to be taken literally, how could these organizations possibly appear before it?

These remarks are necessary to indicate the perspective of this review, in which, first and foremost, I have attempted to formulate a line of thought acceptable to workers and farmers as members of the political society in Quebec, rather than as members of a specific ethnic group. I leave the pursuit of properly nationalistic ideologies to so-called 'national' or patriotic organizations. Such a role would be unsuited to labour or agricultural associations whose primary function is promoting the social or economic interests of workers. Should these organizations – or the state itself for that matter – direct the whole of their action towards obtaining the specific good of one ethnic group, thus becoming the vehicles of ethnocentric ideologies, they would inevitably be moving in the wrong direction.

This is not to say that the state must disregard cultural or linguistic values. Among the many values that a political society must protect and develop, these have high priority. It is therefore entirely desirable that a state ensure, through its constitution and legislation, the protection of such values. Moreover, it is inevitable that its policies will serve the interests of ethnic groups, and especially of the majority group in proportion to its numbers; but this will happen as a natural consequence of the equality of all citizens, not as a special privilege of the largest group.

Similarly, private organizations must consider the rights of the French-speaking group to which the majority of its members belong. Because the main object of the present review is to discuss the social and economic repercussions of our country's political structures upon the working classes, the reader should not conclude that I am indifferent to the other problems arising from the fact that two great linguistic communities have co-existed in Canada for the past two centuries. Not only am I far from indifferent about this matter, but I greatly fear that if, through stubbornness, indifference, or fanaticism, no adequate solution to these problems is found in the near future, Confederation will face serious difficulties. Canada must become a truly bilingual country in which the linguistic majority stops behaving as if it held special and exclusive rights, and accepts the country's federal nature with all its implications.

It seems quite evident to me that the English-speaking majority has behaved, historically, as though French Canadians were merely one of the country's ethnic minorities, with a few special privileges. The most striking example of this attitude occurs in the federal civil service, where English is, to all intents and purposes, the only working language. In the past, the Department of External Affairs has built up an image of Canada as a unilingual, English country. I could almost say the same of other departments and Crown corporations. The federal capital is an English capital. The Canadian army is an English army in which French Canadians have to overcome serious handicaps, especially from a linguistic point of view.

With regard to language and education, French Canadians in other provinces do not enjoy rights comparable to those of Quebec's English Canadians. This is true even of New Brunswick, where Acadians constitute two-fifths of the population.

The C.B.C., despite all its efforts in the past few years, has not yet managed to extend its French radio and television network from coast to coast.

Many companies established in Quebec have not respected the language and culture of their employees, nor those of the population. French Canadians have been and often still are in an inferior position as far as hiring or promotion are concerned.

On the other hand, sometimes by agreement and sometimes not, the federal government has often encroached on areas of provincial jurisdiction. It took advantage of wars and crises to seize the lion's share of tax revenues; and it also took advantage of the negligence or weakness of the provincial government in Quebec, which did not always defend its jurisdiction (the best way would have been simply to occupy it), and which did not secure a large enough share of revenues to be able to fulfil its constitutional obligations.

Where should a solution to all these problems be sought? In my opinion, it would be an illusion to look for it in sweeping constitutional changes. A constitution by itself cannot provide adequate protection against the enormous influence exerted by the great mass of Anglo-Saxons that occupies most of North America and penetrates deeply even into Quebec. This influence is not merely the result of our powerful modern means of communication; it comes from the fact that we have at our doorstep a country that is the richest in the world, the most advanced industrially, and strategically one of the poles in our planet's military equilibrium.

In such a situation, legal guarantees by themselves are far too fragile to ensure the survival of French language and culture. People who think such guarantees are enough may be the most dangerous enemies of the traditions we wish to safeguard and perpetuate.

I do not consider a state's political structures or constitutional forms to have absolute and eternal value. But it would be wrong to think that I am merely reluctant to touch the constitution. History teaches us that diversity rather than uniformity is the general rule in this land. With the exception of a certain number of basic principles that must be safeguarded, such as liberty and democracy, the rest ought to be adapted to the circumstances of history, to traditions, to geography, to cultures, and to civilizations.

Thus I am neither shocked nor astonished that individuals and groups are advocating constitutional changes in Canada. There are dozens of ways of thinking politically about the country, from Quebec separatism to the idea of a unitary Canadian state. If we were confronted with a population that had just immigrated to a new territory, several hypotheses would be possible and they could be the subject of heated debate. But this is not the case. Even though our country is young, it has a history, and has lived through some profound experiences which have left their mark upon it, and which it would be vain and childish to ignore.

May I make a comparison with trade unionism? The unions know that they have a relatively large freedom to manoeuvre when the first collective agreement is negotiated; but this no longer holds for subsequent renewals. They cannot, for the mere pleasure of it, play around with those sections of their contract that have not given rise to difficulties. Nor does the opposition come solely from the employer's side: the workers themselves are not prepared to engage in battles simply to obtain a contract that would be theoretically more satisfactory.

I want to make these points at the very beginning of this article, to emphasize that I am far from disagreeing with many of the complaints brought before the Constitution Committee by individuals or organizations. What I do dispute is the validity of the solutions proposed, especially those simplified, unrealistic formulas designed only to inflame existing passions.

In any case these briefs have not, generally speaking, paid much attention to the fate of the working classes and the consequences for them of the proposed constitutional transformations. The main characteristics of these proposals are the emphasis constantly placed upon so-called 'national' questions and the almost total lack of discussion of their effect upon the working classes as such. I am afraid that excessive preoccupation with the future of the language has made certain people forget the future of the man speaking it. A working man may care about his language and cultural values; he also cares very strongly about having a decent life without the risk of losing the little he has through some misguided political adventure. This is why, in the present article, I shall often insist on economic realities; these realities constitute one of the main preoccupations of the working class.

Apart from their professional and sometimes even ideological differences, the various working classes occupy more or less the same position in their political society: the position of people whose material security is quite precarious, and whom the slightest illness or economic recession can plunge into misery.

(a) The prosperity of the agricultural class, since it includes producers, is related in the long term to that of urban workers. All these people contribute in complementary ways to the same general economic activity. The farmers of Quebec, for example, spent $41,250,509 in 1963 for agricultural equipment alone. This economic interdependence becomes even more evident in times of crisis. The mobility of labour, which has long been expressed in Quebec as an exodus from rural areas, means that in effect the two classes are lumped together on the employment market; one group's unemployment impoverishes all the others; and though they may be stricken at different times, they are all left perilously close to actual destitution.

(b) It is in the interests of all labouring classes, as consumers, to have a sound economy capable of supporting a high standard of living. They are aware of the dangers of closed commercial policies which may give a temporary advantage to one class or to a certain percentage of workers, but which in the long term carry the risk of impoverishing the entire population.

In short, labouring classes, whether urban or rural, will be the more or less immediate victims of any political or economic mistakes that might be made by the governing classes. It is characteristic of these victims, however, that their social and economic situation renders them incapable of protecting themselves adequately against the consequences of such mistakes. They are therefore the first to be concerned in constitutional discussions that claim to define new instruments of power within society. It is time people realized that in a democratic country the constitution is the shield protecting the weak from the arbitrary intervention of power.

These preliminary points having been made, I would now like to examine the problem that the Constitution Committee has been set up to resolve: the kind of constitution that would best promote the full development of those values considered important by the political society of Quebec.

The Basic Facts of the Problem

The first law of politics is to start from given facts. The second is to take stock of the real relationship between forces that may divide or unite the existing political factors. Thus, it will soon become evident, even to the least acute of Quebec observers, that no constitutional reform – indeed not even a declaration of independence – could make French a major language of business and industry in North America, or make Quebec a state capable of dictating its terms to the rest of the continent.

The basic facts of the constitutional problem faced by Quebec are, in brief, as follows:

(a) *Economic facts.* The economy of Quebec is closely linked with that of Canada and both are largely dominated by the economy of the United States. This means that Quebec workers cannot discuss their prospects without taking into account the fact that they are integrated into a continental economy. For better or worse, Quebec is linked to the most powerful economic giant the world has ever known: a giant with whom its territories are contiguous. Capital, employment, and technology tend to cross the border as a result of legislation favourable to them.

(b) *Linguistic facts.* In North America, French is the mother tongue of five or six million people, while English is the mother tongue of one hundred and eighty-two million. The only considerable territory in the Western hemisphere in which French-speaking people are grouped in sufficient numbers and are sufficiently attached to French for this language to be a political society's first idiom is Quebec, a province with a population of 5,260,000 in a country of 18,240,000 and on a continent of 233 million. Even if New Brunswick were eventually to be added to it, the two provinces would still have fewer than six million people. In Quebec, the number of persons *speaking only French* tends to increase in absolute numbers (2,016,000 in 1941 and 3,255,000 in 1961) and even, it seems, as a percentage of the total population (60.5 per cent were in this category in 1941 and 61.9 per cent in 1961). In New Brunswick, the absolute number increased from 82,000 to 112,000 during the same period, and the percentage from 18 per cent to 18.7 per cent. In the rest of Canada, the percentage of persons *speaking only French* is insignificant, reaching a maximum of 1.5 per cent in Ontario. Everywhere in North America, except in Quebec (and perhaps New Brunswick, Prince Edward Island, and the Yukon), the phenomenon of cultural assimilation tends therefore to reduce the importance of French as a language used by the population.

These economic and linguistic realities result in a certain balance of power that no amount of exhortation – even incorporated into a constitutional document – can change. The world might be a better place if Quebec were economically self-sufficient, or if a hundred million French-speaking people lived in North America. But politics cannot take into account what might have been; and any constitutional reform based on such suppositions would lead only to disillusion and disaster. On the other hand, an objective appraisal of the basic facts allows one to make the best possible use of these facts and, over a long period, to bring forces of change to bear upon them so that new policies become not only desirable, but possible.

These forces of change are many and various, acting sometimes on men and sometimes on things. For example, it was a search for religious freedom that touched off the immigration of the Puritans to New England, and of the Doukhobors to Canada. Another example is that the demand for independence in Indonesia caused a flow of European capital away from that country. And a final example: in an attempt to escape from misery, Irishmen have fled to England, Englishmen to Canada, and French Canadians, by the tens of thousands, to the United States – proof that faithfulness to one's language and native soil cannot long withstand urgent economic pressures.

It is important to look more closely at how these variations occur. Let us for this purpose consider three areas in which forces of change may affect the basic facts of reality.

MEN

The search for a better life, which has been at the root of nearly all migrations in the world since the beginning of time, is one of the forces also motivating the people of Quebec. But it must be borne in mind that the idea of a better life can be interpreted according to many different standards. If the only pressure is an economic one, workers will tend to go wherever they can obtain the highest wage or salary, and this is also where their contribution to society will be greatest. This may express itself in a change of linguistic allegiance, as when many French Canadians in the West forget their mother tongue; or by a physical displacement of population, as when the awakening of Quebec attracted civil servants from Ottawa but was unable to prevent some forty unemployed workers at Thetford from emigrating to the United States (as happened in 1964). On the other hand, economic pressures may be counterbalanced by moral, patriotic, or sentimental forces. These sometimes affect the mobility of workers, making them accept situations that are economically less rewarding, but more satisfactory on another scale of values: compensation for accepting lower salaries will be found, for example, in the genuine pleasure of speaking French or of living among their own people.

The forces influencing human decisions are, therefore, many and varied. And this is precisely where political factors become important.

The state may resist certain pressures, but not others; it may work to transform the basic situation so that migrations go in one direction and not in another. But the state must take great care not to infringe on the conscience of the individual. I believe that, in the last analysis, a human being in the privacy of his own mind has the exclusive authority to choose his own scale of values and to decide which forces will take precedence over others. A good constitution is one that does not prejudge any of these questions, but leaves citizens free to orient their human destinies as they see fit.

CAPITAL

The richer a country, the more it can save, and consequently invest; the more it can invest, the greater the profits it can make, and consequently the richer it becomes. This explains, roughly, why the economic lead that the United States has over other countries tends to increase rather than decrease. From another point of view, a very wealthy country, with an over-abundance of capital available, is always looking for profitable investments. Left to its own devices, capital will tend to go wherever it can obtain the highest return. Thus it happens that American invest-ment (limited in its own country by anti-trust laws) is naturally attracted to such countries as Canada and the nations of Western Europe, which have social stability and an industrial economy sufficiently advanced to support a high level of consumption. The result is a sort of economic dependence which is sometimes described in such emotional terms as 'colonialism' and 'coloniza-tion'. This may give rise to simplified solutions: as Cuba has demonstrated, it is easy enough to get rid of American capital. But one must be prepared to accept the consequences. And there are no indications that a friendly country would be ready to supply Quebec with $300 million a year as Russia did for Cuba.

The answer here is not to chase away foreign capital, since the standard of living must then be lowered so that foreign capital can be replaced by indigenous capital. The answer, in the first place, is to use foreign capital within the framework of rational economic development; and secondly, to create indigenous capital and direct it toward the key sectors of the future: computers, services, and industry in the age of nuclear energy. Movements of capital, like movements of people, are sensitive to political decisions. I must therefore repeat what I said earlier: in a commendable attempt to change economic facts, the state must never use legal or moral violence against its citizens. A sound economic policy must never be based on the assumption, for example, that workers would be ready to accept a drastic lowering of standards of living for the mere pleasure of seeing a national middle class replacing a foreign one at the helm of various enterprises. Governments must remember that sentimental campaigns to promote the purchase of home-produced goods, or appeals to racial feeling, are often subterfuges hiding the desire of owners of business and industry to protect their profits against foreign competition.

On these matters as well, a constitution of free men must be free from bias.

TECHNOLOGY

In an age when industrial development is dependent on science and technical inventions, economic facts are subject to pressures from technology as well as from capital. Because of this, France was recently unable to prevent the takeover of Bull Equipment by General Electric; at that point, it was not lack of capital that prevented France from retaining control over these crucially important industries; it was lack of scientific knowledge. This deficiency resulted from the fact that France was, and still is, unable to finance research on the scale required by our current industrial revolution. Twenty billion dollars a year are now being spent to finance research in the United States, and this is nearly twenty times as much as in France, and 3.3 times as much as in the eighteen countries of the Organization for Economic Co-operation and Development (O.E.C.D.) put together.[1] The consequences of this are striking: 'In the case of France alone, there is one patent sold for every five we buy from the States, whereas three years ago we sold one for every three.'[2]

[1] *Le progrès scientifique*, 1/9/64, published by the Committee on Scientific Research.
[2] Michel Drancourt, in *Communauté européenne*, November 1964.

And Mr. Louis Armand, one of the greatest experts on technology in France, states:

> Before the last war, if you had raw materials, manpower, capital and energy, you could be an industrial country, whatever your human or financial potential. This is no longer the case. The only material that counts now is grey matter. That is to say, the number and quality of research workers ceaselessly contributing to the progress . . . of science and technology. What these researchers need is not blackboards, but equipment that costs billions of dollars, and quickly becomes obsolete. To meet the needs of a new economy based on science, it is no longer enough merely to be wealthy: you must be colossally rich. Actual needs destroy the idea of nations; they imply – and impose – great industrial complexes, and a sharing of manpower, markets and capital. . . . There are no longer any solutions on a national scale.[3]

These last sentences lead us to think that the role of politics is even more delicate regarding technology than it is regarding population or capital. For if laws and constitutions create a situation that is not favourable to the entry and development of technology and technicians, the country will be hopelessly outclassed economically, and its industries soon outdated and inefficient. On the other hand, if technology is free to enter, the country must irrevocably step into the era of great communities, of continental economies. It will have to pay the price in terms of its national sovereignty. And its constitutional law will have to take this factor into account.

We have now seen what basic facts are at the root of our constitutional problem in Quebec; we have seen that forces of change can affect these facts; and lastly we have seen that political power itself can influence these forces of change. In other words the state – which embodies political power – can play a crucial role in guiding the destiny of Quebec.

One might be tempted to conclude that a weak state would be unable to put up much resistance to demographic, economic, and technological pressures, whereas a strong state would be able to counterbalance them with forces of another order. For such a proposition to be tenable, however, two things must be considered:

(a) The expression 'strong state' can only be applied to the United States and to the Soviet Union, other states being out of

[3]*Réalités*, January 1965.

the race altogether. The latter may certainly pass laws to intervene in the movement of men, capital, and techniques; but far from applying political pressure to these factors, the states themselves are often forced to yield to economic and, especially, to technological laws. For example, France could have passed legislation to prohibit the introduction of processes based on English and American patents into the country, but then it could not have built the Caravelle. As soon as France had decided to build the Caravelle, with its English jet engines and American electronics system, however, the French state was no longer free to sell the plane as it wished: 'The Caravelle cannot be exported to China due to an American licence on the pressurization system.'[4]

(b) The notion of sovereignty is not the most important one to help us appreciate, in these circumstances, the relative strength or weakness of various states. For example, Guatemala, which enjoys complete legal sovereignty, is at an even greater disadvantage when faced with foreign economic pressures than is Quebec, despite the fact that Quebec shares its sovereignty with the federal state.

Another way of expressing this would be to say that states are free to intervene in the action of demographic, economic, and technical forces, but they must pay the price of their intervention.

However, the price to be paid is not the same for all categories of the population. In the case of France, Michel Drancourt, in the article quoted above, expressed it as follows:

[For most people] the fact of becoming a Ford employee may seem bearable even though one would have preferred to remain the employee of a French company. It is at the administrative or governing level that the change is felt most painfully, but then how can one take into account administrators or directors who have failed to retain any real power?

Nevertheless, there is a plausible (and, personally, I think it an extremely probable) alternative: a national reaction along socialist lines.

To combat 'American imperialism', a few countries, and France in particular, would engage in a kind of enlightened 'Castroism'. This would not help the material prosperity of Frenchmen, since it would imply a return to a certain autarchy

[4]B. Goulet, 'Brevets industriels et indépendance nationale', *Economie et Humanisme*, December 1964, p. 40.

and considerable sacrifice on the level of consumption; but they might be 'sold' such policies by persuasion, or indeed by force.

In the case of Quebec, state intervention in demographic, financial, and technological variables, and its results, can take the form of either of two extreme alternatives:

(a) We can demand that Quebec be given complete sovereign powers, thereby saving Quebec particularism by subordinating all other needs to it. So much the worse if the economy is slowed down and the standard of living lowered as a result. That is the price we must pay to end the cultural alienation of a conquered and demoralized nation. When this nation has gained new confidence in itself, it will at last be able to take vigorous and economically valid action.

This alternative is most attractive to those people who are discontented with their situation, but possess some kind of economic security. Since they are not on the verge of misery, they – as well as young people not yet concerned with such matters – may more easily risk a lowered standard of living. In addition, they have more to gain from a separate Quebec, for, in fact, this group will provide the new ruling class.

(b) We can minimize the importance of the state's sovereignty, obtain the maximum advantage from our integration into the American continent, and make Quebec an ideal province for industrial development. So much the worse if the particular qualities of Quebec (including language) must suffer: this is the price that must be paid if the people of Quebec are to attain a higher standard of living and of technical development. Their improved material position will later enable them to affirm more strongly what remains of the French fact in North America.

Those who live in slums and are already on the brink of destitution or unemployment, as well as those who have no reason to fear international competition – for example, true scientists or true financiers – tend very often to favour this second alternative. From their point of view, it is better first to free man through technical progress: to liberate him from physical misery so that he may then concern himself with culture.

Between these two extreme options there is, of course, a whole range of intermediary positions. But it seems clear that each person's constitutional or political options depend upon his particular scale of values and the priorities he attributes to the various objectives he wishes to attain. In the next section, I shall examine a few options that have traditionally been adopted in Quebec. After this, in section IV, I shall outline the objectives that I think present themselves today to the working classes of Quebec. Lastly, in section V, I shall state what constitutional alternatives, in my opinion, result from these objectives.

By way of conclusion to the present section, however, I want to affirm the following. Basic facts as well as the variables that may affect them seem to require the people of Quebec to commit themselves to realistic policies. Whatever constitutional direction we may decide to take, the destiny of our province will be shaped by a balance of forces in which, acting alone, we would have very little weight. Quite apart from our constitutional arrangements, the government of Quebec has but limited power to intervene in capital or technical markets; consequently, it must use these powers wisely and economically, and always in sectors advantageous to the entire population.

Traditional Constitutional Options

If there was any constant factor in Quebec policies from Honoré Mercier to Maurice Duplessis, it was the state's passive attitude toward capital investment. From mines to forests, from hydroelectric resources to urban property, there was scarcely a resource that could not be exploited by private investment without political difficulty. This was also true in the fields of manufacturing and services. True, the state could be bothersome at times, and partisan politics were not above imposing taxes on money-lenders. But on the whole, the main characteristic in Quebec's economic history over the past hundred years has been the absence of any coherent policy on private investment; and the same could almost be said of public investment as well.

With regard to technology, the state of Quebec maintained more or less the same policy of non-intervention. Contractors were free to introduce whatever techniques they liked, in whatever way they liked. With very few exceptions (such as working on Sunday), it never occurred to the government to direct technological movements in any way. It would be an understatement to say that the state did not think of being generous in its support of scientific research: it did not even plan for technical schools (which were supported by Ottawa). As for promoting the formation of French-speaking industrial management, there was no question of it, since no effort was made even to protect the language itself against the invasion of foreign technical vocabulary.

Nor can Quebec governments be said to have done much more to direct the movement of manpower. In matters of immigration, Quebec's attitude was consistently the negative one of refusing to exercise its constitutional powers. In matters of emigration, the state was at first indifferent about the exodus to the United States. When it finally decided to act, it did so as a result of emotional rather than purely rational considerations. To take possession of the soil was presented as an eminently patriotic and moral duty: a great deal of energy and a fair amount of money were spent gaining access to territories that could be colonized, and establishing settlers upon them. It is obvious that had these efforts been directed instead toward consolidating viable agricultural enterprises, establishing industries, and training contractors and skilled workers, we would now be much closer to having first-hand control over our own affairs.

It should be pointed out that, by contrast, the central government as well as certain other provincial governments were much more interested and skilful than ours in directing economic, technical, and demographic forces. A glance at Macdonald's 'National Policy', C. D. Howe's Crown corporations, provincial policies concerning education, health, immigration, nationalization, and social security, makes it obvious that English-speaking Canadians had a much greater awareness of the state's interventionist role.

The recent history of Quebec serves to illustrate the following paradox: despite the fact that our ideology recognized the primacy of spiritual over material matters and that our constitutional powers enabled us to uphold this primacy, economic forces were allowed free reign to influence the destiny of our society. We believed ourselves to be guided by a providential mission bolstered by patriotic motives; but by reducing the powers of the state to a minimum or by badly directing its action, we cleared the way for the most relentless kind of economic liberalism: capital was allowed to enter, manpower to leave, and the technology we obtained was of the sort attracted by docile, ignorant, and cheap labour. Worse still, the language and culture to which we attached such importance became debased, since they were identified with a people placed in a condition of inferiority.

It would, however, be a childish error to condemn our entire past as an unmitigated disaster. For one thing, we must remember that our political strength was at best quite modest. Then too, it may be a consolation to think that one result of the play of economic forces is that our province has attained a relatively high level of industrial development and now possesses relatively important technical equipment.

These last two considerations may serve as a warning against the opposite extreme: absolute subordination of economic forces to political forces.

In recent years a segment of opinion in Quebec has been rushing in the direction of this extreme, thus rejoining a form of protest that often crops up among us. The state was nothing in Quebec: now it must be everything.

So that the state can indeed be everything, one line of thought rejects federalism, and goes so far as to advocate complete independence for Quebec. People speak of the principle of nationalities, affirm the right of these nationalities to govern their own destiny, and conclude that, for reasons of dignity and pride, French Canadians (Quebeckers) must have their own national state endowed with more or less complete sovereignty.

I recognize the right of nations to self-determination. But to claim this right without taking into account the price that will have to be paid, and without clearly demonstrating that it is to the advantage of the whole nation, is nothing short of a reckless gamble. Men do not exist for states: states are created to make it easier for men to attain some of their common objectives.

Therefore, people who wish to undermine or to destroy the Canadian federal system must define clearly the risks involved and demonstrate that the new judicial and political situation they want to establish would be in the general interests of our people.

Far from doing that, this school of thought is content to affirm that independence would not *necessarily* involve a drastic drop in our standard of living – although it recognizes that we do not have enough facts at the moment to be entirely sure. Such people admit that a 'free' Quebec might be dominated by a backward and authoritarian *bourgeoisie*; yet they are prepared to take the risk. They fully expect that a sovereign state will put an end to the real or imagined sense of cultural alienation that afflicts some Quebeckers; but they admit that to achieve this Quebec may have to suffer through a period of stagnation. They do not condescend to show how all this constitutes a necessary step to helping people who live in slums or vegetate on farms. And by way of consolation they assure us that after independence, the mistakes we make will at least have the advantage of being our own!

It seems to me that, faced with such attitudes, the working classes must feel the need of entering the debate. For in the end it is always they who have to pay; it is they who would suffer most from a lowering of the standard of living, who would be hardest hit by a period of political and social stagnation, and who would be the first to suffer from unemployment and destitution. In short, the consequences of whatever mistakes 'our' ruling classes might make would be borne mainly by the working Confederation.

This is not to say that representatives of labour should systematically oppose constitutional reform. They are certainly not people to be frightened of change; but they must be convinced that any particular change is for the better, not the worse. They also want the most urgent matters attended to first. Under our present constitution, the government of Quebec is free to undertake economic and social reforms that seem more important and certainly more urgent than revision of the very foundations of Confederation.

The working man knows very well what benefits he might derive from a better organization of justice, a system of health insurance, better labour or agricultural legislation, or policies promoting low-cost housing. That is why he attaches priority to these reforms, knowing that they will create conditions more favourable to cultural development. And before diverting considerable amounts of time and energy into Quebec separatism – or into annexation to the United States for that matter – he wants to know, *in a concrete way*, what is involved.

In theory, of course, everything is possible. In theory, an economist can demonstrate perfectly well that separation would be entirely to Quebec's advantage. All he needs to postulate, for example, is that if Quebec were independent, foreign contractors and technologists would bring in capital and inventions at an increased rate. (On the other hand, what an odd way to 're-possess' our economy!) Or again, that our markets – including English Canada – would buy even more agricultural or indus-trial products from an independent Quebec than they do now. Or that our governments and all our institutions would over-night become miraculously progressive and well adapted to the technological revolution. Or, finally, that our middle class, after independence, would suddenly discover that its talents lay in high finance instead of ambassadorial service.

If in practice it turned out that these postulates were ground-less, however, the whole adventure would end in disaster. Another economist might justifiably postulate that Quebec's independence would result in loss of both capital and markets, in technological stagnation, and in administrative inefficiency. Nor is it entirely impossible that our rising middle class would discover that it still had less taste for finance than for diplomacy.

Clearly, an economist alone cannot tell us what the future would hold for an independent Quebec. To his knowledge must be added sociology, political science, history, and, if at all possible, a gift for prophecy. Faced with such contradictory and uncertain possibilities, a man by himself may decide to take the plunge. From dignity and pride – or even in the hope of raising his own social rank – he may declare himself ready to try national independence, especially if he has intellectual or financial reserves to fall back on should the adventure miscarry.

But this does not hold for those people who have, at best, a precarious economic security. Organizations concerned with the working classes in Quebec would plainly be irresponsible to scuttle Confederation with an attitude of 'Come what may!' These associations must give the benefit of the doubt to estab-lished political institutions that have helped Canadians attain the second or third highest standard of living in the world. Let the burden of proof fall upon people who would lead an entire nation into an unknown speculation.

In my opinion, nothing said before the Constitution Com-mittee or published in the province has been sufficient to under-mine confidence in the federal system. It is true that in practice the system has not been free from inequalities and injustices; for example, all Canadians do not have a reasonable share of our highly praised standard of living. On this point, however,

Quebec's position is not the worst, and if it were a question of economic colonialism, the Maritimes would have far greater right to complain than we.

It is clear, then, that the position I am outlining here is not at all based on smug satisfaction. In the past, popular movements have worked for economic, social, political, or even, when there was need, for constitutional changes; and they will continue to work for them. But, for reasons I have just explained, and for other reasons which will become apparent in subsequent chapters, the fact remains that an open federal system is the aim assumed in this review.

Objectives

The function of a state is to ensure the establishment and maintenance of a legal order that will safeguard the development of its citizens. This order, as I conceive it, must be based on a certain number of objectives which, for convenience, I shall class as economic, social, and cultural.

ECONOMIC OBJECTIVES

What counts for an economist is not the size of a country, but the size of each inhabitant's income. Thus, the United States' particular virtue is not that it possesses extensive territory or a large population – in these China is far richer – but that it has the highest per-capita income in the world. At the other extreme, Switzerland, which is a small country on the basis of both territory and population, nevertheless has a standard of living that classes it among the four most prosperous countries on earth. It seems, therefore, that a country's wealth is not necessarily related to the size of its home markets, but may just as well result from its capacity to produce goods and services that are competitive everywhere in the world. For example, the most interesting aspect of the European Common Market is not the Market as such, but the gradual abolition of protective tariffs between member countries, which will force each one of them to develop greater efficiency if its standards are to be maintained.

As is well known, neither Sweden nor Switzerland depends on the Common Market for its high standard of living; they have achieved it partly by keeping out of European wars and partly by adapting to their own needs the very latest developments of technology and finance over the past fifty years. (In 1963, for example, the balance of payments on manufactured goods between France and Switzerland was eight to one in favour of Switzerland.)

Looked at solely from the point of view of economic objectives, the important question is not whether Quebec will become a sovereign state, remain integrated with Canada, or be annexed to the United States, although these options are not unrelated to the kind of political means used to attain economic goals. In the last resort, what really matters is that the per-capita income be increased as quickly as possible. To achieve this, the economy of Quebec must become extremely efficient, technologically advanced, quite specialized, and capable of offering the best products at the best prices in all the markets of the world.

In practice this means that the economy of Quebec must not be isolated, but open to the whole world, for then it will find new markets as well as the competition it has to expect.

Whatever may be said to the contrary, it seems clear that a large part of the constitutional upheaval so fashionable in our province at the moment would in fact tend to isolate Quebec. It is proposed, for example, that Quebec be given exclusive jurisdiction over banks, immigration, manpower placement, foreign trade, customs duties and tariffs, and many other things as well. The stated aim – to regain control over our economic destiny – seems very laudable. But all the evidence indicates that the motive for using these legal instruments is to protect our capital, businessmen, and the top ranks of management from foreign competition. And this is precisely the way to render them inefficient, and to make certain that our products are rejected in foreign markets. Quebec would then have to oblige its consumers to 'buy French Canadian'; and farmers and workers would have to pay more – either in prices or in subsidies – for these products. This argument applies to steel as well as to blueberries, and it would be a mistake to think that the working classes would derive any long-term benefit from being turned into a captive market.

The objection is sometimes made that this is not at all what is intended; far from wishing to isolate Quebec once it has gained the constitutional powers mentioned above, the government will seek to integrate it within some kind of common market. A most peculiar line of thought! For in general, such a common market would require Quebec to abandon its autonomy on the migration of capital, techniques, and manpower, as well as on such matters as the value of currency, external trade, customs, and tariffs. In other words, from an economic standpoint a 'new' Quebec would have more or less the same sovereign powers, the same measure of independence, and probably the same competitive protection if it joined a common market as it does at the moment within the Canadian Confederation.

As producers and consumers, therefore, the working classes in Quebec must strive for an economy based on world-wide markets and as competitive as possible. That is the only way for Quebec to become richer in the long run; and that is why we must reject constitutional reforms that not only give no indication of increasing economic efficiency, but seem to imply protectionist and isolationist policies the benefit of which will be measured in terms of increased prestige and dividends for propertied classes.

On the whole, our present constitution allows the provinces – and therefore Quebec – extensive jurisdiction over the means of achieving the objectives mentioned above. Provinces are responsible for education, and it is mainly through education that labour and administrators will acquire the financial and scientific knowledge they need in order to act efficiently at a time when industry is so dependent upon research, and production techniques upon computers. Furthermore, provinces have jurisdiction over land and resources, which allows them to develop the land, complete the network of industrial support (roads, bridges, electricity, services, and the rest), and develop resources, each according to its own pace and set of priorities.

On the other hand, the fact that the provinces do not have jurisdiction over tariffs and international commerce could only be inconvenient for Quebec in these two particular cases:

(a) If Canada's policies were more protectionist than Quebec wished them to be, there would be a danger of fostering a 'hot-house' culture, unable to face outside competition. I can only say that this is highly unlikely. As far as we can judge from the attitudes and slogans adopted by Quebec opponents of Confederation, it seems certain that free trade would find greater (if still inadequate) support from the federalists. In any case we must not forget that, protection being equal, Canada would still have an advantage over a separated Quebec, first because its markets are three times as large, which means economizing through larger-scale production, and second because its competition is three times as strong, which stimulates efficient production.

(b) If Canada's tariff system were detrimental to Quebec products as compared to other Canadian products, it is clear that Quebec would be justified in demanding control over its tariffs and external commerce. This hypothesis is just as improbable as the first. In the past, Canadian tariff regulations have on the whole worked against the West and the Maritimes. And it is difficult to see how in the future an alert, and, more important, a knowledgeable Quebec could be victimized by adverse tariff regulations from Ottawa. There are too many vested interests – and not only French Canadian – involved in the matter.

It would certainly be an advantage if the federal government consulted the provinces about matters that affect them, even if these matters are entirely within federal jurisdiction. I do not see why we could not establish permanent consulting bodies to ensure that our trade, tariff, customs, or monetary policies really reflect the opinions of people throughout the country, and that no province feels undermined by the exercise of central power.

Before turning to the next section, I should like to add one more comment: these objections to economic chauvinism are valid for English Canadians as well as French Canadians. It is always costly and inefficient to choose men or to favour institutions on the basis of their ethnic origin rather than their particular aptitude or competence. Great industries cannot promote maximum efficiency by ethnocentric policies, any more than by nepotism. Now, speaking only of Quebec, no matter how backward the province may have been in its technical and administrative education, neither this backwardness nor pure chance is sufficient to account for the fact that in all levels of industry, from the very top down to the foreman, French Canadians have been poorly represented in proportion to their number. It even happens that a Quebec worker being hired for industry is required to speak English as well as French – a form of discrimination that should be rigorously forbidden by Quebec law.

Quebec does not need to extend its jurisdiction to questions of tariffs in order to condemn the form of protection most harmful to the province: that which operates against French

Canadians in high finance and large industries. There is no doubt that the whole of Quebec suffers as a result of these practices. The number of English-Canadian financiers and industrialists able to compete in our North American big league is pathetically small; and it is almost certain that the inefficiency of the Montreal group is at least partly due to their chauvinism.

The conclusion that must be drawn is this: from the point of view of its economic objectives, Quebec will find Canadian Confederation not only an acceptable system, but indeed the one most conducive to its full development.

SOCIAL OBJECTIVES

Economic forces operating in the way I have outlined – that is to say, according to certain laws but unhampered by administrative red tape or territorial barriers – will tend to enrich the community as a whole. For this wealth to be fairly distributed within the community, however, a certain number of social objectives must necessarily be pursued.

In a very general way, these consist in so organizing a political community that all its members have the essential before a few are allowed to enjoy the superfluous. Of course, the concepts of the 'essential' and the 'superfluous' will be defined variously in different countries and at different times; and even in one country at any given time they will be defined according to each person's social philosophy. As for labour organizations, they also have their own definition of these concepts and have frequently elaborated them in the briefs they regularly submit to their governments. This side of the question therefore need not be re-examined in detail by the Constitution Committee.

It must be pointed out, however, that social objectives sometimes conflict with economic objectives; and whereas the latter can only command limited state intervention, the former can command a great deal. For example, automation is good for the progress of industry but bad for the labourer who becomes redundant as a result; and a state that allows automation must also be responsible for workers affected by it.

The conflict is not always easy to resolve. It would be a great oversimplification to adopt the attitude: social needs first, then economic. For, as I mentioned in section II, it is a rare state that can disregard economic or technological laws with impunity. A government trying to do so, even though for excellent social motives, would so impoverish its economy that its social goals became unattainable. In fact, unless the economy is fundamentally sound, a strong, progressive social policy can be neither conceived nor applied. All social security measures, from family allowances to old age pensions, from free education to health insurance, must remain theoretical if the economic structure is incapable of bearing the cost. Even the right to work remains no more than a pious hope if economic cycles or the stagnation of business creates unemployment for industrial labourers, or prevents farmers from selling their products profitably.

In the matter of social objectives, then, we must begin by applying the same constitutional considerations that I outlined for economic objectives in sub-section A. This means in effect that we must oppose the dismemberment of our country, because the result would be to weaken the economy of Quebec and therefore to some extent prevent the province from pursuing social objectives or being able to assume the cost.

From another point of view, our Canadian constitution gives provinces the widest possible jurisdiction in matters of social security. This permits the government of each province to apply whatever social philosophy is best suited to its own population. The resulting diversity can create a healthy rivalry between provinces on matters relating to taxation and to the benefits to be derived for the various taxpayers. In the Canadian federal system, therefore, a citizen has a multiple choice, and this increases his democratic freedom: within the Canadian economy as a whole, manpower and capital will tend to move toward whatever balance of fiscal charges and social services suit them best. Obviously, because of language considerations, a French Canadian will be relatively less mobile; this is merely another reason why the government of Quebec must choose its fiscal and social policies with great care and in the most democratic way possible.

To the foregoing considerations must be added these three observations:

(a) First, the rivalry mentioned in the preceding paragraph carries some risks: for example, a province might be tempted to attract capital and industry by adopting anti-cooperative and anti-union laws, as well as by reducing its expenditures for social purposes to a minimum. This can constitute a real danger for labour and agricultural workers who, lacking other means of protection, will wish to transfer some constitutional jurisdiction over these matters to the central government. I would consider this kind of centralization to be a last resort, however, and would prefer to retain, as far as possible, the freedom and diversity arising from federative decentralization. This is why I consider it so urgent to negotiate interprovincial agreements establishing certain minimum standards of social legislation, at least in the larger industrial provinces.

Within this context, I can only consider premature and inappropriate the preoccupation in certain circles with constitutional reforms designed to give provinces the right to conclude treaties with foreign powers without consulting the federal government. As long as Quebec has not negotiated agreements with other provinces regarding trade union legislation, can it be very urgent, or indeed economically wise, for the province to sign treaties that would bind it to standards established in other countries?

Similarly, the province has recently concluded certain agreements with France, without overstepping the bounds of constitutional legality. I am not one of those who greeted this initiative with great enthusiasm; to be quite frank, I am not all that preoccupied with the 'image' that Quebec as a province projects on the international scene. As for the future, I am of the opinion that Quebec has better things to do than, for example, to be seen at every meeting of UNESCO, especially considering that it has not even begun serious negotiations with a neighbouring province about the education of that province's French minority.

(b) My second remark concerns provinces that are too poor to achieve minimum standards of social security by themselves. Under our present constitution, the central government can remedy this lack by equalization grants, and this is a system that must continue. From this point of view, I find it regrettable that Ottawa and Quebec should have quarrelled about the division of federal tax revenues. A concept of tax sharing that does not take into account the beneficiary's needs, and which seems to claim that any given group of taxpayers must receive as benefits at least the equivalent of what it pays in taxes, makes a mockery of the equalizing function of taxation and identifies itself as completely reactionary. – And speaking of taxes, it is perhaps not inappropriate to denounce another idea widespread in Quebec: that the province should recover from Ottawa the funds drawn from it in the last World War. I shall content myself with saying that this was a political, never a constitutional matter; and that on a political level, Mr. Duplessis and after him Mr. Lesage established ways of allowing Quebec to receive a far greater proportion of personal and corporate income taxes, and succession duties, than was ever yielded during the war.

(c) My third remark concerns planning and anti-cyclical policies, both of which presuppose some form of state intervention in economic mechanisms for social purposes such as full employment or rational development. It would not be appropriate to go very deeply into such technical concepts in this review. I shall merely say that in the Canadian constitutional system, these two kinds of policies presuppose a measure of co-operation between the federal and provincial levels. The federal government is of course mainly responsible for the economy of the whole country, but its action cannot be efficient unless it has the support of the provinces.

Both planning and anti-cyclical policies have very great priority for the agricultural and working classes. If a federal régime made these goals harder to attain, these classes might be obliged to advocate reforms leading to greater centralization. It is precisely to prevent the necessity of such a move that I am suggesting, instead of constitutional modifications, a more systematic recourse to consultation and to federal-provincial agreements.

In conclusion, it appears that from the point of view of social objectives federalism is the form of government that can best serve the interests of the Quebec community.

CULTURAL OBJECTIVES

We have seen that the state must occasionally intervene in the play of economic forces to better ensure the pursuit of social objectives. But it must not stop there; if it does, we could find ourselves promoting the development of a community that was rich, technologically advanced, equitably structured, but completely depersonalized. We would be struck with the disease that threatens every society in an advanced stage of industrialization. Technology, which brings abundance and material happiness, presupposes an undifferentiated mass of consumers; it also tends to minimize the values that let a human being acquire and retain his own identity, values that I am grouping here under the vague term 'cultural'. The political order created by the state must struggle against this kind of depersonalization by pursuing cultural objectives.

The state must use its legal powers to compel the economic community to favour certain values that would otherwise be destroyed by the pressure of economic forces. In other words, just as the state intervenes in economic matters to protect the weak through social legislation, so it must intervene to ensure the survival of cultural values in danger of being swamped by a flood of dollars.

This principle does not create problems when it is a question of intervening in favour of painting, music, films, the 'Canadian content' of radio or television, and other similar matters. But it may be useful to recall that even this kind of cultural investment is only achieved at some cost, not only economic, but also cultural. For it supposes that the state knows better than the citizen what is 'good' for him culturally, and such a hypothesis must always be applied with utmost prudence and consideration. More than any other, this kind of value is international and common to all men; in the long term, then, the state should ideally promote an open culture. There is also a danger that cultural protection, like its economic counterpart, would tend eventually to produce a weak, 'hot-house' culture.

Having made this point, I must now turn to the much more difficult question of cultural values directly related to ethnic background; or, to be more precise, the values for which the French language is the vehicle in Canada and in Quebec.

Let us start by recalling the facts: 28 per cent of all Canadians speak French as their mother tongue, and 58.4 per cent speak English. (The next largest percentage is German, with 3.0 per cent.) And of those whose mother tongue is French, 83 per cent live in the province of Quebec.

Because of this last fact, many people are tempted to consider Quebec the 'national state of French Canadians'. But, as I mentioned in the Introduction to this review, I believe that a definition of the state that is based essentially on ethnic attributes is philosophically erroneous and would inevitably lead to intolerance. Moreover, this definition seems to me strategically unacceptable. If Quebec defines itself constitutionally as the 'national state of French Canadians' on the grounds that it contains the majority of French-speaking Canadians, the same logic – the logic of numbers – would lead all the other provinces, and indeed the federal state itself, to define themselves (at least pragmatically) as the national states of English-speaking Canadians. French Canadians would then have gained nothing and have lost a great deal: they would be neither more numerous nor more cultured, and it is most improbable that even in Quebec they could succeed in noticeably reducing the use and influence of the language that dominates North American life so completely. On the other hand, French Canadians in all other provinces – and in Ottawa as well – would have to abandon for ever the hope of being anything but a minority among – or after – many others. No longer would there be any question of English and French Canadians possessing equal linguistic rights within Confederation.

The idea of a national state is thus unacceptable both in theory and in practice to any person who does not wish to see French Canadians withdraw from the Canadian scene and limit themselves exclusively to Quebec.

I have shown that the option of withdrawing from Canada, with its attendant constitutional reforms, is inadmissible from an economic or social point of view. I now wish to demonstrate that the same is true from a cultural point of view.

Let me make it very clear from the beginning that the issue at stake is not the mere survival of the French language and of the cultural values relating to it. Their survival is already assured. French is spoken in Quebec by an ever increasing number of persons. If one discounts the possibility of genocide or of some major cataclysm, it seems certain that in this part of America French will continue to be spoken regardless of what happens to the constitution.

The problem is therefore to stimulate our language and culture so that they are alive and vital, not just fossils from the past. We must realize that French will only have value to the extent that it is spoken by a progressive people. What makes for vitality and excellence in a language is the collective quality of the people speaking it. In short, the defence of the French language cannot be successful without accomplishments that make the defence worth while.

Given these facts, should French-speaking people concentrate their efforts on Quebec, or take the whole of Canada as their base? In my opinion, they should do both; and for the purpose they could find no better instrument than federalism.

If French Canadians are able to claim equal partnership with English Canadians, and if their culture is established on a coast-to-coast basis, it is mainly because of the balance of linguistic forces within the country. Historical origins are less important than people generally think, the proof being that neither Eskimo nor Indian dialects have any kind of privileged position. On the other hand, if there were six million people living in Canada whose mother tongue was Ukrainian, it is likely that this language would establish itself as forcefully as French. In terms of *realpolitik*, French and English are equal in Canada because each of these linguistic groups has the power to break the country. And this power cannot yet be claimed by the Iroquois, the Eskimos, or the Ukrainians.

This reality is sometimes expressed in Canada by the 'two nation' concept. In my opinion, this concept is dangerous in theory and groundless in fact. It would be disastrous if – at the very moment when French Canadians are at last awakening to the modern world and making their presence count in the country – their politicians were to be won over to anti-federalist policies. The consequence would be that French Canadians in Ottawa, Washington, and all capitals of the world would represent a country of five million inhabitants, and could expect to exert an influence in proportion to this population. On the other hand, if Quebec were part of a Canadian federation grouping two *linguistic* communities as I am advocating, French Canadians would be supported by a country of more than eighteen million inhabitants, with the second or third highest standard of living in the world, and with a degree of industrial maturity that promises to give it the most brilliant of futures.

This is what *could* happen. But on two conditions:

(a) First, French Canadians must really want it; that is to say, they must abandon their role of oppressed nation and decide to participate boldly and intelligently in the Canadian experience. It is wrong to say that Confederation has been a total failure for French Canadians; the truth is rather that they have never really tried to make a success of it. In Quebec, we tended to fall back upon a sterile, negative provincial autonomy; in Ottawa our frequent abstentions encouraged paternalistic centralization. If we lack the courage and the strength to launch out in Canadian politics, where at worst the odds are only two to one, how can we claim that we should be confronting the world, where the odds would at best be a hundred to one?

(b) The second condition is that the dice are not loaded against French Canadians in the 'Confederation game'. This means that if French Canadians abandon their concept of a national state, English Canadians must do the same. We must not find Toronto or Fredericton or, above all, Ottawa exalting the *English*-Canadian nation. On the contrary, when either the federal or provincial governments intervene in the economy to protect cultural values, they must apply the same rules of equity toward the French as Quebec has always applied toward the English segment of its population.

Just as the central state invests tax funds in such various enterprises as railways, radio and television, and the flag, in order to develop that non-commercial value, a specifically Canadian identity; and just as provincial governments are ready to patronize the arts in the hope of enriching the lives of their citizens; so these governments have the duty to intervene in favour of certain linguistic values whose preservation constitutes a *sine qua non* for the existence of Canada.

The Canadian community must invest, for the defence and better appreciation of the French language, as much time, energy, and money as are required to prevent the country from breaking up. Just as the federal government can use equalization grants to impose a just sharing among the provinces in economic matters, so the constitution must without delay extend these concepts of just sharing to the cultural field.

In practice, this can be achieved by a constitutional amendment granting French minorities in other provinces, as well as in Ottawa, the same rights and privileges as the English minority in Quebec. I shall have more to say on this point in the recommendations presented at the end of this article.

In the last analysis, those who clamour for French Canadians to be heard in the concert of nations should be glad that our community, despite its limited number of voices, has, in Canada, an enormous sound-box, and, in Ottawa, an excellent amplifier.

Precisely because they are such a tiny minority in North America, French Canadians must refuse to be enclosed within Quebec. I am opposed to what is called 'special status' for these two reasons, among others: first, I would not insult Quebeckers by maintaining that their province needs preferential treatment in order to prosper within Confederation; and second, I believe that in the long run this status can only tend to weaken values protected in this way against competition. Even more than technology, a culture makes progress through the exchange of ideas and through challenge. In our Canadian federal system, French-Canadian cultural values have a good balance of competition and protection from a fairly strong state.

But the fact remains that French-Canadian strength is concentrated in Quebec. And as I wrote in section II: 'The only considerable territory in the Western hemisphere in which French-speaking people are grouped in sufficient numbers and are sufficiently attached to French for this language to be a political society's first idiom is Quebec.'

It is clear that the way in which a nation is governed is part of its culture, in the widest sense of the word. The anatomy and physiology of political institutions constitute one of the most important characteristics of a nation, and serve to distinguish it from its neighbours.

On this basis as well, Canadian federalism is ideal. The federal system obliges Quebec's political culture to stand the test of competition at the federal level, while allowing Quebec to choose the form of government best suited to its needs at the provincial level. Under our present constitution, Quebec may modify its own constitution (except in those sections relating to the function of the Lieutenant-Governor) and create the political institutions its people desire. It is true that in the past the people did not really desire very much: witness the survival of the Legislative Council! But this was due to the people themselves, not to any lack of freedom.

Consequently, there is no need to evoke the notion of a national state to turn Quebec into a province 'different from the others'. In a great number of vital areas, and notably those that concern the development of particular cultural values, Quebec has full and complete sovereignty under the Canadian constitution.

I believe in provincial autonomy. I think it was important for French Canadians to have had a place of their own in which to learn the art of democratic and responsible government. But I hope that our people and their leaders will soon have developed sufficient political maturity to no longer feel the need of engaging in purely symbolic battles. Doubtless it is still important to resist the central government's paternalistic tendencies, or to block massive use of joint planning. But we can be mature and responsible without rejecting out of hand every form of administrative co-operation with Ottawa. After all, our human resources are not so unlimited that we can afford to systematically refuse help in carrying those burdens we share with the rest of the country. Nor are we short of work to do in Quebec.

First and foremost, on a strictly material level Quebec must assert itself as a society undergoing rapid economic development. Otherwise some of our workers will emigrate and lose their maternal language, while others will stay but will be ashamed of a language identified with an economically weak people. As we have seen, however, federalism is a system that can be extremely advantageous to Quebec on the purely material level.

On a spiritual level Quebec must assert itself as a province that fosters moral, intellectual, artistic, scientific, and technical values. When Quebec has produced or attracted a sufficient number of real philosophers, real scientists, real film directors, real economists, real experts in computer technology, and a large enough number of true statesmen, the 'French fact' will prosper in North America, and will have no need of the separatist crutch. These values on the whole are developed through education and through interaction with other cultures; from this point of view as well, our present constitutional institutions are satisfactory for the province since they give it complete jurisdiction over education. Consequently, it is up to Quebec to put its population in the forefront of progress in such matters. And as the majority of French Canadians live in this province, it is up to us to assure the triumph of French cultural values. (As for French minorities in other provinces, they can only have a future if Quebec establishes itself as a strong, progressive force *within* Confederation; if Quebec withdraws into itself or secedes, these French minorities will have approximately the same rights and the same influence as cultural groups of German origin in Canada.)

To sum up, the political culture of French Canadians will be what they decide to make it. As a group, they are free to direct provincial policies as they wish; and those who complain of a colonial mentality need to see to their own political re-education. Naturally, this education will still have to occur in a hostile world; but the world is not likely to be any less hostile simply because Quebec has revised its constitution. In the field of political culture, no less than in other fields, our institutions do not deserve to survive at all unless they can successfully survive external competition. And Canadian federalism is a closed field in which the French-Canadian province can seek to rival other provinces in political maturity and administrative efficiency, on a more or less equal footing. It is not at all certain that were Quebec to find itself isolated on the North American continent, it would find the game any easier, or its rules any more favourable.

The Elements of a Solution

In attempting to specify the goals to be sought by political communities, we have seen that for some purposes it is desirable that the state be limited in size, while for others a larger territory is definitely preferable. For example, in social or cultural matters, where needs often vary from region to region and where a citizen must feel that he can communicate directly with the source of power, there is an advantage in limiting the territorial jurisdiction of the state. In other areas, such as economic matters, it is much more efficient for the geographical unit to be considerably extended. In still other areas, such as peace or trade agreements, the trend will be toward international political groupings.

The ideal state would therefore seem to be one with different sizes for different purposes. And the ideal constitution for it would be one that gave the various parts, whatever their size, the powers they needed to attain their own particular objectives.

In practice, the federal state comes closest to this ideal. Its advantage is to be able to create a state that fits the dimensions of the problem; there are two levels of government, and the measure of sovereignty each one has is dictated by necessity.

For these reasons, the present writer opts for federalism. And, in particular, our own form of federalism seems to me the system best suited to French Canadians, for it allows them to take full advantage of the province, country, and continent in which they are destined to live. Under our present constitution, the federal government has jurisdiction over foreign affairs, defence, criminal law, navigation, railways, and postal and telegraph services, as well as over most areas required to establish a large and stable basis for sound economic development: international trade, customs, financial institutions, currency, and statistics. It is important to notice, however, that with the possible exceptions of marriage and broadcasting, federal jurisdiction covers only those areas having minimal cultural content. In these matters it is safe to assume that, except in times of crisis, linguistic factors will not be involved, and public opinion will be governed by criteria in which ethnic considerations play very little part.

Provincial governments, on the other hand, have jurisdiction over all matters of a purely local or private nature; over education, natural resources, property and civil rights, municipalities, roads, social and labour legislation, and the administration of justice; and more generally over all matters relating to cultural development or development of the land.

With regard to agriculture and immigration, the federal and provincial governments have concurrent jurisdiction. For all practical purposes, the powers of any government in matters concerning the levying and spending of taxes are limited only by the fact that politicians are ultimately answerable to their taxpayers.

This division of powers no doubt results in a constitution that is less than perfect, and in this respect the fundamental law of Canada is just like any other human institution. Industrialists or businessmen might prefer to see greater power vested in the central government; jurists or men of letters might wish that the provinces had more extensive jurisdiction. But any discussion between these two sides would soon make it clear that each was basing its argument solely on its own particular point of view. The former attach very little importance to purely social or cultural values; the latter often neglect to take account of the most elementary laws of technology or political economy.

If we look at all aspects of the problem, therefore, I think we shall find the general spirit of Canadian federalism quite acceptable. I should be very surprised if real statesmen, given the facts of the problem, arrived at the conclusion that our constitution needs drastic revision.

At the one extreme, I have said enough in sections III and IV to indicate why I believe Quebec must resist the temptation to isolate itself. Granted the province would then be safe from competition or other dangers, but it would also be quite safe from any form of progress!

At the other extreme, I would be opposed to either merging our province with Canada if the country were to become a unitary state, or allowing it to be absorbed by the United States. I cannot believe that a pan-Canadian or pan-American form of nationalism would be any less prone to chauvinism than the French-Canadian form.

In terms of personal or political maturity, a citizen of Quebec – especially if he is French-speaking – does not stand to gain anything from total assimilation within a continental or semi-continental macrocosm. On the contrary, faced as we are by the gigantic complexes forced upon us by our third industrial revolution – that of thermo-nuclear energy and computers – it is absolutely vital that we maintain psychological equilibrium as well as democratic responsibility by strengthening local ties and keeping regional governments on a human scale as much as possible.

To my mind, neither Canada's present constitution nor the country itself represents an eternal, unchangeable reality. For the last hundred years, however, this country and this constitution have allowed men to live in a state of freedom and prosperity which, though perhaps imperfect, has nevertheless rarely been matched in this world. And so I cannot help condemning as irresponsible those people who wish our nation to invest undetermined amounts of money, time, and energy in a constitutional adventure that they have been unable to define precisely but which would consist in more or less completely destroying Confederation to replace it with some vague form of sovereignty resulting in something like an independent Quebec, or associate states, or a 'special status', or a Canadian common market, or a confederation of ten states, or some entirely different scheme that could be dreamt up on the spur of the moment, when chaos at all levels had already become inevitable.

That the Canadian federal system must evolve is obvious. But it is evolving – radically – and has been for a hundred years without requiring any fundamental constitutional reform. In our history, periods of great decentralization have alternated with periods of intense centralization, according to economic and social circumstances, external pressures, and the strength or cunning of various politicians. A recent factor in politics, which is also a verifiable law in most industrial countries, is that the state must nowadays devote an ever increasing proportion of an ever increasing budget to purposes that in Canada are the constitutional responsibility of provincial governments. In other words, Canadian federalism is presently evolving in the direction of much greater decentralization.

Since the end of the Second World War, Canada has undergone profound transformation. The rapid growth of our school-age population has created hitherto unknown needs at all levels from elementary schools to universities and technical colleges. At the same time, the proliferation of services, combined with an unprecedented industrial growth, has resulted in an urban concentration that is increasing at perhaps the fastest rate in the world and thereby creating many new needs at the municipal level: the need for expansion of welfare services; public health programs for slum areas; control of air and water pollution; development of low-cost housing; extension of urban transport; provision of better facilities for police and fire departments, hydro, water supplies, electricity, and telephone; development of new recreational facilities such as parks, libraries, green belts; and many others.

At the same time as these new needs were being created by the evolution of external circumstances (and this includes the substantial rise in incomes throughout the country), another transformation was taking place in the minds of men ('the revolution of rising expectations'). In our province, this transformation expressed itself in terms of increased public action: the various social movements, especially labour unions and agricultural organizations, brought increasing pressure on the state to intervene in such fields as education, medical and hospital services, welfare, the development of natural resources, and social, agricultural, and industrial legislation.

Our present constitution places all these needs and services without exception under provincial jurisdiction. Already the situation has produced the following statistics (for the years 1953 to 1963): during this decade, provincial expenditure for goods and services rose from 3 per cent of the gross national product to 4 per cent; similar expenditures at the municipal level (which also falls within provincial jurisdiction) increased from 5 per cent to 8 per cent; while federal expenditure fell from 10 per cent to 7 per cent. This realignment of state expenditures has naturally brought about changes in the division of tax revenues between the central and provincial governments. So much so that from 1961 to 1963, for example, provincial income and corporate taxes rose from $655 million to $1,144 million, while federal taxes increased only by $114 million.[5] This trend towards decentralization is even more striking if one compares the gross general revenue for 1954 and 1962: at the federal level, it rose from $4.44 to $6.6 billion; at the provincial level, from $1.58 to $4.24 billion; at the municipal level, from $1.02 to $2.11 billion. In brief, then, the total revenue increased in those eight years by 48.6 per cent for the federal, as opposed to 144.2 per cent for the provinces (including municipalities).[6]

The phenomenon becomes even more obvious when one considers the total sum of government expenditure, excluding intergovernmental transfers. 'Final' expenditure at the federal level rose from $4.198 billion in 1954 to $6.550 billion in 1964, which represents an increase of 56 per cent. During the same period, provincial and municipal expenditure went from $2.652 to $8.065 billion, which is an increase of 204 per cent.[7]

Clearly, an enormous amount of power is being transferred to provincial governments by the natural operation of demographic, social, and economic forces, without the necessity of amending a single comma of the constitution. In the circumstances, it seems rather surprising that some Quebeckers should choose this very moment to clamour for a new constitution. Twenty years behind the times as usual, they are at last coming to terms with the reality described in the Rowell-Sirois *Report* of 1940, and preparing to charge the centralizing dragon just when it has stopped breathing fire.

The error, especially in terms of strategy, is glaring. For anyone who really wishes a return to greater centralization will be only too glad – despite some feigned reluctance – to reopen constitutional negotiations. No doubt a few legal gestures would be made in the direction of Quebec's particular characteristics, but in all probability, Quebec would receive less than it is

[5]The Bank of Nova Scotia, *Monthly Review*, September 1964.
[6]*House of Commons Debates*, February 22, 1965, p. 11, 565.
[7]*National Accounts, Income and Expenditure*, Table 37. Data revised in July 1965.

gradually obtaining through the force of circumstances. Meanwhile, the modifications we had thus introduced into our constitution might well alter our entire economy: it is a well-known fact that the slightest change in the letter of constitutional law would be sufficient to annul a hundred years of constitutional precedent and judicial decisions – most of which tended on the whole to favour the provinces. And therefore I must repeat: is this the time for such action, since both the letter and interpretation of the law are presently so favourable to provincial autonomy?

I must confess that, seen from this angle, the Fulton-Favreau formula for repatriation and constitutional revision does not fill me with wild excitement. I can certainly appreciate its many merits: it is no mean achievement to have finally found a compromise allowing our constitution to become a completely Canadian document, as well as a way of placing checks upon the arbitrary use of power permitted under the 1949 clause of Section 91(1) of the B.N.A. Act.

In my opinion, however, these merits are not so great, nor the reforms proposed so urgent, that they can entirely override the following considerations:

I consider it illogical that the Legislative Assembly should commit Quebec to an irrevocable constitutional move before it has even had time to hear the report of its Constitution Committee. It is not true, as some have claimed, that the Fulton-Favreau formula (where it relates to constitutional revision) merely expresses in precise terms an existing body of custom and accepted practices. Quite the contrary, the formula represents a radical innovation, and one that would be practically irreversible.

In the first place, the formula provides that the jurisdiction of Parliament may be extended in certain matters if this is supported by two-thirds of the provinces, representing 50 per cent of the population. Furthermore, the federal government and four provinces may proceed to delegate legislative powers relating to several fundamental matters between the two levels of government.

It is my fear that in the present situation, the two-thirds formula and the technique of delegating powers will serve on the whole to weaken the theory and application of federalism in Canada; my reasons follow.

We have seen that, within the framework of our present constitution, natural forces are now tending to strengthen provincial autonomy. If we wish this situation to continue, there is no need for the new amendment formula. Indeed, its effect, if any, would merely be to allow a certain number of provinces to increase the legislative jurisdiction of the central Parliament. The two-thirds amendment would permit Ottawa to invade certain legislative fields; and, although provinces would theoretically retain their right to act (according to the Honourable Mr. Favreau, *Le Devoir*, March 5, 1965), very few would in practice wish to duplicate federal action. In addition, the technique of delegation would mean that some groups of provinces abandoned their autonomy in certain matters while other groups abandoned it in other matters. This process would, of course, be reversible; but we must not delude ourselves that provinces would be particularly keen to re-establish abandoned ministries or government services.

Thus, the two new elements of the Fulton-Favreau formula would tend systematically to weaken the reality of federalism in most provinces, to break the opposition of the provinces as a whole to centralization, and to create divisions between them along lines that are not yet clear, but that would probably depend on the relative wealth or poverty of the provinces, their leaning toward right-wing or left-wing politics, or their ethnic composition.

It must be obvious that this kind of blurring of the boundary lines between the two levels of government could only be disastrous. Parliament's jurisdiction over Canadian citizens would vary depending on the area in which they lived; during federal elections, voters in provinces that had chosen to remain autonomous would be called on to judge the way in which the government had administered the public good in other provinces; Members of Parliament would have to take a stand and vote on laws not applicable to their own constituents; and taxpayers would have to finance the application of laws from which they themselves could derive no benefit.

Moreover, considering our present political climate, there is reason to fear that above all this kind of confusion would tend to isolate Quebec. Our province would in fact achieve a 'special status' constitutionally, but only at the cost of deriving least benefit from the situation. After other provinces had used the two-thirds and delegation formulas in order to modify the constitution for their own benefit and to suit their own needs, Quebec would be left with what remained of the B.N.A. Act. And then where would we be with our right to veto?

In brief, it seems almost certain that if the Fulton-Favreau formula were put into effect, Quebec would tend to evolve, at least in practice, toward the formation of a national state that would have every reason to disparage whatever remained of federalism. As I have already made clear, I prefer the federal system for economic, social, and psycho-cultural reasons. In my opinion, politicians or commentators on public affairs who encourage other provinces to establish interprovincial or federal-provincial relationships that differ from those used for Quebec, thereby fostering the isolation of this province, do a very great disservice to the country they claim to serve.

Our existing constitution, skilfully exploited, modified if need be (but in such a way that the division of power between the two government levels is the same in all provinces), creates a country in which Quebec may call upon the support of nine allies to protect provincial autonomy, and yet still feel that it struggles against even – not overwhelming – odds in its attempt to develop French culture in North America.

At the same time, this constitution prevents Quebec from becoming a closed society, which could only spell extinction for French Canadians living outside Quebec, and the development of a ghetto mentality for those living within it.

And this is the constitution our innovators want to change! Let them first come up with a system in which the rules of the game are really more favourable than the present one, and then we shall perhaps listen to them with greater interest.

Conclusion and Concrete Proposals

Essentially, a constitution is designed to last a long time. Legal authority derives entirely from it; and if it is binding only for a short period it is not binding at all. A citizen – to say nothing of a power group – will not feel obliged to respect laws or governments he considers unfavourable to him if he thinks that they can easily be replaced: if the rules of the constitutional game are to be changed in any case, why not right now? A country where this mentality is prevalent oscillates between revolution and dictatorship. France, once it had started down the slippery path, gave itself eighteen constitutions in 180 years.

I do not believe that Quebec is powerful enough to afford such waste. Our province must have a long period of constitutional stability if it is to establish a sound basis for the great economic, social, and cultural development it wishes to achieve. Furthermore, the rest of the country would refuse to negotiate seriously with us if it had reason to suspect that any constitutional concession granted to Quebec would merely lead to new and greater demands. This means that the 'revision of the Canadian constitution' mentioned in the mandate of the Legislative Assembly's Constitution Committee must be interpreted as taking place over several generations.

All the evidence seems to indicate that at the moment Quebec is not ready to say precisely what constitutional system of government it would like to have during the next half-century. When it comes to constitutional matters, political thinking in Quebec tends on the whole to be vague and self-contradictory. For example, our public opinion has long maintained that provincial unanimity should be required for any constitutional amendment; now that the idea of unanimity is embodied in the Fulton-Favreau formula, however, it is rejected as an obstacle to Quebec's 'special status'! One need only glance at the briefs presented to the Constitution Committee to realize just how various and fluctuating our public opinion can be. It is now fashionable to be for change – but for *what* change, exactly? That, alas, is where there is a complete lack of consensus.

To my mind, this only goes to prove that we must not meddle with the constitution just yet. The real danger is that all these constitutional debates will provide an escape valve for our energies, and useful diversionary tactics for those who fear the profound social reforms advocated by the progressive element in our province. Worse still, if we did succeed at this stage in imposing a new constitutional framework, we would merely fetter this progressive element instead of giving it greater freedom of action.

If it is indeed true that Quebec is on the march, let us first find out just where it wishes to go, and where it in fact *can* go. There will still be ample time for lawyers to incorporate both what is desirable and what is feasible into the law.

All these reasons, taken together, lead me to exercise great restraint in suggesting constitutional reforms; and they account for the fact that in recent years I have appeared as a supporter of the constitutional *status quo*. As I have demonstrated in previous sections, the constitution has very little to do with the state of economic, technical, and demographic inferiority in which the French Canadians of Quebec find themselves today. I am not in a frantic hurry to change the constitution, simply because I *am* in a frantic hurry to change reality. And I refuse to give the ruling classes the chance of postponing the solving of *real* problems until after the constitution has been revised. We have seen only too often how, in the past, discussions centring on ideas such as the form of the state, nationhood, provincial autonomy, and independence have served to conceal the impotence of the ruling classes when faced with the profound transformation of our society by the industrial revolution. All I ask of our present ruling classes is that they stop being so preoccupied with the hypothetical powers an independent Quebec might have, and start using the powers the real Quebec does have a bit more often and a bit more wisely.

In the economic field, it is infinitely less important to dream up new constitutional phrasing that would allow Quebec to recoup a larger percentage of federal taxes (this is already happening under our present constitution) than it is to move our province to the forefront of industrial progress (the result of which would be to increase substantially the very basis of provincial taxation).

Similarly, in the social and cultural fields, it is infinitely less important for Quebec to modify the constitution so as to acquire an international judicial identity, than to invest immense energy in agrarian reform and better urban planning, and concentrate all the strength it can muster upon educational reforms.

It should not be concluded from what I am saying that I am less aware than others of imperfections in the B.N.A. Act and the rules of federalism embodied in it. There is nothing easier than proposing constitutional reforms, and I could very easily outline several points that would some day have to be taken into account by a new constitution. For example:

(a) A Bill of Rights could be incorporated into the constitution, to limit the powers that legal authorities have over human rights in Canada. In addition to protecting traditional political and social rights, such a bill would specifically put the

French and English languages on an equal basis before the law.

(b) The protection of basic rights having thus been ensured, there would be no danger in reducing the central government's predominance in certain areas (for example, by abolishing the right of reservation and disallowance); at the same time, this would have the advantage of getting rid of some of the constitution's imperial phraseology.

(c) The organic law relating to the central government could be revised in order to give it a more authentically federal character. In particular, conflicts in jurisdiction between federal and provincial levels could be judged by an independent body deriving its authority directly from the constitution. The Senate could also be reformed so that it represented the provinces more directly. Far from diminishing the authority of Parliament, such a measure would increase provincial confidence in the legislation that emanates from Ottawa (for example, in matters of tariffs or macro-economic policy).

These points are certainly important, and no doubt Canadians will have to face them some day – perhaps following the repatriation of the constitution. But I refuse to propose them formally at the moment, for the reasons I have already given, which I would like to summarize briefly once again:

Natural forces are presently favouring provincial autonomy. It is the centralizers who should be pressing for constitutional changes. If Quebec negotiators were cannier, they would affect supreme indifference, saying blandly: 'Oh, the constitution isn't all that bad after all. . . . We are so busy trying to change the social and economic *status quo* that we simply haven't time for constitutional reforms just at the moment. . . . But if you are really keen about it, of course we are prepared to discuss revisions with you – say in a few months' time, or perhaps next year?'

Meanwhile, decentralization would have continued apace, the strong provinces would have established competent administrations which would be difficult to dislodge, and Quebec would have found several allies in its struggle for an improved federal system. Better still, our progress in the province would have raised the prestige of Canada's entire French-speaking population.

And so when constitutional negotiations finally began – at the instigation of other provinces! – Quebec could concentrate all its bargaining power on the most crucial point, which I have called in section V 'a very small constitutional modification'. In conclusion I should like to make a few comments on this modification.

It is obvious that most of Canada's constitutional crises, like the present one, arise from ethnic problems, and more precisely from the question of the rights pertaining to the French language. As I have said earlier (in section III), the French language will be able to express progressive values only if North Americans who speak it are themselves in the forefront of progress, that is to say if they compete on an equal basis with English-speaking Canadians.

But the competition *must* be on an equal basis. Otherwise, the French population is in danger of becoming paralysed by an excess of defensive mechanisms. We shall develop the mentality of a beleaguered people, withdrawing into Quebec the better to sustain the siege. In other words, French Canadians may be forced by *English*-Canadian nationalism to push Quebec nearer to a national state and sooner or later to independence.

On this matter as on many others, the Fathers of Confederation showed great wisdom. Although they may have suspected that French Canadians would *in fact* always remain a linguistic minority, it seems that they wished to avoid making them feel a minority as far as *rights* were concerned. To put it in another way, while recognizing that French Canadians might always feel more at home in Quebec, they attempted to prevent the law from fostering in them a sense of inferiority or from giving them any excuse to feel like aliens in other parts of Canada.

According to Section 92 of the constitution, education became the responsibility of the provinces, as French Canadians had wished. The first paragraph, however, made it unconstitutional for provinces to interfere with confessional schools; and it is mainly through these, as is well known, that French Canadians develop and transmit their particular cultural values. Moreover, the last two paragraphs gave the central government power to rectify infringements upon 'any right or privilege', including linguistic rights, of the (religious) group that includes almost all French Canadians.

Section 133 gave the French language official status for the exercise of the following political rights:

(a) At the federal level, the two languages were placed on

an absolutely equal basis for all legislative as well as judicial functions. There was no mention of executive functions, but very likely this was due partly to the fact that in 1867 there was a much smaller number of people involved in the military and civil services, and partly to the fact that the cabinet was not defined by the constitution, but by custom; and in practice custom has gradually ensured that the number of French Canadians in the cabinet is more or less proportionate to their population. In so far as federal political institutions are concerned, then, the intention seems to have been to place English and French on an equal basis throughout Canada, and consequently to give the central government a genuinely bilingual character.

(b) In so far as provincial political institutions are concerned, the French language obtained equal rights only in those provinces where there was a considerable number of French Canadians. In practice, this meant Quebec; but the future was left open – for, according to Section 92, paragraph 1, each province could give the French language a position corresponding to the size of the French-Canadian population in that province. The spirit in which this was intended is evident if one considers that three years later, when the central government created Manitoba, whose population contained a large percentage of French-speaking people, French was placed on a par with English in this province.[8]

In substance, then, the Canadian constitution created a country where French Canadians could compete on an equal basis with English Canadians; both groups were invited to consider the whole of Canada their country and field of endeavour.

Unfortunately, for reasons that I cannot go into here, but that on the whole reflect less credit on English than on French Canadians, the rules of the 'constitutional game' were not always upheld. In the matter of education, as well as political rights, the safeguards so dear to French Canadians were nearly always disregarded throughout the country, so that they came to believe themselves secure only in Quebec.

Worse still, in those areas not specifically covered by the constitution, the English-speaking majority used its size and

[8]The *Manitoba Act*, Section 23. See also Section 22, relating to education.

wealth to impose a set of social rules humiliating to French Canadians. In the federal civil service, for example, and even more so in the Canadian armed forces, a French Canadian started off with an enormous handicap – if indeed he managed to start at all. This was true also in finance, business, and at all levels of industry. And that is how English became the working language, even in Quebec, and at all levels from foreman to bank president.

These social 'rules of the game' do not lie within the mandate of the Constitution Committee. But a complete transformation of these rules is most urgently needed. And I have already described, especially in section IV, the conditions that are necessary if French Canadians are to revise these rules so that they operate in their favour.

The Constitution Committee, however, must propose amendments to the constitutional rules. The constitution must be so worded that any French-speaking community, anywhere in Canada, can fully enjoy its linguistic rights. In practice, this means that for the purpose of education, wherever there is a sufficient number of French-speaking people to form a school (or a university), these people must have the same rights as English Canadians in the matter of taxes, subsidies, and legislation on education. Of course, the concepts of 'sufficient number' and 'equal rights' will often have to be defined judicially or administratively; but both judges and administrators have as a guide the fact that these concepts have been applied for the past hundred years in remote areas of Quebec wherever there lived a 'sufficient number' of English-speaking Canadians.

(a) At the federal level, the two languages must have absolute equality. With regard to legislative and judicial functions, this is already theoretically the case, according to Section 133 of the constitution; but the theory must be completely incorporated into actual practice so that, for example, any law or ruling is invalid if the English and French texts are not published side by side. Like the United States, we must move beyond 'separate but equal' to 'complete integration'.

With regard to the executive functions, innovation is clearly required. Of course, it would be difficult to test the bilingualism of ministers of the Crown, and no doubt the whole thing will rest upon which men the voters decide to elect. (But it might also be decided by the fact that unilingual ministers would become frustrated when decisions were sometimes taken in French, and sometimes in English within the cabinet.) Everywhere else, and notably in the civil service and the armed forces, the two languages must be on a basis of absolute equality. This concept of equality must also be put into effect by management and by the courts. A simple, fair way of doing this might be to institute reciprocal rules: for example, if an infantry corporal or a minor Post Office official is exempted from knowing French because his functions bring him into contact with only a small percentage of French-speaking people, the same rule should apply to English when English-speaking people constitute the same small percentage. Or, to take another example, if a knowledge of English is required in the higher echelons of the civil service, then the same should be true of French. It is obvious that if such rules were applied overnight, they would result in a great many injustices and might indeed bring the state machinery grinding to a halt. But the introduction of such reforms must nevertheless be carried out according to a fixed schedule set by law (we could take the example of the Supreme Court of the United States which, in matters of racial integration, bases its decisions on the spirit, the general tendency, and to some extent upon the chronological intentions of the legislation brought before it).

(b) At the provincial level, similar reciprocal rules must be applied. In principle, the language of the majority will be the only official one. However, when a province contains a French or English minority larger than, say, 15 per cent, or half a million inhabitants, legislative and judicial functions must be exercised in such a way that the two languages are given absolute equality. It is very doubtful whether the same rule could be applied to the executive function; regardless of the size of its minorities, a province will therefore be able to remain unilingual on this point, provided of course that any citizen has the right to an English-French interpreter in his dealings with officials. (In practice, this could lead to the establishment of a bilingual civil service in those provinces where there was a sufficiently large and concentrated French or English minority.)

Such reforms must certainly be incorporated into constitutional law. It would not be very realistic to rely upon good will or purely political action. For example, in a province containing a greater number of Canadians of Ukrainian origin than of French origin, it would be rash to think that an elected provincial legislature would risk giving French schools privileges that Ukrainian schools did not have. Nor is it wise to rely entirely upon federal intervention: the ill-fated 'remedial legislation' of 1896, relating to Manitoba schools, taught us to be cautious on this score.

The reforms I am proposing must therefore be written into the constitution itself, and must be irrevocably binding upon both the federal and provincial governments. As I suggested earlier, the guarantees contained in Sections 93 and 133 of the constitution must be extended and incorporated into a clear, imperative text which could be worded more or less along these lines: 'Any law passed by the Parliament of Canada and relating to its executive, legislative, and judicial functions, as well as any law on matters of education passed by a provincial Legislature, or any constitutional text, will be invalid if it does not place the English and French languages on a basis of absolute judicial equality.' And also: 'In any province where there is a French or English minority exceeding 15 per cent or one-half million inhabitants, no law relating to legislative or judicial functions will be valid if it does not place the English and French languages on a basis of absolute judicial equality; however, a number will not be considered to exceed 15 per cent or one-half million inhabitants, unless it has been so established at two successive decennial censuses.' And lastly: 'It will be the right of every citizen to have an English-French interpreter in his dealings with any level of authority either in the central or the provincial governments.'

Those are more or less the comments I wished to make about the constitution. The reforms I am proposing may seem quite modest in comparison with the vast upheaval favoured by so many Quebeckers these days; but this is because I want to keep to what I consider to be the absolute essential. This essential, however modest, implies an immense transformation of attitudes and of what I have called the social rules of the game. If this is achieved, sterile chauvinism will disappear from our Canadian way of life, and other useful constitutional reforms will follow suit without too much difficulty. If, on the other hand, the essential is not achieved, there is really no point in carrying the discussion any further; for this will mean that Canada will continue to be swept periodically by the storms of ethnic dispute, and will gradually become a spiritually sterile land, from which both peace and greatness have been banished.

NOTE: This essay was written during February, March, and April of 1965, while I was at the Institut de Recherche en Droit Public at the University of Montreal. It was meant as a working document for some private organizations that wanted to submit a brief to the Constitution Committee of the Quebec Legislative Assembly. As this essay has already been widely circulated, I have decided to publish it under my name. It goes without saying that my opinions are not necessarily those of the Institut de Recherche en Droit Public or the private organizations I have mentioned above.

Translated from the French by Joanne L'Heureux.

A Constitutional Declaration of Rights

(An address to the Canadian Bar Association, Sept. 4, 1967)

OF ALL the problems that Canadian public opinion is currently concerned with, the one that is most frequently debated, the one that brings forth the strongest expressions of view, is that of constitutional reform.

Although the subject is one of serious proportion, it is nevertheless one on which I should like to express some thoughts to you. There is no more appropriate forum, no place where this topic can be treated with more objectivity and serenity, than that composed of the members of the Canadian legal profession.

Your Association – I should say *our* Association, because you have done me the great honour of making me your honorary president – is a meeting place for those whose profession it is to examine the law and to ponder its application. We must recognize that the constitution is the country's fundamental law, the law on which our entire judicial system is based. If the constitution of a country collapses, or if its authority is seriously challenged, ordinary law loses its power to command and society itself is propelled toward anarchy.

For this reason men who are free – and who are anxious to remain so – do not lightly undermine the constitutional framework of a democratic country. They only approach it 'with fear and trembling'. For this reason, among others, I have personally resisted what, if it has not become a mania, might be termed a fashion of constitutional iconoclasm. At a time when every last trooper believed he had a new constitution in his bags, I quite willingly classed myself among those who began by asking questions: asking what new society would be replacing the old; asking whether the new legal norms would ensure the same degree of peace, of liberty, and of prosperity as the old. While I wished to reflect upon the matter, it was not the possibility of change itself that displeased me. On the contrary, I have always been convinced that we, men of the law, should not only advocate respect for the constitution, but also encourage its development.

In a submission presented to the Tremblay Commission in 1955, I wrote:

> The Province [of Quebec] could well declare herself ready to accept the incorporation of a declaration of human rights in the constitution on the condition that the rights of disallowance and reservation be done away with. The Province could suggest a precise plan for repatriating the Canadian constitution, including in it a method of amendment, on the condition that the Senate be turned into a body more federalist and less unitary and on condition that the organization of the Supreme Court be made to depend directly on the Canadian constitution rather than solely on federal law.

Six years later, in *Social Purpose for Canada*, I again took up the same kind of propositions. And ten years later, at the beginning of 1965, in a paper prepared for eventual presentation to the Committee of the Quebec Legislature set up to examine the constitution, I made similar suggestions, adding:

> I do not accord an absolute and eternal value to the political structures or the constitutional forms of states. . . . With the exception of a certain number of basic principles that must be safeguarded, such as liberty and democracy, the rest ought to be adapted to the circumstances of history, to traditions, to geography, to cultures and to civilizations.

As Thomas Jefferson said about the Constitution of the United States: 'Nothing then is unchangeable but the inherent and unalienable rights of man.'

Nevertheless, I have always wished to assure myself that the changes would be for the best and not for the worst. It has become commonplace to repeat that constitutions are made for men and not men for constitutions. However, one tends to forget that constitutions must also be made *by* men and not by force of brutal circumstance or blind disorder. In this area, more than any other, one must know where a policy leads.

And this is what prompts me to say a few words about the policy of the present Liberal government in constitutional matters.

You will recall that over a year ago the Prime Minister informed the House of Commons that a special committee of senior federal officials had been formed to examine and to prepare studies on particular constitutional questions. This work had progressed to the point where, shortly after becoming Minister of Justice, I felt that a broader and more comprehensive review could be undertaken by these officials working jointly with persons outside the public service. Accordingly, I appointed Mr. Carl Goldenberg, Q.C., Special Counsel on the Constitution and have attached to his office, as advisers, some of the most eminent constitutional authorities in the country. They are now examining a variety of constitutional matters; for example, the constitutional problems arising from various federal-provincial arrangements and our system of final adjudication, particularly as it relates to the constitutional field. Studies on other major constitutional issues, such as treaty-making powers and related international matters, are very well advanced. Moreover, the government is awaiting the report of the Royal Commission on Bilingualism and Biculturalism which will undoubtedly make important recommendations calling for action in many areas within, or bordering upon, the constitution.

We have not confined our activities in the constitutional field to these studies. While this work has been going on, ministers and officials have been looking for the best basis on which to begin a dialogue on constitutional reform between the federal government and the provincial governments. We have reached the conclusion that the basis most likely to find a wide degree of acceptance, and one that is in itself a matter calling for urgent attention, is a constitutional Bill of Rights – a Bill that would guarantee the fundamental freedoms of the citizen from interference, whether federal or provincial, and that would have a high degree of permanence in that neither Parliament nor the Legislatures would be able to modify its terms by the ordinary legislative process.

As lawyers, you will appreciate that the adoption of a constitutional Bill of Rights is intimately related to the whole question of constitutional reform. Essentially, we will be testing – and, hopefully, establishing – the unity of Canada. If we reach agreement on the fundamental rights of the citizen, on their definition and protection in all parts of Canada, we shall have taken a major first step toward basic constitutional reform.

At a meeting with the provincial premiers held in July of this year, the Prime Minister stated that he would issue an invitation to them to attend a conference to discuss the possibility of adopting a constitutional Bill of Rights binding on both the federal and the provincial governments. This invitation has been issued, and it is hoped that a conference can be held early in 1968.

Much useful work has already been done in the field of civil rights in Canada, particularly in connection with the enactment of the Canadian Bill of Rights in 1960. We are now aiming at a new Bill which will be broader in scope and will be firmly entrenched in the constitution. The Canadian Bill of Rights sets out the legal rights of the citizen in respect of life, liberty, and the security of the person, and such basic political rights as freedom of speech and of the press, freedom of religion, and freedom of assembly. There are also various provincial statutes affording protection against discrimination and invasions of human rights. All of these measures are, however, statutory in character and they do not preclude future encroachments on these rights by Parliament or the Legislatures. They may be amended in the same way as any other statute. Moreover, they do not cover certain rights which are of special concern to a country like Canada, founded on two distinct linguistic groups.

Accordingly, we envision a Bill of Rights that will be broader in scope than the existing legislation. We all agree on the familiar basic rights – freedom of belief and expression, freedom of association, the right to a fair trial and to fair legal procedures generally. We would also expect a guarantee against discrimination on the basis of race, religion, sex, ethnic or national origin. These are the rights commonly protected by bills of rights. They are basic for any society of free men.

But there are rights of special importance to Canada arising, as I have said, from the fact that this country is founded on two distinct linguistic groups. While language is the basic instrument for preserving and developing the cultural integrity of a people, the language provisions of the British North America Act are very limited. I believe that we require a broader definition and more extensive guarantees in the matter of recognition of the two official languages. The right to learn and to use either of the two official languages should be recognized. Without this, we cannot assure every Canadian of an equal opportunity to participate in the political, cultural, economic, and social life of this country. I venture to say that, if we are able to reach agreement on this vital aspect of the over-all problem, we will have found a solution to a basic issue facing Canada today. A constitutional change recognizing broader rights with respect to the two official languages would add a new dimension to Confederation.

If we agree on the general content of a constitutional Bill of Rights, a number of important questions will remain to be resolved. These will be important for everyone but, from a technical point of view, they will be of special concern to those who, like ourselves, are trained in the law. Should the rights be declared generally, or defined precisely with exceptions clearly specified? For example, if we guarantee freedom of speech without qualification, will this invalidate some of our laws which deal with obscenity, sedition, defamation, or film censorship? Is freedom of religion compatible with compulsory Sunday-closing legislation? What of a constitutional guarantee of 'due process of law'? In the United States, this phrase has, in the past, created many problems because of its vagueness. At times, the courts have construed it so broadly as to invalidate some social legislation which we would now accept as essential. Should we avoid the possibility of such an interpretation of 'due process' in Canada by using a more precise term to guarantee the rule of law? What of the right to counsel? Should this 'right' impose a duty on the government to provide counsel for those who cannot afford it? If we recognize the right of every person to use and to be educated in either of the two official languages, should we limit the exercise of this right to places where there is a con-centration of one or the other language group?

These are some of the questions which will arise as we try to develop a constitutional Bill of Rights. I mention them here, not because I expect immediate answers, but to illustrate the complexities involved in any basic constitutional reform. I hope that the Canadian Bar Association will study some of these problems and in due course give us the benefit of its advice, in the light of its long-standing interest in the protection of human rights.

I envision a Bill of Rights that will not only be broader in scope than the existing legislation but will also be firmly entrenched constitutionally. The Canadian Bill of Rights of 1960 is a statute binding only at the federal level of government. Even at that level, the courts have shown some reluctance to interpret it as having an overriding effect. Also, it obviously does not apply to the exercise of provincial powers. Moreover, the effect of most existing human rights legislation in Canada is rendered uncertain by the present division of legislative powers. It is not clear to what extent Parliament or the Legislatures can validly act in the protection of human rights. We will face this problem as long as we try to protect human rights by ordinary legislation. It is for these reasons that I believe the time has come to place the necessary safeguards in the constitution.

I am thinking of a Bill of Rights that will be so designed as to limit the exercise of all governmental power, federal and provincial. It will not involve any gain by one jurisdiction at the expense of the other. There would be no transfer of powers from the federal Parliament to the provincial Legislatures, or from the provincial Legislatures to the federal Parliament. Instead, the power of both the federal government and the provincial governments would be restrained in favour of the Canadian citizen who would, in consequence, be better protected in the exercise of his fundamental rights and freedoms.

I have already said that agreement on a process whereby a Bill of Rights would be entrenched in the constitution will raise other basic constitutional issues. First, what procedure is to be followed in amending the constitution? How is the Bill to be entrenched? Shall we ask the Parliament at Westminster to enact the necessary changes in the British North America Act? Or will we finally agree on a formula for amending our constitution in Canada? It is inevitable that discussion of an entrenched Bill of Rights will lead to a renewed attempt to agree upon an amending formula – something we have failed to achieve after years of effort. I can think of no better occasion for seeking to find a solution to the problem of developing a Canadian constitution in Canada – of finally 'patriating' our constitution – than when we have reached agreement on constitutional protection of the basic rights of the citizen.

We shall also face other constitutional issues. A constitutional Bill of Rights would modify even further the concept of parliamentary sovereignty in Canada. Once fundamental rights are guaranteed, they will be beyond the reach of government at all levels. This will confer new and very important responsibilities on the courts, because it will be up to the courts to interpret the Bill of Rights, to decide how much scope should be given to the protected rights and to what extent the power of government should be curtailed. This will inevitably bring us to consideration of the system of final adjudication in the constitutional field by the Supreme Court of Canada, as the latter is presently constituted.

A Bill of Rights entrenched by an amending formula that 'brings home' the constitution, and applied throughout Canada by our supreme constitutional tribunal, will open the door to further constitutional reform. For example, will not the powers of reservation and disallowance of provincial legislation lose their meaning once a Bill of Rights has been entrenched in the constitution? Are there not other antiquated features of the British North America Act which might well be reconsidered at that time?

You will now see why I said, at the outset, that the adoption of a constitutional Bill of Rights opens the door wide to necessary constitutional change. I believe that, once we have agreed on a Bill of Rights, an amending formula, and a system of final adjudication, little would stand in the way of a general constitutional conference to discuss such other particular changes as may be necessary to adapt our constitution to the requirements of our day. We look forward to such discussions. Our policy is flexible enough to allow for consideration of any reasonable initiative or proposal.

From the foregoing remarks, it should be apparent that the government's policy in regard to the constitution has been consistent and progressive throughout. It has been, and remains, a policy of *controlled development*, one which does not fear change. Indeed, our policy even fosters change, provided that it maintains the integrity of Canada. Our aim is the maintenance of a strong federal government and strong provincial governments. That is what federalism means.

That, then, Mr. Chairman, is more or less what I wanted to say on the question of constitutional amendment.

It is certainly correct to infer that during a certain period the federal government has not manifested much enthusiasm for public discussion of the Canadian constitution. We realized that a federal system was a delicate machine, easier to throw out of kilter than to start off again; and, in the capacity of the central government, we felt that we had a great responsibility for the maintenance of harmony among so many culturally and geographically distinct regions. Also, we wished to give the country time to reflect upon and to adjust to the new relationship of political, cultural, social, and economic forces that have been developing in the dawn of our second century.

I believe that this course was wise. Several governments have set up committees charged with preparing for constitutional discussion. Politicians and public opinion have had ample opportunity to measure the importance of the problem and the difficulties inherent in its solution. The time is ripe.

The federal government declares itself ready to discuss any constitutional changes that are proposed.

As I said in Parliament on the twenty-third of June last, when asked about certain constitutional amendments: 'I have not received any representations asking for such an amendment, Mr. Speaker. If I do, I shall look carefully into them.'

We are not going to be caught in a posture of immobility. But we do desire that any changes shall take place in an orderly way and under the guidance of governments responsible to the people. That is why the federal government has taken the initiative with concrete propositions. (Besides, one must not forget that for one hundred years, when it came to the question of modifying the text of our constitution, it has almost always been the federal government that has taken the initiative.) We have not supported vague and contradictory formulas designed to change everything all at once without really knowing what would follow. Quite simply, we propose that the discussion be begun with essentials: precise and limited they may be, but all the rest can follow.

If the Fulton-Favreau formula for the amendment and repatriation of the constitution has failed, it is probably because what was sought was unanimous agreement on the technical details rather than on the substance. Today, we are beginning with the substance. We say to all Canadians, from all provinces: let us first agree on the basic freedoms, on the fundamental rights that we wish to guarantee. After that, we will deal with the mechanism.

The challenge, Mr. Chairman, is an imposing one. Are there any higher bidders?

This article is the text of an address delivered
to the 49th Annual Meeting of the
Canadian Bar Association in Quebec City on
September 4, 1967.

Part Two

De libro, tributo…
et quibusdam aliis

In DECEMBER 1952, deploring our lack of political consciousness, I wrote: 'It seems to us that emotional bias rather than
serious reflection prevails in discussions of, for example, the
role of law or the function of a national fiscal policy.'[1]

A year later, a law relating to that very matter – fiscal policy
– proved me right, more so than I wanted to be: since January
15, 1954, when Mr. Duplessis announced his legislation to
'ensure that the Province has the revenue necessary for its
development', the political atmosphere in Canada has been
emotionally charged to an extent that is completely excessive.
So-called 'national' societies rose to the defence of this newest
'last rampart of our language, laws, and rights'. Public opinion
was mobilized in other provinces against Quebec's step towards
secession(!). Hysteria on an international scale was followed
by threats to move the headquarters of I.C.A.O. elsewhere. In
Toronto, professors professed that Quebec had no right to adopt
such legislation. In Quebec, legal experts (*quaere*) supported
the untenable theory that the provinces have an exclusive right
to the field of direct taxation.

In the midst of this hullabaloo appeared a perfectly serene
and remarkably intelligent book on Canadian federalism.[2]
Naturally, our fantastic élite lost no time in impressing upon

[1]*Cité Libre*, No. 6, p. 56.
[2]Maurice Lamontagne, *Le fédéralisme canadien: évolution et problèmes*,
  Laval University Press, 1954.

the author that he had been unbearably pretentious to mention ideas in an argument about race. Condemned, before it had even been written, by the man who remains (in spite of all) our most lucid journalist,[3] disowned by the then rector of Laval University,[4] misunderstood yet opposed by a professor of History at the University of Montreal,[5] this work received the only fate it could expect at the hands of our official intelligentsia.

No one in Quebec should be surprised at these latest symptoms of a disease so often diagnosed: it goes without saying that the top levels of our society suffer from paralysing inertia. But I am not convinced that the disease is incurable, and I therefore propose to examine four different aspects of our present fiscal muddle.

Mr. Lamontagne's Book

Mr. Lamontagne is the first to publish a book in French surveying Canadian federalism from the standpoint of modern economics, and this approach is what gives his work its great value.

There are, of course, other elements in the book: some good, some bad, some indifferent. For although it is well planned, the second half often lacks balance and bears the mark of excessive haste. For example, the long discussion of labour-management relations (pp. 205–14), although of the greatest interest, is

[3] *Le Devoir*, editorial page, in the early part of the year.

[4] According to a Canadian Press report of June 2, 1954, Mgr. Ferdinand Vandry felt himself obliged to dissociate Laval University from ideas which (according to him) 'tend to sacrifice the essential freedom of the province'. I find this rather amusing, since in their concern for the freedom of provinces, our magnificent rectors are forced to sacrifice freedom of thought. For, as the report continues, 'the universities of Quebec have been heavily subsidized through provincial taxation'.

[5] A talk by Michel Brunet on Radio-Canada, June 11, 1954, and reprinted in *Le Devoir* and *Notre Temps*. It is evident that Mr. Brunet has not understood Mr. Lamontagne's economic propositions when he states that 'Mr. Lamontagne contradicts himself constantly' and supports this serious accusation with a single example, which proves nothing but Mr. Brunet's complete incompetence in the matter of public finance. Mr. Brunet himself must feel that he is on shaky ground, since he hastens to add: 'the most serious charge one could make against Mr. Lamontagne is that he has forgotten he is a French Canadian from Quebec.' It is inconceivable that a true scholar should use such means to discredit another scholar's work. And this is what makes me think that Professor Brunet, whom I do not have the honour of knowing, must, in his courses, occasionally mingle fancy with fact.

irrelevant to the problem of federalism. On the other hand, the little lecture on 'collective security and defence costs' (pp. 157–60) is nothing but a collection of clichés on neutralism, the cold war, and communism; like most official arguments, these are rather unsatisfactory and only tend to prove what the author elsewhere denies (p. 252): that federal expenditures are far more difficult to reduce than provincial expenditures. As examples of elements that are entirely indifferent, I would gladly cite those little excursions into statistics and marginalia (pp. 113, 117) by which many may be misled but only the naïve will be impressed.

It is clear that the author had many valuable things to say. But circumstances forced him to put them all hastily into one book; and that is why one finds in it so many half-developed and irrelevant facts. Because of this, I cannot help regretting that Mr. Lamontagne did not publish more, although I do not blame him for it: he was living in a province where professors have, alas, neither the right nor the means to think out loud. Such is the bondage in which intellectuals are held that the unfortunate rector of Laval believed himself 'obliged [sic] to declare that his university took no responsibility for the personal opinions' of a man who was no longer in any way under its jurisdiction. Why did he not fire the former professor *retro-actively* as well? We would then have seen the true face of the 'Unique Chancelier' who has control, when all is said and done, over every university[6] in the province.

One major lesson that emerges from Mr. Lamontagne's argument is that 'there is no simple solution which is valid for all times.' (p. ix) Each new era must set up its own workable economic policies – that is, policies that meet the requirements of the present reality. And the author himself is truly creative when he relates facts to economic theory. This is what makes the reading of his historical chapters so lively and instructive and permits him to make such brilliant excursions into the field of international trade. And this is also what lets him give original and penetrating views on a great variety of subjects,

[6]Even McGill's Board of Governors is beginning to feel the yoke; it was quite a revelation to them when they received their share of university grants, a sum of several million dollars, in the form of a cheque made out, not to the Chancellor, nor to the Principal, nor to the Board of Governors, nor to the Treasurer, but to a member of the Union Nationale!

from technological and seasonal unemployment to the incidence in Canada of direct and indirect taxation, the control of monopolies and combines, the law against margarine, the civil service, social security, and so on.

All this is discussed in terms of the Canadian federal system, and results in an irrefutable demonstration of the absolute necessity for intergovernmental co-operation. To co-operate is not to give in, and press reports slanderously distorted the author's ideas when they reported him as saying that Quebec had lost the struggle for autonomy. Quite the contrary, Mr. Lamontagne indicates several areas in which the provinces, by themselves or with the help of the federal government, could have greater autonomy: the development of natural resources, the extension of public works, and the struggle against technological unemployment, for example. He goes so far as to recommend a constitutional amendment to give provinces 'the same powers as the federal government in the field of sales taxes'. (p. 259) As for the foremost problem of fiscal co-operation, he demonstrates (p. 270) – no doubt with greater virtuosity than realism – that the whole system of fiscal agreements could disappear without anyone being the worse off for it. *What more do autonomists want?*

I find Mr. Lamontagne lacking in realism on this point, simply because he suggests replacing fiscal agreements by subsidies that would be determined unilaterally by the federal government; this solution, he claims (p. 270) 'would avoid . . . long discussions and the dissensions which these tend to create'. Now, quite apart from the fact that the economic efficiency of this formula would depend on the provinces' perfect submission to federal coercion (a risky assumption!) it seems to me rather strange that an author who has so knowledgeably established the absolute necessity for federal-provincial co-operation and declared that 'the new orientation of the Canadian federation is . . . irreversible' (p. 284) should come up, at the end of his book, with a solution to the most crucial problem that 'avoids discussion' between governments, forgets all about co-operation, and is in the most outdated of 'Canadian federal traditions'. According to this theory, the federal government, which 'must be entitled to use *all* means of taxation' (p. 192) and which must 'have access to *all* levels of expenditure' (p. 197), 'could simply advise the provinces that it was offering them an un-

conditional annual subsidy' (p. 270), and the whole fiscal
question would be settled! 'Should any of the provinces manifest
ill will, thereby threatening the national program of economic
stability, the central government could always take measures
against it. . . .' (p. 271)

No thank you, this is too much like arbitrary power for my
taste. I can understand perfectly well that Mr. Lamontagne
should be out of all patience with the crass ignorance so characteristic both of Quebec's economic policies and of the political
opinion that produces them; I can even admire the fact that in
spite of this he managed to write a treatise that is calmly
scientific. This does not, however, justify our putting the future
of Canadian federalism entirely into the hands of federal
economists.

To start with, they are not infallible, a fact that Mr. Lamontagne misses a golden opportunity (among others) to demonstrate when he places blame for post-war inflation on 'the
principal private groups'. (p. 199) However, the economic
policies of the federal government were based on the expectation
of a recession following the war, and in fact it is to this fortunate
error that we owe the anti-deflationary measure of family
allowances. Second, the gentlemen in Ottawa like to govern a
bit too much; this is the only explanation I can find for their
using, during a period of *inflation*, spending powers that could
only be justified legally or economically in times of recession:
for example, university subsidies. And finally, their moral sense
is rather pliable; indeed, had it not been for Mr. Duplessis's
coup and the startled reaction of French Canadians, they seemed
unscrupulously prepared to accept a plan that would have drawn
hundreds of millions of dollars from the French-Canadian
province over a period of five years and redistributed the money
among provinces as rich as Ontario, Alberta, and British
Columbia.

Die Realpolitik Duplessis

When one considers that the principle of fiscal agreements has
undergone, in the past ten years of research and experiment,
over half a dozen different forms of implementation, it is impossible to attribute to anything but hostility the sudden desire
of Ottawa to regard these agreements as unchangeable; espe-

cially at the very moment when our province – after all the others – requested some modification to end the costly discrimination levelled against us.

The federal attitude seems to me even more untenable because, from the beginning of Confederation down to our day, the system of federal subsidies and payments has undergone more than twenty modifications of every kind. For example, although Section 118 of the British North America Act ruled that certain subsidies should constitute 'a complete settlement precluding all future demands', Nova Scotia obtained preferential treatment as early as 1869; Quebec and Ontario followed suit in 1873; then, at the Interprovincial Conferences of 1887 and 1902, all the provinces requested higher subsidies; next, in 1906, Manitoba, Alberta, and Saskatchewan tried to have their subsidies increased, and the Premier of British Columbia even went to London to press his claim; in 1907 a constitutional amendment completely revised the subsidy basis contained in Section 118; in 1930 Saskatchewan and Alberta obtained new concessions; the continued complaints of the Maritimes finally won them preferential treatment in 1932; and last, in 1949, Newfoundland made the federal government pay dearly for its entry into Confederation.

In brief, then, each province in turn applied all kinds of pressures on Ottawa to increase its share of the subsidies, and obtained all sorts of concessions until at last, in 1952, every province except Ontario and Quebec had signed agreements. At this point Finance Minister Abbott came up with yet another form of agreement which, as he said, 'proved useful only for Ontario'. Ontario having then signed, the question seemed to be closed as far as Ottawa was concerned. And so between 1947 and 1954 Ottawa took exclusive control of income taxes in all provinces *including Quebec*, and in return paid various sums to all provinces *except Quebec*.

I am well aware that this state of affairs resulted from the Duplessis government's total incompetence in economic matters; that is why I rarely missed an opportunity of blaming his systematic and obstinate refusal to take better advantage of the principle of tax rental agreements. But you cannot plead the victim's stupidity as an extenuating circumstance for the thief; and I notice that the federal government and its clever civil servants accommodated themselves only too easily to a system that, at least until 1954, amounted to a manifest defrauding of the Quebec taxpayer.

In the circumstances, I cannot entirely condemn Mr. Duplessis's *coup*. I am not aware of many instances in which the central government took the initiative to redress an injustice committed against French Canadians. Ottawa has never really believed in Canada's bicultural character;[7] and our minor victories in this field have always been obtained as the direct result of manoeuvres that made Ontario tremble because of our electoral strength.

Now Mr. Duplessis, by transforming what had been an abstract conflict of constitutional rights into a heavy burden on the taxpayer, suddenly managed to unite the entire electorate of Quebec against Ottawa. From this position of strength he then proceeded to ask the federal government to modify its fiscal policy by allowing provincial income taxes to be deducted from the federal income taxes. His negotiations were despicable, and probably cowardly: devoid of manners or dignity, achieved through press conferences and through forms unworthy of even the U.N. Security Council. But negotiate he did: he asked that Quebec retain in the form of tax deductions a lesser sum than the one offered by Ottawa in its tax rental agreements!

Had the federal economists been more equitable and the federal Liberals more intelligent, they could have used Mr. Duplessis's proposal against him. They could have pointed out that the tax abatement he requested was for a sum and for a period of time that were perfectly consonant with those originally planned in the fiscal agreements; and that this constituted tacit acknowledgement that decisions about the funds needed for macro-economic stabilization came under the jurisdiction of Ottawa. Assuming this acknowledgement, they could have accepted tax deductibility *in principle*, leaving Mr. Duplessis with the task of framing a law that would turn deductibility into an administrative feasibility.

[7] I cannot resist the opportunity of reminding the reader of the perceptive, courageous talk given by Murray Ballantyne on the English network of the C.B.C.: 'We [English Canadians] cannot have it both ways. Either we limit the life of the minority to a single province, in which case we cannot blame French Canadians for putting that province first; or else we accept their right to their language and their schools wherever they are. Are we, or are we not, prepared to consider Canada a fundamentally bilingual and bicultural country? That is the question that I leave you to answer.' Quoted in *Le Devoir*, June 25, 1954.

But Messrs. Abbott, Lesage, and their federal colleagues,[8] together with the satellite provincial party, found it easier to cross swords with Mr. Duplessis than to provide remedies for Quebec's real ills. Not that it did them much good. Two months later, while the Young Liberals gathered in national convention were still seconding their chiefs with all the enthusiasm of flunkeys and yes-men, Mr. St. Laurent made a speech which, as J.-T. Larochelle noted in an excellent article (*Notre Temps*, June 5, 1954) 'indirectly made the point that the nucleus of the Quebec delegation had displayed short-sighted conformity'. The Prime Minister, in fact, made it clear that he no longer considered the fiscal agreements to be the ultimate in perfection, declaring that his 'government would continue to study means of sharing taxation revenue in the fairest way possible . . .'. On June 23, Mr. St. Laurent went so far as to declare that there would be, that very autumn, a conference of federal-provincial experts to study amendments needed in the fiscal agreements. Finally, on July 1, he even specified that meetings could be held with the individual provinces.

The Liberal Prime Minister ended where he should have begun; but in any case he showed himself to be more flexible (through fairness or through political flair?) than his entire party put together. Moreover, he gained a strategic advantage over Mr. Duplessis. For if the latter refuses to negotiate on the grounds that his committee of experts (the Tremblay Commission) will not be ready to report before 1955, he will lose the support of the taxpayer burdened by double taxation in 1954; if, on the other hand, he agrees to negotiate in the autumn, he will be unable to benefit from the expert knowledge of his Commission, and thus will render part of their work futile.

The Solution Proposed by the Fédération des Unions Industrielles du Québec

Many organizations have maintained that the formula of tax deductibility could put an end to our present fiscal muddle – organizations as different from each other as the Quebec Conservative and C.C.F. parties, the Montreal Chamber of Commerce and the Canadian Catholic Congress of Labour, the

[8]It is to Mr. Lacroix's credit that he was the only Liberal to vote against Mr. Abbott's budget.

Gazette and *Le Devoir*. But to my knowledge, only the Fédération des Unions Industrielles du Québec (C.C.L.) has demonstrated that the requirements of economic stabilization and provincial autonomy could be reconciled by integrating the tax deductibility formula into the system of fiscal agreements.[9] I therefore wish to quote at length from this brief, which demonstrates that federal-provincial fiscal co-operation must rest upon three concurrent principles:

1. *The principle of proportional fiscal resources*: Each government, whether federal or provincial, must have, over the taxable matter territorially under its control, a right to impose taxation that is proportionate to the responsibilities under its jurisdiction. . . .

This first principle is based on the concept of sovereignty: a sovereignty whose essential function is to safeguard the common good. In a federal system, however, the exercise of sovereignty is divided between a central government and regional governments, each of which must protect some part of the common good. The total revenue at the disposal of the sovereign authority must thus be divided among various governments in such a way as to allow each one to best develop that part of the common good within its own competence.

. . . Consequently, if a government disposes of surplus revenue in such a way that it contributes to the common good in fields that *do not lie within its jurisdiction*, the suspicion arises that this government controls more than its share of taxing powers. . . . Should a province undertake to give regular subsidies to military hospitals or to set up its own army on the grounds that Ottawa is too poor or not doing a proper job; or should Ottawa regularly provide funds for the building of schools simply because all the provinces need more money or do not care enough for education, these governments would be violating the first principle of fiscal collaboration. Graver still, they would be attacking the very basis of the federal system, which does not give a government the right to interfere with the administration of other governments in those areas not under its own jurisdiction. . . .

2. *The principle of financial equalization*: The federal and provincial governments must be jointly responsible for ensuring that each government has at its disposal sufficient revenue to enable it to carry out its functions adequately. . . .

This principle also stems from the concept of federalism discussed above. The very existence of the Canadian federa-

[9]Brief presented by the C.C.L. to the Royal Commission on Constitutional Problems, on March 10, 1954 (especially pp. 27–33 and 38–49). (Editor's note: This brief was conceived and written by P. E. Trudeau.)

tion depends upon the economic ability of each government to safeguard that part of the common good for which it is answerable. This is not to suggest that all provinces must be financially equal, but at least each provincial government must be in a position to ensure that its particular electorate enjoys a standard of life approaching the Canadian norm on all essential points.

The political cohesion of society depends in fact upon its desire to secure the essential minimum for *all* its members, regardless of their geographical situation. If it happened, therefore, that one province (in contrast with all the others) was too poor to provide adequate administration for its citizens, it would no longer be to their advantage to stay in a federal system, and they would rightly press to have the *entire* common good become the responsibility of the central government.

It seems therefore that the central government must be responsible for equalization policies, since it can rise above the diverse and contradictory claims of the provinces. . . . And only the central government can be held responsible at the polls for equalization policies. For the electorate of each province, taken separately, could easily let itself be convinced that it had 'done its share', which would be a way of avoiding the fact that the distribution had been inadequately done. The central government, on the other hand, is answerable to all the citizens of the country: mathematically, the less fortunate provinces would have a greater chance of being treated fairly, and the federal system itself would thus be reinforced.

3. *The principle of economic stabilization*: No government should be able to prevent counter-cyclical fiscal policies from being carried out if these policies are the wish of most Canadians. . . . It is good political theory to locate responsibility clearly for such important matters as economic stabilization and (cyclical) unemployment, so that voters know who is responsible for what. This responsibility cannot be located at the provincial level, since the machinery for dealing with economic stabilization is federal, and since the electorate in each province could not hold its own regional government responsible for national results. Consequently, economic stabilization and general employment must be included in that part of the common good within federal jurisdiction. Of course, successive governments in Ottawa may not necessarily be of the same mind as to what constitute the best counter-cyclical policies, but each will know that its chances of being re-elected will depend on the success of its theories. . . .

In periods of inflation: . . . [The federal government] must accumulate more money than it spends, in order to reduce the over-all demands of society and combat inflation.

For this to be effective, however, the federal government must be sure that its fiscal policies are not nullified by the action of a provincial government taking advantage of prosperity to increase expenditure and reduce taxation. The federal government has therefore proposed agreements with the provinces by which it takes absolute control over the principal sources of provincial taxation. . . .

The Fédération des Unions Industrielles du Québec believes that the formula for agreements now being proposed by the federal government must be modified in order to combine their stabilizing influence with greater fiscal autonomy for the provinces. The modifications proposed are:

1. The sums offered to the provinces, to induce them to withdraw from the fields of personal income tax, corporation taxes and succession duties, should be based solely on the principle of fiscal need; rich provinces could no longer, as they do now, opt for a formula based on taxable capacity. In this way the fiscal agreements would incorporate the principle of financial equalization.

2. The amount offered should be high enough to make it rewarding (from a financial point of view) for all provinces to sign the agreements.

3. The federal government should give the provinces the following right: either to withdraw from the stated fields of taxation and receive the stated subsidy, or else to take exclusive control of the fiscal field up to the level of the stated subsidy, and receive nothing from the federal government.

4. From the point of view of the federal government, the result would be the same; it could never be called upon to grant tax deductions higher than the amount it was already prepared to pay the province in the form of subsidies. And in one way or another, the federal government would have achieved its goal of reducing the provinces' inflationary surplus of buying power.

5. Finally, it must be added that the provinces that had chosen to retain their fiscal autonomy would not be able to use this power in a way likely to promote inflation. For if they taxed more than the deductible amount, they would thereby help to reduce inflation; and if they taxed less, the federal government would receive the difference.

. . . Obviously, it would be an extremely delicate and important matter to determine in a just way the size of the subsidies (or the percentage of provincial taxes deductible from the federal). But the responsibility for this decision would be clearly established, and the voters would henceforth know how to judge it and who to thank for it. There would in fact be little danger of the federal government's setting excessive subsidies or deductions; and if they were too low, this would soon become apparent, in that the federal government would have money to

spend for that part of the common good not within its competence, while the provinces would have to tax too heavily in
order to finance themselves adequately. . . .

Having completed the demonstration for the case of inflation,
the brief proves by parallel reasoning that the proposed modifications of the system of fiscal agreements would make these
equally applicable and effective in times of recession or stability.

I do not think this solution involves insuperable administrative difficulties. True, the size of the subsidies varies from year
to year and from province to province, according to provincial
population and the gross national product; this would require a
similar adjustment in the figures allowed for tax deduction. But
this could be taken into account in the agreements by stipulating
that federal law on taxation authorize the taxpayers (in any
given province) to claim deductions at a rate set for that
province and that year; this would mean that the estimated total
deduction would be equivalent to the grants the said province
would have received had it not levied the said taxes. Naturally,
the more a province varies its fiscal program, the greater will be
the chance of making incorrect estimates; but in any case errors
could be corrected in the rate of deductibility set for the following year, or more simply by the use of a joint compensation fund.

Besides being economically feasible, the solution proposed
by the F.U.I.Q. has the advantage over other theoretically
possible formulas of being politically acceptable to the governments now at loggerheads; it is acceptable because it is based
on their respective claims: it retains Ottawa's mechanism of
fiscal agreements, and it accepts Quebec's principle of provincial
tax deductibility.

It proposes temporary agreements that do not necessitate
constitutional amendment and that may be re-examined
periodically in the light of changing economic circumstances
and new political requirements. Moreover, this solution calls
for federal-provincial co-operation; it permits the provinces to
help each other and to present a common front during discussions of the percentage of taxation the federal government
should give to the provinces. Once the combined governments
have reached agreement about the figures that should govern
tax sharing, each provincial government will decide whether to
take its share by accepting subsidies, or by collecting its own
taxes, with the heavy administration costs which this entails.

On this subject, it seems appropriate to suggest that the terms now used in fiscal agreements could be improved by being modified to better express the spirit of the F.U.I.Q. solution. There should no longer be any question of who controls specific tax fields, no question of rents, grants, or subsidies paid by the federal to the provincial governments. What a province would receive by virtue of these agreements would be the taxes paid by its own taxpayers. And in cases where the province did not wish to levy its tax directly (using the privilege of tax deductibility for its taxpayers), it would officially request the federal government to levy, *on its behalf*, the maximum annual amount provided for in the agreements.

In this way, each government is answerable to its own electoral body for taxation and the uses to which it is put. If a provincial government finds that the rate of taxation set by the agreements is too high, it can always relieve its taxpayer in other ways by reducing his other taxes (permits, gasoline taxes, sales taxes, and the rest). If, on the other hand, a provincial government finds that the tax-sharing formula accepted by the majority of the governments is not equitable, or does not bring it sufficient revenue, it is always free to levy its own taxes at whatever rate it wishes; these, by virtue of federal laws, are deductible up to the amount stipulated in the agreements; if the amount were exceeded, the taxpayer in that province would be subject to a double imposition.[10] He would then be in a position, when the next election came round, to support either one government or the other; and to guide his judgment he could use the principles of equalization policies and proportional fiscal control, along the lines described above.

The Tremblay Commission

Neither this article, the F.U.I.Q. brief, the whole body of other briefs, nor even Mr. Lamontagne's book has done more than

---

[10]This could be economically inconvenient in periods of recession if a province were so poor that its rate of taxation was very much higher than the existing federal rate. But this danger seems to me only theoretical. For in practice the government of such a province would know that it was gaining through equalization policies; and its taxpayers would be sure to make the point that it would be folly to impose exorbitant taxes only to receive a slight increase over what would be received anyway, and painlessly, through federal deficit budgeting.

scratch the surface of the immense problems of political economy that must be faced by the Canadian federal system. This merely shows what a lot of work has to be done by the Tremblay Commission before it can publish its report.

I do not wish to elaborate here on the Commission's handicaps; the tree must be judged by its fruit. The Commissioners are men of integrity, and it is certain that in dealing with matters of such vital importance to the province, they will hold themselves above personal controversy and political bias. I also hope that they will take into account that major document, the Rowell-Sirois *Report*, not to contradict it but to fill in its gaps.

For, although political and economic thinking in Ottawa may be miles ahead of that in Quebec, it would be a mistake to consider it in the least bit adequate. And I am not speaking merely of statistics, I am thinking of the innumerable questions to which the actual state of our political, economic, and social knowledge does not allow us to give an answer. To give a few random examples: What would be the reaction to an intergovernmental fiscal commission set up to collaborate on the preparation of fiscal agreements, and to outline anti-cyclical policies in the field of public works? What about an intergovernmental credit organization to make it easier for provinces to adopt deficit budgeting in times of recession? Could Canada adapt the New Deal's Reconstruction Finance Corporation? What would be the advantages of the Massachussetts Formula for provinces sharing corporate income taxes? To what extent do the conditional subsidies proposed by the federal government encourage the provinces to spend above their means and to tax at a deflationary rate? Should a farmer, in his tax calculations, not include the farm products consumed on his farm? And should a home-owner's income not take into account the real-estate value of his home? There is a procedure that indicates to the taxpayer what part of his tax is used to finance old age pensions. Could this same procedure not be used to advantage in order to indicate defence costs? What studies should be undertaken to determine the maximum economic size of townships, municipalities, parishes, and so on, from the point of view of such services as religion, health, education, police protection, roads, and recreation? To what extent is the cost of municipal services (order, transport, water supply, sewer system) borne by the city dweller while benefiting other users who are tax exempt (parasitic suburbs, industries, religious communities, civil service, etc.)?

All these unanswered questions at least serve to underline the extreme paucity of our knowledge on federal matters, and our gross incompetence in the management of the *res publica*.[11] It would be futile to hope that the Tremblay Commission will do very much to extend the range of our knowledge. But we have a right to expect that it will at least recognize the immensity of our ignorance, at least in comparison with the rest of Canada, and suggest concrete measures to reduce it.

With regard to the main questions at issue, the Commissioners must in conscience adopt scientifically unassailable positions on them, and propose solutions that are administratively feasible. For example, they must not shirk discussion of the Keynesian concepts held by federal economists.[12]

[11]I would be delighted to know what economic principles inspired the Honourable Onésime Gagnon when he brought down deficit budgets during our recent years of inflation; but was the Honourable Douglas Abbott that much more clever when, during these same years, he gave as excuse for the size of his surpluses the difficulties of exact calculation?

I am, moreover, completely out of patience with Mr. Duplessis when, having systematically obstructed federal policies designed to provide full employment, he declares (last July 2) that the problem of unemployment is a federal concern and that 'Ottawa should immediately provide remedies to the situation'; on the other hand, what kind of courage has been shown by the King and St. Laurent governments which, after nineteen years of attempting to extend, in the name of stabilization policies, their centralizing control of the national economy, have never yet declared themselves responsible for cyclical unemployment?

[12]If I insist on this point, it is because our wretched crew of nationalists have given us some insight into their methods in their reaction to Mr. Lamontagne's book. Not one dared to confront directly the economic theories that form the substance of his book, but every one tried to demolish the author by attacking him on side issues.

I have spoken above of Professor Brunet. As for Mr. Léopold Richer (*Notre Temps*, July 10, 17, 24, and 31), he alleges that 'the framework of these articles does not permit him to deal specifically with the problem of economic stability'! But his reference to the gravity of cyclical policies reveals just enough of his knowledge to let us understand why he has been content to refute the ideas of the economist, Mr. Lamontagne, simply by taxing him with the fact that he had not written a book on patriotism like Mr. Minville, or on the workings of the Stock Exchange, like Mr. Montpetit.

In fact, it is once again our old friend Gérard Filion who has initiated discussion in the most courageous way. (*Le Devoir*, July 21–4, 1954) I agree with him when he declares that it is dangerous to 'build what Mr. Lamontagne calls the new Canadian federalism upon economic theories which will probably be outdated within a generation'. But economic problems have to be resolved today with the economic knowledge

Finally, the Commissioners could write nothing more deadly than a narrow, provincial report concerned mainly with the valour of French Canadians who defend their 'language, faith, and rights' against a centralizing oppressor. Six men have it in their power to bring to an end the era in which Laurier could rightly say: 'French Canadians do not have opinions, they merely have emotions.' And in the eyes of future generations, Messrs. Tremblay, Minville, Parent, Arès, Rowat, and Guimont will have much to answer for.

---

we currently possess. And that is what Mr. Lamontagne attempted to do; whereas Mr. Filion, when he concludes that the financial crisis will be settled 'when each government looks after its own patch of garden', makes us think that he has spent longer in the company of André Le Notre than in that of John Maynard Keynes.

Cité Libre, October 1954. Translated from the French by Joanne L'Heureux.

Federal Grants
to Universities

... of Denmark.
HAMLET

SOMETHING is wrong somewhere. On the question of university grants, I find myself in disagreement with my friends and with people whose ideas I usually find congenial. On the other hand, I quite approve of some of the attitudes taken by Mr. Duplessis and the nationalists, with whom I am not in the habit of agreeing.

In an attempt to explain my position to both sides, I should like to make a few preliminary points.[1]

A fundamental condition of representative democracy is a clear allocation of responsibilities: a citizen who disapproves of a policy, a law, a municipal by-law, or an educational system must know precisely whose work it is so that he can hold someone responsible for it at the next election.

For unitary states such as the United Kingdom, this condition is a relatively easy one to meet. Since Parliament has absolute sovereignty, *all* the country's laws emanate from it, and its members are answerable to the electorate not only for what they accomplish for the general welfare, but also for what they fail to achieve despite their complete legislative powers.

In a federal state such as Canada, the situation is more complex. The exercise of sovereignty is divided between a central government and ten regional governments which, taken together, constitute the *Canadian state*, and each of which must

---

[1] I have already developed these ideas in another form, in the brief presented to the Tremblay Commission by the Fédération des Unions Industrielles du Québec. (March 10, 1954; see more particularly section IV.) But who reads briefs presented to royal commissions?

ensure a certain part of the general welfare. Since the same citizens vote in both federal and provincial elections, they must be able to determine readily which government is responsible for what; otherwise the democratic control of power becomes impossible.

Responsibility is delegated by the constitution itself: the government of a province must safeguard the common good of its people in all matters that relate to Section 92 (among others) of the British North America Act, and the central government has a similar responsibility for matters outlined in Section 91. But the corollary is that no government has the right to interfere with the administration of other governments in those areas *not within its own jurisdiction.*[2]

Thus a provincial government would go beyond its jurisdiction if it tried to meddle in foreign affairs (for example in the question of aid to underdeveloped countries), since this is clearly a matter under federal control. On the other hand, a provincial government with sufficient tax resources is answerable *only to its electorate,* never to the federal government, for the regulation and financing of education, and this would be true no matter how ruinous its policies.

From these principles it inevitably follows that the total resources available to the Canadian Treasury must be divided among the federal and provincial governments in such a way as to allow each government to look after its share of the common good *as it sees fit.* The implementation of this principle could be difficult for extremely poor countries; when tax revenue is not great enough to support both central and local governments, a question of priorities arises, as to whether the central good (e.g. foreign affairs) should take precedence over the local good (e.g. education). Fortunately, this question need not arise in Canada.

Consequently, if a government has at its disposal such a surplus of funds that it can undertake to support a part of the common good that *does not lie within its jurisdiction,* one may suspect that this government controls more than its share of taxation. The suspicion is not always warranted, of course. The

[2]This principle of federalism would seem to entail discussion of several other points, notably the right to disallowance. But as they do not enter into the present question, I shall not burden the reader with a show of my knowledge (?) of constitutional law.

government of Quebec may, for example, give funds to the University of Ottawa, claiming that this money does not come from taxation and that education in Quebec benefits directly from its use. Similarly, the federal government can use blocked funds in Europe for educational purposes on the grounds that these funds, by virtue of both origin and their use, are being used for the benefit of all Canadians in the field of international relations. It will then be up to the electorate – of Quebec in the first example, of Canada in the second – to judge whether or not each government has taken more than its share of taxation.

On the other hand, there are cases where the suspicion of encroachment is justified. If, for example, a province began to tax its electorate for the purpose of financing the Canadian army, giving as its excuse that Ottawa was too poor to protect us from the threat of Russian invasion; or if Ottawa regularly subsidized the construction of schools in all provinces on the pretext that the provinces did not pay sufficient attention to education, these governments would be attacking the very foundation of the federal system, which, as I have pointed out, does not give any government the right to meddle in the affairs of others.[3] Here again, it is up to the voters to elect, at the federal level, a government that will do its duty as far as national defence is concerned, and, at the provincial level, men who will give education the priority it requires.

These principles having been posited – and accepted, I hope, since otherwise we would not agree even on the meaning of the word 'democracy' – I now wish to examine the arguments so many people use to justify their support of federal grants to universities.

1. THE ARGUMENT BASED ON THE POLICY OF EQUALIZATION

The political cohesion of a society depends on its desire to secure the essential minimum for *all* its members, regardless of their geographical situation. Consequently, if a province is too

[3]If this principle needed further support I would refer to the letter written to the Montreal *Gazette* (October 25, 1956) by the federal Minister of Justice, Mr. Garson, in which he notes his agreement with the Rowell-Sirois *Report* when it affirms 'the right of each province to decide the relative importance of expenditure on education and expenditure on other competing services. . . . Hence, we do not think that it would be wise or appropriate for the Dominion to make grants to the provinces ear-marked for the support of general education.'

poor to provide university services that approach the Canadian average, it has a right to federal grants. (See, for example, J. Perrault, *Vrai*, November 10, 1956.)

My answer to this argument is that I believe in equalization grants so long as they relate to that part of the general welfare that is under federal jurisdiction. But this argument is beside the point here. For equalization grants take the surplus from the wealthier provinces and redistribute it among the poorer; while at present federal grants are offered to universities in *all* provinces regardless of their respective wealth, and according to a single schedule of payment. In other words, the federal government collects funds from all ten provinces and redistributes them to all ten provinces, to finance a service that is not within its jurisdiction. This may be called centralization, but certainly not equalization.

2. THE ARGUMENT BASED ON MACRO-ECONOMIC STABILIZATION

'Taxation is one means of curbing inflation; . . . [consequently] there will be surpluses . . . which represent a portion of the national revenue which federal authorities are disposed to redistribute.' (G. Picard, *Le Devoir*, November 8, 1956)

I recognize that the function of stabilizing the economy belongs primarily to the federal government. But the anticyclical theory referred to by Mr. Picard in fact militates *against* university grants. For since 1951 (when the federal government first offered university grants), Canada has been undergoing a period of inflation; this means that the federal government should tend to *reduce its expenditure*, and use the surplus (for example) to diminish the national debt. Given the state of our economy, the federal grants are indefensible on these grounds, and have been since their inception.

3. THE ARGUMENT BASED ON JOINT JURISDICTION OVER THE UNIVERSITIES

'Are the provinces responsible for university education?' wonders Léon Dion, after an ingenious summary of the situation. And he answers: 'The university should not fall . . . under any sphere of influence, whatever it may be.' (*Le Devoir*, November 5, 1956)

Unless this answer is designed to lead us away from accepted theories of legal sovereignty into some kind of pluralistic anarchy, it boils down, as I understand it, to the same position as that adopted by Maurice Blain: '[Must not] our universities, caught between two inexorable masters, . . . satisfy their economic needs by maintaining a constant balance of power between the federal and provincial levels?' (*Le Devoir*, November 2, 1956)

I am not saying, *a priori*, that education (at least university education) should never fall under concurrent federal jurisdiction: it might well be in the general interest for the central state to undertake immediately an enlargement of our cultural horizons, or to co-operate in the large-scale production of technicians to come to grips with our own underdeveloped state, our economic rivals, and our ideological enemies. But this needs to be proved. Above all, as a citizen I would require that such a revolutionary interpretation of our constitution be made the object of a conscious choice. I would demand that political parties take a clear stand on the matter, and make their reasons public, thus allowing the electorate to decide with full knowledge of the issues involved.

In a widely acclaimed article, Gilles Mercure wrote: 'The only condition needed to modify the constitution, either at once or gradually, is the existence of dynamic forces capable of winning public opinion to their side.' (*Le Devoir*, November 17, 1956) I agree completely, and certainly do not intend to be caught napping. However, these dynamic forces must be put into play openly and publicly before the sovereign people – and this the federal government could have done in the present case, either by requesting an amendment to the constitution, as it did for unemployment insurance and old age pensions; or even by having recourse to Section 92 (10) (c) of the constitution to maintain that the universities constitute a 'service . . . contributing to the general good of Canada'.

On the contrary, the federal government took great pains to make it clear that it did not wish to be responsible for universities at all. Mr. St. Laurent even devised the scheme of making the university grants via the National Conference of Canadian Universities in order to dispel the fear that there was any move toward an 'encroachment upon the provincial legislature's exclusive jurisdiction in the field of education'. (Speech at the University of Sherbrooke, October 17, 1956) And in another speech on November 12 of the same year, Mr. St. Laurent reiterated that 'Provincial authorities have the exclusive right to legislate in matters of education. . . .'

Therefore, no argument based on a new federal jurisdiction over education could possibly be used at present to justify the grants.

4. THE ARGUMENT BASED ON FEDERAL COMPETENCE

'The federal state is the Canadian state: it is our state,' wrote Pierre Dansereau. (*Vrai*, November 3, 1956) Similarly, Gérard Picard declared: 'We must stop thinking of Ottawa as a foreign government.' (*loc. cit.*)

Again, I am in total agreement; but here, too, the argument itself misfires, as must be clear from my preliminary points and my answer to the previous argument. I cannot express it more concisely than F.-A. Angers: 'In general, the Canadian state is not the central government, but the central and the provincial governments taken together. . . . In matters of education the Canadian state is the provincial state, and none other.' (*Vrai*, November 10, 1956)

5. THE ARGUMENT OF ANCILLARY POWERS

Ancillary powers, as defined by our courts of law, are the right of a government possessing authority over a certain field to legislate as well on matters implicitly related to that field. Are we to understand that Mr. J. Perrault (*loc. cit.*) was referring to the theory of ancillary powers when he wrote: 'The federal government has the right to be concerned in education for these three constitutional reasons . . .'; or when he said that federal jurisdiction over international, military, and criminal affairs permits the central government to ensure that citizens 'obtain the knowledge and training to develop their personality', and so on?

In my opinion, it would be a mistake to believe that Mr. Perrault was referring to ancillary powers. Such an interpretation would be the very negation of federalism, since the central government could for the same reasons intervene in municipal affairs, the performing of marriages, the civil code, the administration of justice. Are these institutions not equally important for the prevention of 'juvenile delinquency' or of ignorance among military personnel, and for the development of our future 'cultural attachés'?

In any case, Mr. Perrault himself affirmed even more strongly than Mr. St. Laurent that: 'Culture, education, and teaching on all levels are the exclusive prerogative of provincial governments.' This makes it clear that the 'ancillary powers' referred to in the above argument are not meant to be taken literally. It is not a question of 'legislating on' but of 'giving to'. And this is what I now wish to examine.

6. THE 'POWER OF THE PURSE' ARGUMENT

'There is nothing in the constitution to prevent the Canadian government from making gifts to any group or institution whatsoever. This is exactly what is happening in the case of university grants,' writes J. C. Falardeau (*Le Devoir*, October 23, 1956). And Mr. St. Laurent, in his speech of November 12, declared:

> The federal government has the absolute right to use indirect taxation for any purpose, and the right to impose direct taxation provided that it is destined to increase Canada's Consolidated Revenue Fund. With the approval of Parliament, it can then use this money to make gifts or grants-in-aid to individuals, institutions, provincial governments, or even foreign governments. This is a royal prerogative which our constitution does not limit in any way.

Note that Mr. St. Laurent argues that *any* tax is allowed provided it is destined to increase the Consolidated Revenue Fund; and that *any* grant is allowed provided it is drawn from these funds. I am emphasizing this because it is this argument alone that I wish to refute in the following paragraphs. (The right to give money that does not come from taxation is an entirely different matter, and I shall deal with it later.)

To support his theory, Mr. St. Laurent quotes from a statement by Mr. Justice Duff, without indicating that the opinion was not accepted either by a majority of Justices of the Supreme Court or by the Privy Council. Mr. St. Laurent nevertheless clings to the resulting verdict, and quotes from Mr. Justice Kerwin and especially from Lord Atkin:

> That the Dominion may impose taxation for the purpose of creating a fund for special purposes, and may apply that fund for making contributions in the public interest to individuals, corporations or public authorities, could not *as a general proposition* be denied.

But, as was noted by Mr. Duplessis (who, though he may

not read much, seems to remember everything!), Mr. St. Laurent was giving only part of the Privy Council's judgment. For Lord Atkin continued:

> But assuming that the Dominion has collected by means of taxation a fund, it by no means follows that any legislation which disposes of it is necessarily within Dominion competence. It may still be legislation affecting the classes of subjects enumerated in s. 92, and, if so, would be ultra vires. In other words, Dominion legislation, *even though it deals with Dominion property*, may yet be so framed as to . . . encroach upon the classes of subjects which are reserved to Provincial competence. . . . [In such a case] the legislation will be invalid. To hold otherwise would afford the Dominion an easy passage into the Provincial domain. (1937 A.C. 367)

From this it follows that the fact of creating by means of taxation a federal fund for the purpose of making donations is not *in itself* ('as a general proposition') *ultra vires*. It becomes illegal, however, when the federal government disposes of these funds through legislation that encroaches upon provincial jurisdiction. But Lord Atkin does not tell us whether, in his opinion, a budgetary law would so encroach if it merely made grants (with certain conditions and in certain areas) to institutions that are under provincial jurisdiction; or whether encroachment occurs only when there is a specific attempt to legislate in these areas. It is, moreover, impossible to know whether his 'general proposition' is merely a tautology; or whether it is intended to authorize grants to institutions that are not under the exclusive control of either the federal or provincial governments; for example, relief funds for victims of disasters, etc.

These points should be referred to the Supreme Court for elucidation. In the meantime, we may gain some light on the subject by considering the university grants from the point of view of where the money comes from. Let us try to understand the concept of 'Dominion property' mentioned by the learned Lord Atkin. Is any tax levy permitted provided that it is destined to increase the Consolidated Revenue Fund, as St. Laurent claimed? Or, to borrow the terms used in another Privy Council decision, can the federal government add to the Consolidated Revenue Fund by means of taxation when the taxation is not 'confined to Dominion taxes *for Dominion purposes*'? (1924, A.C. 1004) The answer is no. This is made clear in the case of direct taxation: the Canadian Parliament may 'impose a Dominion income tax *for Dominion purposes*'. (*loc. cit.*) When it comes to indirect taxation Mr. Justice Phillimore places his trust in the federal government, and considers it unnecessary to pronounce judgment on an issue unlikely to occur: 'the not very probable event of the Parliament of Canada desiring to raise money for *provincial purpose* by indirect taxation'. (*loc. cit.*) Consequently, if there is federal legislation to grant taxation money for provincial purposes, this legislation is illegal for the excellent reason that the federal government cannot by law have money in its coffers which it then claims should be used for provincial purposes. *Nemo dat quod non habet.* This is so clearly true that if in its next session the federal government decided to raise taxes on the understanding that the increase would be given to universities, there would be a general uproar among the electorate. It is one of the mysteries of life that a similar revolt does not occur when the Dominion does exactly the same thing by diverting the surplus from current taxation into the universities.

It remains the duty of each government to ensure that it does not collect taxes for that part of the public interest not within its jurisdiction. If the federal government has a surplus of funds large enough to give grants to all the universities, and if it cannot justify its action by claiming that it is an equalization measure (since it gives grants to *all* universities) or an anti-cyclical measure (since we are in an inflationary period), this government is plainly guilty of infringing the principle of the proportional division of fiscal resources that underlies any federal system: it has levied for education, which is not within its competence, funds that – had the matter been left to the provinces – might or might not have been used for universities, depending on the wishes of the provincial electorates and their respective governments.

The fact that Quebec is not raising enough tax revenue to meet its educational needs is entirely beside the point. The mere fact that a government does not exploit its full share of the fiscal field does not mean that it no longer has the right to do so. Otherwise each government would always have to tax to the maximum in order to retain its prerogatives, a situation the taxpayers would never tolerate. As the Province of Ontario declared (despite the fact that it supported the validity of the federal law for unemployment insurance): 'It is *not* conceded that the Dominion may tax everything everywhere and that the provinces are left solely with what is left.' (1937 A.C. 361)

Unsupported by the highest judicial authorities,[4] condemned by the theory of federal tax systems, Mr. St. Laurent attempts to use the idea of customary practice (from what he calls the 'already distant past') to justify his university grants. In his talk of November 12 to the National Conference on Higher Education, he cites as precedents the grants-in-aid made to universities by the federal departments of agriculture, fisheries, and so on, for *specific purposes*. There is no precedent here. In these areas the federal government has (concurrent) constitutional jurisdiction: so that there can be no question of denying its right to give grants, or even to legislate in these areas, any more than in the establishing of military colleges.

The Prime Minister also pleads that the grants 'arise from a national cultural policy', citing as precedents the establishment of a National Museum, the Public Archives, the C.B.C., etc. This illogical reasoning is unforgivable. It is recognized (sometimes as a result of judicial decisions) that the federal government can legislate on these institutions; no one therefore could contest the fact that the federal government can also give them funds. However, according to Mr. St. Laurent himself, the federal government *cannot* legislate on universities. And so his right to give them grants does not relate to anything.

In any case an argument based on precedent is worthless as far as constitutional rights are concerned. Otherwise, Mr. Duplessis's acceptance of grants in 1951–2 could be used against him now. But no precedent can stand against a written constitution. This is why the Lemieux Law, adopted by the federal government in 1907, was ruled *ultra vires* by the Privy Council in 1925, although it had been accepted by the provinces for eighteen years.

Mr. St. Laurent then attempts to compare the grants with the right of 'individuals and private industry' to make donations to universities although they cannot legislate upon them. This is begging the question. For individuals and industries can only give donations *within the limits of the law*. (For example, the

[4]I had not meant this phrase literally, but I realize that it is true, even in its literal sense! In the Privy Council decisions I have quoted above, Mr. St. Laurent was counsel for the losing party.

Civil Code, Article 1265, prohibits certain donations between married people.) Similarly, our governments may give donations only within the limits of the constitution; and it is precisely these limits, stemming from the theory of federalism and defined by the Privy Council, that must be respected.

But apparently Mr. St. Laurent wants to deny the very existence of these limits. His reasoning amounts to saying that the fact of making donations belongs, by its very nature, to that part of the general welfare under both federal and provincial jurisdiction. And to strengthen his argument, Mr. St. Laurent in effect claims that 'Provincial legislatures also possess the same royal prerogative', which consists in the right to make grants *without set limits* from moneys raised by taxation. With all due respect, therein lies the error. It is certain that making donations (the power of the purse) is a prerogative of the Crown; and the exercise of that prerogative creates no problems in a unitary state. But in a federal country the situation is entirely different: the question is *who* may exercise *what* prerogative. It is obvious, for example, that a province may not appoint ambassadors, even though this is a royal prerogative. It is therefore always necessary to refer to the constitution.

According to the constitution, however, each of the federal and provincial governments is sovereign in its own sphere. 'Within these limits [of Section 92] the local legislature is supreme, and has the same authority as the Imperial Parliament, or the Parliament of the Dominion. . . .' (1883–4, 9 A.C. 132) Consequently, the various governments must exercise their prerogative of making grants from tax revenues only within their area of jurisdiction. Probably both Ottawa and Quebec may make grants-in-aid of this kind to individuals, or to organizations such as the Red Cross, since there is always some aspect of their function by which they fall under federal jurisdiction (e.g. war and peace), and another by which they fall under provincial jurisdiction (e.g. works of charity). But universities are in an entirely different category, since, according to Mr. St. Laurent, they fall *exclusively* under provincial jurisdiction.

Let us carry the reasoning to its absurd conclusion. If under the royal prerogative provinces have the power to make unlimited donations, it must follow that the very fact of giving, irrespective of its aim or recipient, constitutes a purpose that provinces are justified in pursuing; donating funds is a 'provincial purpose' in the sense of Section 92 (2 and 9) of the constitution. This section, which allows the provinces to levy direct taxation *for provincial purposes*, must therefore authorize provinces to collect taxes in order to finance (for example) the postal system, military service, federal civil service, penitentiaries, and the Department of External Affairs. When this point has been reached, the two largest provinces have only to combine and take complete control over direct taxation for the central government to be reduced to the point of bankruptcy and impotence and for the constitution to be totally destroyed.

Mr. St. Laurent's theory is, as has been shown, the direct negation of federalism: it can only lead to anarchy.

In the meantime, we may well ask why the federal government does so little, so late. Since it has the right to give as it wishes – since giving is a *Dominion purpose* (in the sense defined by Lord Phillimore) – how can one explain the fact that, from a budget of five billion dollars and a surplus of hundreds of millions, it can only find a mere sixteen million for the universities? Since the National Research Council's function is to develop scientific research in Canada, how is it that the federal government has only spent twenty-five million for this purpose in the last forty years? Since the federal government wants to be responsible for a national program of health, why has it only spent four million in the last eight years?

Come now, gentlemen, a mere sixteen million for the universities you claim to consider so important – surely you are joking? And since your power of giving is unlimited, why not provide a few grants for the provincial civil servants, who are so badly paid? On their side, provincial governments could offer a bonus to federal civil servants who could demonstrate that they were bilingual. And so everyone would meddle in the affairs of others; citizens who were discontented with their provincial government would go to Ottawa to find solutions, and vice versa.

Mr. St. Laurent's party would then have managed to demolish the two most fundamental principles of our constitution, the first being that 'no provincial Legislature could use its special powers as an indirect means of destroying powers given by the parliament of Canada' (1921–2 A.C. 91); the second that 'the Parliament of Canada could not exercise its powers of taxation so as to destroy the capacity of officials lawfully appointed by the province'. (1924 A.C. 1006) Universities would have to be in desperate need, to subscribe to the theories of federalism proposed by Mr. St. Laurent!

7. THE ARGUMENT OF NEED

'We cannot afford to wait,' writes Pierre Dansereau, 'the need is too urgent.' Doctor Robillard adds: 'Does a starving man consider the colour of the hand offering him bread?' (*Vrai*, November 3, 1956) This is basically Vianney Décarie's argument as well: the safeguarding of French-Canadian culture requires that the grants be accepted by universities 'whose desperate needs stare everyone in the face'. (*Le Devoir*, November 24) And finally this comment from Mgr. Lussier: 'The universities of Quebec . . . are in very great need of assistance.' (*Le Devoir*, November 15)

I must admit this is a moving argument. Who am I to pass judgment on a starving man? What standards could I use? Someone dying of hunger is justified in seizing whatever food he can find, regardless of the laws governing property. Similarly, the refinements of political or constitutional science may seem entirely irrelevant when a dying culture suddenly finds itself faced with the very thing that may save it.

In answer, allow me to distinguish between men and culture. I give sincere praise to men who have made a career of teaching – at what cost only God and their families know – in a society that has constantly shown them contempt and, very often, hostility. I can well understand their favourable reaction to a patron who suddenly begins to show some regard for higher education. But when we come right down to it, we are not dealing with a case of *literal* starvation. For unless I am mistaken, Professors Angers, Minville, and Brunet, who are opposed to the grants, are no better off than anyone else in the teaching profession.

We must therefore be dealing with a case of 'dying culture'. But shouldn't we rather speak of suicide? From a judicial point of view, education is strictly the responsibility of the Quebec government; from a democratic point of view, this government is entirely the responsibility of that valiant people filled with true patriot's love and standing on guard forever by the great waters of the St. Lawrence, tra-la, tra-la. Which is to say that if teaching is scorned and intelligence humiliated in our noble province, the fault lies very specifically with those who live in it. Under the circumstances, the very thing we must *not* do is run and beg Ottawa to alleviate our famine by giving us a bit of our own tax money. Once again we would be avoiding our duty as citizens of a (provincial) state responsible for education. There is a kind of unconscious but specious paternalism in the attitude of our intelligentsia, for it wants to save French-Canadian culture – and yet it does not see that the necessity for this operation must be convincingly demonstrated to the people, whose culture it is and on whom provincial elections depend.

Two and a half years ago, some local labour unions were wondering whether they should request the federal government to disallow two harmful bills, 19 and 20. These bills meant something worse than starvation: they meant the end of some unions, among them the admirable Alliance des professeurs de Montréal. After serious consideration, the unions decided against this action: they decided not to request Ottawa to repeal laws passed by Quebec deputies, as Ottawa is allowed to do by the constitution. In true democratic fashion, the trade unionists realized that the solution was a political one and lay in their power to achieve, by electing deputies and a government that would be less anti-union. All other procedures would simply mean shuffling the problem around and postponing the day when people finally took their destiny into their own hands.

I wonder whether intellectuals in general, and academics in particular, have a similar consciousness of their responsibilities, as well as the courage to face up to them. Mme Françoise Lavigne explained that the reason intellectuals do not become involved in necessary political reforms is that they are too disgusted with a society that either ignores or despises them. (*Le Devoir*, November 23, 1956) But had trade unionists shown such reticence, they would long ago have lost all freedom.

Take up the cudgels, for goodness' sake! If our culture is in such pressing danger that you feel justified in bypassing the constitution, why not begin by ignoring the law: go on strike, refuse to pay your taxes, or, better still, demand that the federal government grant a tax reduction applicable solely to university professors. (We shall soon see whether Mr. St. Laurent cares so much for culture that he would be prepared to confront the rest of the taxpayers with this kind of preferential budget legislation! Yet it would be entirely constitutional.) To state one's position is at least a first step, and to my mind this explains the surprising report from six professors of social science who finally cracked their faculty's ideological monolith. (*Le Devoir*, November 29) Now is the time to act, to write articles, to go on the hustings, to engage in political action. If the opposition parties are not suitable, there is always the Rassemblement.

For democracy has its logic, and freedom its requirements. An increasing number of academics are beginning to understand this, and I admire them for it. But it must be recognized that this is a recent, and still a rather uncertain phenomenon. I do not think I am far wrong in saying that, for quite a number of years now, the trade unions, and the C.C.L. in particular, have, through their briefs to the government and their work in trade schools, done more than professors[5] to impress on public opinion the urgency of problems relating to all levels of education.

Moreover, I feel that even in their wise judgments, our intellectuals tend to introduce too many prudent elements. Last September, at the meeting of the Institute of Public Affairs dealing with education, for example, there was not a single speaker who had not firmly adopted self-imposed limitations from the very beginning. No one came down unequivocally for free tuition at all levels, and for salaries for students. No one proposed the appointment of laymen as university presidents. No one proposed to break the clerical monopoly over secondary education. And (despite the report in *Notre Temps*) no one even proposed a ministry of education.

Unless I am mistaken, it was left to someone like Roger Duhamel (who does not exactly have a reputation for being *avant-garde*) to make the point that the title of Monseigneur did not necessarily carry a teacher's certificate with it. It was left to a nationalist like Michel Brunet to write that 'the first reform needed . . . is the immediate establishment of a true

[5]Mr. Esdras Minville is of the same opinion: 'It is proper to inquire what the universities have done to enlighten the government and to encourage it to set up a comprehensive educational policy.' (*Le Devoir*, November 19) It is a good question. . . . But in point of fact, has Mr. Minville himself not been the director of a school and the dean of a faculty for many years now? His answer is: 'Our institutions of learning have until now wrapped themselves in the most complete silence, as if they were indifferent to the functioning of everyday life.' He also deplores 'the absence of political thought in this province'. How is it then that the dean's faculty still has no department of political science?

Ministry of Education.' (In *Alerte*, a bulletin of the Saint-Jean-Baptiste Society, October 1956, p. 232. The entire article has great value, and is very courageous – since it is, alas, the fashion to praise the 'courage' of people who are simply thinking for themselves.)

With regard to the grants, it was left to the Ligue d'action nationale to reveal the central government's hypocrisy in giving taxation money to the universities (which is forbidden by the constitution) while refusing to help minority schools (which it is obliged to do by the constitution). (*Le Devoir*, November 19) It was left to Father Arès to point out that 'the debate over the universities is no more than an episode in a conflict between Quebec and Ottawa that has been going on for the past ten years, with the issue at stake being the future of the Canadian federal system.' (*Relations*, December 1956) Before crying: 'truism!' everyone had better examine his thoughts to make sure he has not adopted two contradictory positions on the questions of grants and provincial tax deductibility. After all, if the tax deductibility formula was a good one three years ago, why does it not remain a fair solution for taxpayers of provinces wishing to refuse the university grants?

Decidedly, the nationalists will surprise me in the end! For the moment, however, I must in all loyalty make it clear that I am not in agreement with the motives that lead most of them to reject the university grants. They still seem to believe that Ottawa has a deep, dark plot against their faith, language, and rights. They are against this, because they have always been against everything: against old age pensions, unemployment insurance, family allowances, fiscal agreements, medicare, the National Film Board, C.B.C. radio and television – in short, against what they call 'English, Protestant money'.

The federal government is still preparing (and has been since 1919!) a medicare program; when it is completed, you will see nationalists protesting that it should really come under provincial jurisdiction. You might think that in the meantime they would clamour for rapid provincial action to prevent terrible cases of deprivation. But do they? Not a bit of it: they claim that health is not the business of the state at all, but of 'intermediary bodies'.

Why, then, are they so disgruntled about university grants? Mr. St. Laurent offers them a corporate solution, for the

National Conference of Canadian Universities, which is to administer the grants, is nothing more than their 'intermediate body'. The truth is that they are disgruntled because they are against state intervention in any field: in education, social security, family welfare, economic stability, natural resources, private enterprise, housing, health, and all the rest. They believe that they are against socialism: but at a time when the only acceptable control over a heavily industrialized society is a strong, democratic government, they are simply against progress and reforms.

St. Augustine taught that education is a function of the state and as such is the responsibility of the people as a whole. But this is beside the point in French Canada where, for historical reasons admirably summed up by Professor Brunet (*loc. cit.*), teaching has become the private property of the clergy, and their exclusive responsibility. After 1867 this state of affairs had no reason to continue, since the provincial government – composed of a large majority of Roman Catholic French Canadians – became constitutionally responsible for education. At this point, the Church could have stopped filling a temporary need and rendered unto Caesar the rights and obligations belonging to education – especially since, as it happened, the democratic state was also, in the nature of things, Roman Catholic.

Nevertheless the clergy, forgetting as always that the Church is also composed of laymen, preferred to keep education as their own private inheritance. They preferred to negotiate their parsimonious subsidies behind closed doors, rather than let the needs of education be discussed in the Legislative Assembly.

The result? Citizens lost interest in the subject, and politicians never had to give it a thought, except in terms of their campaign funds. . . . Now for the past few years (to be precise, since the Sulpician Fathers were ruined by the 'crash' of the Detroit tram company) financial difficulties have seriously affected the quality of the education dispensed by the clergy. With increasing frequency, they have had to go on secret pilgrimages to the politicians, as a result of which the latter have become rather high-handed. Thus we see a Quebec bishop accepting without protest the humiliation of appearing in public accounts as a . . . supplier![6]

[6]See *The Public Accounts* of the Province of Quebec, among others, for the period ending March 31, 1952, p. 47.

That is why the clergy – falling victim to the secret anti-democratic practices which they themselves originated – are now beginning to demand a magic formula: statutory grants! To which Mr. Duplessis is perfectly right in answering, 'All grants are based on statute.' (*Le Devoir*, November 21, 1956) This simply goes to show once more how confused and incompetent our discussions of political problems can be.

In the last analysis everyone knows that what the clergy want (and here I do not wish to question the integrity or generosity of their administration, but merely its democratic character) is to receive, regularly and automatically, nice fat sums from the state for use in 'their' institutions of learning. What they do *not* want is to let Parliament have any say in how this taxpayers' money is spent. In the circumstances, it is not surprising that the Quebec hierarchy was hesitant in the matter of university grants, and half tempted to accept them. True, the grants would come from an 'English and Protestant' state, but on the other hand what a bargain: the federal government offering funds on a simple, automatic, per-capita basis, with no strings attached, while at the same time recognizing that it lacks the constitutional competence to legislate on the money's subsequent use!

Is this not the context in which one should read the remarks of Mgr. Lussier, a rector who has elsewhere been admirable in his defence of academic freedom?

We suffer at the moment from seeming to be political. . . . The first responsibility for education lies with the parents. . . . The ultimate aims of education are not left to the judgment of the individual. . . . The Church, in matters of religious instruction or the safeguarding of religion, is absolutely the only competent authority. In other matters the Church still maintains its competence to the extent that it considers them related to the previous aims. . . . This philosophy of education recognizes the state's jurisdiction in certain areas; but with regard to the responsibility of parents, it only allows the state a supplementary and assisting role. With regard to the Church, a state composed of a majority of Catholic citizens must facilitate the accomplishment of the Church's mission. (*Le Devoir*, November 15)

I must confess that I find it hard to see what the state is left with or what it can do, except hand out the money blindly. In the circumstances there is no reason why it should give very much, nor can one expect taxpayers to finance institutions that are persistently declared to be none of their concern.[7] The 'Church' will continue to 'fill in' for other authorities, and education at all levels will gradually die of starvation.

Obviously, I do not accept 'official' Quebec attitudes toward education. But I also reject the arguments – especially Mr. St. Laurent's – in favour of federal grants to universities.

There still remains an aspect of the 'power of the purse' argument that no one has mentioned and that I have not yet examined. I have argued that it would be detrimental to our federal system to permit either the central or the provincial governments to donate money *received from their taxpayers* outside the area of their own jurisdiction.[8] The fact remains, however, that these governments may have in their possession money *that does not come from taxation*: funds from the public domain, from war debts, profit from Crown companies, operational earnings from the Bank of Canada, and so on. Of course, no theory of federalism can prevent a government from donating these funds as it sees fit. This wealth is, in a certain sense, the government's private property, since the act of acquiring it did not specifically diminish the share of taxable revenue that belongs to other governments. Nor does it infringe the autonomy of these other governments and cannot therefore be considered an interference in their affairs.

Thus the way in which these funds are acquired would never constitute encroachment. As for the way in which they are spent, only the electors of the donor government are qualified to judge whether or not they were put to good use. The electors of the recipient governments need only decide whether or not their governments were wise to accept. The principles of federation are not called into question.

However, it must be pointed out that in practice a govern-

[7] They are so little their concern, apparently, that the Board of Governors of the University of Montreal (which includes several laymen, as Mr. Perrault would point out) does not feel obliged to inform the public about the use made of tens of millions of dollars subscribed by the public a few years ago.
[8] It is in fact against this very point that Mr. Duplessis has given his only serious argument. On October 19, 1956, he declared: 'When the federal government levies *taxes* ... for purposes within provincial jurisdiction, it goes beyond its proper field of action and its particular field of taxation.'

ment's 'private' wealth cannot be distinguished from funds raised by taxation once it has gone into the Consolidated Revenue Fund. This makes it impossible, in practice, to know what money may be used without limitations for grants, and what money may not. Even if it were possible to know, it would matter very little in the case of a government that, through socialization or the intermediary of Crown companies, filled its coffers with an endless supply of 'private' funds. For then it could make limitless donations.

And so, in three short paragraphs we have managed to get round my long and elaborate argument against Mr. St. Laurent's theory. It appears that a government *can* make grants as it wishes – even in areas for which other governments are responsible – provided it uses its own funds, and does not take the money from the taxpayers of other levels of governments. If there are any readers who have had the patience to follow me to this point, they may well feel like asking, 'And where does all this get us?'

But it does get us somewhere. For we have discovered that even the most scrupulous refutation of every argument put forward in favour of the grants still leaves *one* reason for permitting the federal government to give and the provinces to receive university grants. This ultimate reason is the touchstone of the entire system. If one tries to refute it, one completely paralyses the modern state. If, on the other hand, one exaggerates its scope, one destroys the very notion of a federal system.

In fact, on the one hand, how can either the central or the provincial governments be prevented from having 'private' money in their coffers? To do so, the most basic concepts of liberalism would have to be practised; private enterprise would have to take over the handling of the mail, firemen, highway systems, Hydro, the Liquor Commission, the Bank of Canada, and so on. And even then there would still be operations relating to the public domain: sale of natural resources, maritime fisheries, etc. Then again, how can the various levels of government be prevented from making donations as they see fit from their 'private' funds without also denying the Christian duties of pity and mutual aid?

But if, on the other hand, any government, federal or provincial, decided to abuse its constitutional right to give 'private' funds outside its jurisdiction, it would certainly cause the ruin of both taxpayers and the federal system. In their determination to finance their excesses with 'private' money rather than taxation funds, such governments would in fact engage themselves in a program of complete state control, each government trying to enrich itself at the expense of others in order to prevent others from doing the same at its expense. It would be small consolation for citizens to find themselves 'scalped' as consumers rather than as taxpayers!

Clearly, it is impossible to make a rigorous and adequate division of the total wealth available to the sovereign state between the federal government and the provinces. It is the same country that is governed by the central authority and the ten provinces. The same taxpayers are solicited by the two levels of government; the same consumers depend upon them. Consequently, any attempt to arrange the 'spheres of influence'– or the taxpayer's wallet – into water-tight compartments only leads to absurdity. An excess of logic in one direction leads to meaningless isolationism and to the spiritual wilderness within which our self-styled nationalists wish to immure us; in the opposite direction it leads to an exaggerated, totalitarian centralization that spells death to both culture and democracy. Such logic can only result either in separatism, or in a unitary state; and the stages in its progression are financial strangulation, repeated disallowance by Ottawa of provincial laws, civil war.

It would therefore be futile to avoid one's responsibilities and leave the solution of these problems entirely to the courts. There are areas in which even the courts cannot provide enlightenment: no matter how clear one's rights, the federal system must ultimately rest upon a basis of collaboration. Tensions must be creative; otherwise our country will be destroyed. To avoid this possibility, we must pass beyond the limits of logic and law: we must at all costs enter the field of moral judgment and good will.

To sum up, we may say that it is permissible to make moderate donations even outside one's own jurisdiction. But the nature of the donation must be such that its recipient does not have grounds to suspect that charity is being given to him out of his own pocket. And how can this suspicion be avoided in Canada, when the central government takes such a large proportion of the tax revenue and makes such regular, organized grants outside its own jurisdiction?

There remain only a few practical conclusions to be drawn from this long argument.

THE FEDERAL GOVERNMENT

In offering grants to universities, the federal government could have made a gesture of mutual assistance that would have been constitutionally acceptable.

Instead, it made the mistake of linking its gesture with a conception of the fiscal system that is incompatible with harmonious federalism. It will be recalled how unjust, from the point of view of provincial autonomy, were the results of the first set of fiscal agreements. And it is certain that the federal authorities have not yet shown such regard for the provinces as to make them unmindful of the classical warning *Timeo Danaos et dona ferentes*. It is insulting to the provinces to be offered gifts from what Mr. St. Laurent tells them is their own taxpayers' money. It is fatal for the principles of representative democracy.

Even if the federal government now claimed that the money used for the grants was 'private', its excess of wealth would still be inadmissible in a federal system where the deprivation of provinces and municipalities is precisely the result of federal fiscal concepts.

The federal government must therefore contrive to change its fiscal practices so that provinces and municipalities have at their disposal sufficient tax revenue to allow them to fulfil their obligations.

Until this is done, we shall be justified in suspecting that the federal government's gifts are marred by improper motives, and in remembering it at election time.

THE UNIVERSITIES

Universities could have accepted the grants if they had first managed to make Mr. St. Laurent modify the concepts underlying them.[9]

University teachers and administrators are also voters, and influential ones at that. Had they understood the problem more clearly, they could have benefited from the grants and at the

---

[9]Mgr. Lussier's argument in favour of using the grants only for 'capital expenditure' seems to be a commendable attempt to qualify the donor's 'absolute power'. (*Le Devoir*, November 15, 1956) What a pity that he should have chosen an argument so constitutionally specious!

same time made the federal government accept more sensible views on federal tax systems.

Mr. Duplessis would then have been forced by his own autonomist logic to pass a law preventing universities from accepting federal donations. Discussion of such a law in the Legislature would have meant that Liberals could not have had recourse to the evasive tactics they used on November 20. The voters would have taken a further step toward maturity, and the universities toward a sense of responsibility.

However, it now seems quite certain that secret negotiations have convinced all Quebec universities to reject the grants. This is not in itself fatal, for, by virtue of a clause whose astuteness I cannot help admiring, grants not claimed are not lost: they are to accumulate until one day the very magnitude of the sum offered will force the Quebec electorate to weigh the full strength of a rapacious centralization against merely verbal autonomist policies.

On the other hand, all is lost if universities indulge in secret diplomacy and *combinazione*, as they have already begun to do. The people will be slightly more ignorant of the needs of education, universities will find themselves in new bondage, and the politicians of Ottawa and Quebec will continue to play football with the constitution.

Now is the time, therefore, for people to see what stuff academics, rectors, and chancellors are made of: let them *publicly* challenge the Union Nationale government to set up and put into effect, within the next three years, a plan allowing universities to assume, untroubled by political manoeuvering, their cultural, scientific, and financial obligations. If Mr. Duplessis will not accept the challenge or the time limit, they should set to work to oust him from power. Let them say the same kind of thing to Mr. St. Laurent about his economic policies, and use the same threat of sanctions.

They will not earn our respect in any other way.

THE PROVINCIAL GOVERNMENT

It is not the government's policy of autonomy that we condemn, but the purely negative and narrowly partisan aspect of this policy. Let Mr. Duplessis establish an administration as efficient and honest as the federal government, and we shall then consider the rivalry to be a fair one. Let him give the universities, and indeed the entire school system, the means of fulfilling their role. Let him give so generously in this field that the federal grants will seem insignificant, and therefore acceptable. Let him reply to federal attitudes on tax sharing and the grants with constructive alternatives instead of refusals. Let him be so competent and so full of good will as to put the federal government on the defensive in these matters; he can be as fanciful as he likes provided he achieves results.[10]

Alas, this is mere wishful thinking. Mr. Duplessis believes that we have the cleverest people, the best system of education, and the best government in the world. And the greatest provincial premier since Confederation.

[10]In *Vrai*, December 11, 1954, I suggested to Duplessis a technique to prevent the province from registering a loss every time it refuses to accept federal generosity (university grants, financing for the Trans-Canada Highway, and so on).

Cité Libre, February 1957. Translated from the French by Joanne L'Heureux.

Some Obstacles to Democracy in Quebec

HISTORICALLY, French Canadians have not really believed in democracy for themselves; and English Canadians have not really wanted it for others. Such are the foundations upon which our two ethnic groups have absurdly pretended to be building democratic forms of government. No wonder the ensuing structure has turned out to be rather flimsy.

The purpose of the present essay is to re-examine some of the unstated premises from which much of our political thinking and behaviour is derived, and to suggest that there exists an urgent need for a critical appraisal of democracy in Canada. No amount of inter-group back-slapping or political *bonne-ententisme* will change the fact that democracy will continue to be thwarted in Canada so long as one-third of the people hardly believe in it – and that because to no small extent the remaining two-thirds provide them with ample grounds for distrusting it.

I

French Canadians are perhaps the only people in the world who 'enjoy' democracy without having had to fight for it. Before 1763 they had known only an authoritarian rule, implicitly founded on a belief in the divine right of kingship. The people were subjects of an autocratic monarch and were governed by administrators responsible only to him. Their church was also authoritarian, their seigneurial system was quasi-feudal, and even on a strictly local plane the farmers and townsfolk had

103

never been active participants in public affairs. As Gustave Lanctot demonstrated: 'The *habitants* of New France had no experience of common action in political matters. With no organization whatsoever that could group and direct them they had become accustomed to submitting without question to the ordinances of the intendants, to the orders of the governors and to the edicts of Versailles.'[1]

That whole political structure was challenged in 1760 *by an outside force*. And its gradual replacement by forms of sovereignty which were to give an ever widening place to the principles of self-government was first brought about not by the Canadiens but by the English colonists. It was the latter who protested against the Act of 1774 and demanded an elective assembly; it was the former who circulated petition after petition in opposition to such an assembly. In 1788, Lord Dorchester advised the Colonial Office that only one-fifth of the total population wanted a 'change of laws and form of government';[2] and fully three-quarters of the French Canadians were actively opposed to such a change.[3]

Consequently, when the Constitutional Act of 1791 ushered in – after a fashion – representative government, the Canadiens were neither psychologically nor politically prepared for it. As Durham later remarked, they were being initiated to responsible government at the wrong end; a people who had not been entrusted with the governing of a parish were suddenly enabled through their votes to influence the destinies of the state. And as was natural with a vanquished people, they valued their new form of government less for its intrinsic value than as a means to their racial and religious survival. Thus, though the elections of 1792 failed to evoke much enthusiasm in the Canadiens, they were quick to realize that, though their ethnic group composed 94 per cent of the population, it had elected only 68 per cent of the Assembly; and that furthermore they were in a

[1] *L'Administration de la Nouvelle-France* (Paris, 1929), p. 140. See also F. Ouellet, 'M. Michel Brunet et le problème de la conquête', *Bulletin des recherches historiques* (June 1956), p. 99: 'La société canadienne à l'époque de la Nouvelle-France avait vécu sous l'absolutisme le plus complet.'

[2] Quoted by Mason Wade, *The French Canadians, 1760–1967* (Toronto, 1968), p. 96.

[3] M. Trudel, 'L'Essai du régime parlementaire', *Notre Temps* (Montreal), April 2, 1955.

minority in both the non-elective bodies – the Legislative and Executive Councils, where the seat of power truly rested.

Such a situation, soon to be aggravated by Governor Craig's despotic disposition, stifled what otherwise might have been a nascent belief in democracy. French Canadians felt that they had been deceived by the pre-1791 propaganda extolling the virtues and powers of representative assemblies; and they would forevermore look with distrust at majority rule, so called. True, they soon took to the electoral process like ducks to water; and 1837–8 even found many of them fighting and dying to uphold its logic. But such conduct cannot be ascribed to a sudden miraculous conversion to parliamentarianism. They had but one desire – to survive as a nation; and it had become apparent that parliamentary government might turn out to be a useful tool for that purpose. Consequently, in adopting piece by piece the British political system, their secret design was not merely to use it, but to abuse it if need be.[4]

Such abuse was apparent in the extremism of the assemblies which opposed first Aylmer's and then Gosford's conciliatory attitudes, and brought the racial issue to a head. Though the *Quatre-vingt-douze Résolutions* reflected the republicanism of the leaders of the revolt, there is little doubt that the effectiveness of the document among the people stemmed mainly from the anti-British violence which it contained. And whereas the Mackenzie rebellion in Upper Canada was a clear struggle for democratic self-government, most of Papineau's followers took up their pitchforks to fight for national self-determination. It was because of that issue that Durham observed: 'I expected to find a contest between a government and a people: I found two nations warring in the bosom of a single state: I found a struggle not of principles but of races.'[5]

The Canadiens fought at Saint-Denis and Saint-Eustache as they would eventually rally for electoral battles or parliamentary debates whenever their ethnic survival seemed to be imperilled, as men in an army whose sole purpose is to drive the *Anglais* back. And, as everyone knows, the army is a poor training

[4]See F. R. Scott, 'Canada et Canada français', *Esprit* (Paris) (August 1952); and also P. E. Trudeau, 'Réflexions sur la politique au Canada français', *Cité Libre* (December 1952). I have drawn heavily from this earlier article of mine in a few of the following paragraphs.

[5]*The Durham Report* (Coupland ed., Oxford, 1945), p. 15.

corps for democracy, no matter how inspiring its cause.

That is not to deny the existence of radical currents in French-Canadian political thought. For instance, one cannot ignore the fact that during part of the nineteenth century a significant section of the *bourgeoisie* was notoriously *rouge*. But if historical events are any guide at all to the discovery of underlying ideologies, it seems fair to assert that the dominant ideologies in French Canada turned out to be more nationalistic than democratic. A lengthy study would be necessary to show how French-Canadian radicalism was crushed, mainly by agreement between the English-Canadian governing class and the French-Canadian higher clergy. Quite typical of such a pincers operation was the seizure of *Le Canadien* by Governor Craig, and the approval of that seizure by the Bishop of Quebec. The end result was that, for the mass of the people, the passage from French to British rule was remembered – not unnaturally – more as an enslaving defeat than as a liberation from Bourbon absolutism; regardless of how liberal were the conqueror's political institutions, they had no intrinsic value in the minds of a people who had not desired them, never learned to use them, and who finally only accepted them as a means of loosening the conqueror's grip.

How then were the French Canadians to use the arsenal of democratic 'fire-arms' put at their disposal? There were two possibilities: sabotage of the parliamentary works from within by systematic obstruction which, like the Irish strategy at Westminster, might lead to Laurentian Home Rule; or outward acceptance of the parliamentary game, but without any inward allegiance to its underlying moral principles. The latter choice prevailed, no doubt because the years 1830 to 1840 demonstrated that sabotage would lead to suppression by force. Moreover, a show of co-operation would have the added advantage of permitting French Canada to participate in the governing councils of the country as a whole. Such a decision guided most French-Canadian politicians after the union of Upper and Lower Canada, and continued to do so after Confederation.

Fundamentally, all French-Canadian political thinking stems from these historical beginnings. In the opinion of the French in Canada, government of the people by the people could not be *for* the people, but mainly for the English-speaking part of that people; such were the spoils of conquest. Whether such a belief was well founded (an issue I shall discuss in the following section) is entirely irrelevant to the present argument. So the Canadiens believed; and so they could only make-believe in democracy. They adhered to the 'social contract' with mental reservations; they refused to be inwardly bound by a 'general will' which overlooked the racial problem. Feeling unable to share as equals in the Canadian common weal, they secretly resolved to pursue only the French-Canadian weal, and to safeguard the latter they cheated against the former.

In all important aspects of national politics, guile, compromise, and a subtle kind of blackmail decided their course and determined their alliances. They appeared to discount all political or social ideologies, save nationalism. For the mass of the people the words Tory and Grit, Conservative and Liberal, referred neither to political ideals nor to administrative techniques. They were regarded only as meaningless labels, affixed to alternatives which permitted the auctioneering of one's support; they had no more meaning than *bleu* and *rouge*, which eventually replaced them in popular speech. French Canadians on the whole never voted for political or economic ideologies, but only for the man or group which stood for their *ethnic* rights: even condemnation of liberalism by the Church did not prevent Mercier and Laurier from being elected in 1886 and 1896; and the advantages to Quebec's economy of Laurier's reciprocity did not prevent Bourassa from being returned as an anti-imperialist in 1911.

In such a mental climate, sound democratic politics could hardly be expected to prevail, even in strictly provincial or local affairs where racial issues were not involved. For cheating becomes a habit. Through historical necessity, and as a means of survival, French Canadians had felt justified in finessing at the parliamentary game; and as a result the whole game of politics was swept outside the pale of morality. They had succeeded so well in subordinating the pursuit of the common weal to the pursuit of their particular ethnic needs that they never achieved any sense of obligation towards the general welfare, including the welfare of the French Canadians on non-racial issues. Consequently, apart from times of racial strife such as the Riel Rebellion, the schools question, conscription, the plebiscite, and the like – when the Canadiens banded together avowedly to fight for survival within the national whole – they came to regard politics as a game of every man for himself. In other words, their civic sense was corrupted and they became political immoralists.

The foregoing explanation of the lack of civic-mindedness must not be taken to exclude religious factors. French Canadians are Catholics; and Catholic nations have not always been ardent supporters of democracy. They are authoritarian in spiritual matters; and since the dividing line between the spiritual and the temporal may be very fine or even confused, they are often disinclined to seek solutions in temporal affairs through the mere counting of heads. If this be true in general, it is particularly so in the case of the clergy and laity of Quebec, influenced as they were by the Catholicism of nineteenth-century France, which largely rejected democracy as the daughter of the Revolution.

But there was a quite separate reason why the Church in Quebec was suspicious of popular sovereignty. When Canada passed into British hands, the Church naturally concerned herself with safeguarding the faith by protecting her authority. And, as it turned out, she discovered that her position had in a sense improved. For after the débâcle of 1760 she remained alone as a social beacon to give strength and guidance to a vanquished people, and to the victor she had the potentialities of a formidable opponent. So, after difficult beginnings, both powers found it advantageous to work out a *modus vivendi*. Loyalty was bartered for religious freedom, and the Church was as good as her word. During the wars of 1775, 1812, 1914, and 1939, the Catholic hierarchy preached submission to His Majesty's government; they even launched an appeal against the Fenian raiders in 1870. And at the time of the 1837 rebellion, they used their powers to check the *patriotes*.

When the faith lay safe, no distant call to democratic liberty held much appeal to the churchmen. The reason may have been partly that the torch of freedom so often appeared to be borne by enemies of the faith, as in the case of nineteenth-century revolutionaries whose staple stock-in-trade was anticlericalism. But more profane rivalries are not to be discounted. Until the rise of democratic politics, a French Canadian's only access to positions of command lay through holy orders; but with the coming of the politicians, a career was opened to the Canadiens whereby they might compete with ecclesiastical authority. It is no coincidence that leaders such as Papineau, Mercier, Laurier, and even Bourassa, to say nothing of a host of lesser men, all incurred varying degrees of ecclesiastical censure.[6]

A conquered people therefore not only faced a state which they feared as the creature of a foreign nation, but also belonged to a church which distrusted that state as a rival power and as a child of the Revolution, liable to be dominated by anti-clericals, Protestants, or even socialists. The resulting popular attitude was a combination of political superstition and social conservatism, wherein the state – any state – was regarded as an ominous being whose uncontrollable caprices were just as likely to lead it to crush families and devour crucifixes as to help the needy and maintain order.[7] Electoral processes for the mass of the people remained mysterious rituals of foreign origin, of little value beyond that for which the individual can barter his vote: a receipted grocery bill, a bottle of whisky, a workman's compensation, a contract to build a bridge, a school grant, a community hospital. For it is noteworthy that in Quebec, a school or a hospital is not expected by the citizens as of right, being their due from an obedient government and for which they pay, but as a reward for having returned a member to the Government benches.[8] And many a respectable citizen or prelate who would deem it dishonourable to sell his vote for a keg of beer thinks nothing of advising his *gens* to barter theirs for a load of bricks.

I see little use in illustrating these latter points, not only because that task was excellently done after the last Quebec

[6]P. E. Trudeau in *La Grève de l'amiante* (Montreal, 1956), p. 59. See also the author's 'Obstacles à la démocratie' in *Rapport de la Conférence de l'institut canadien des affaires publiques*, 1954.

[7]That and that alone can explain why nationalist Quebec has never dared to translate into public ownership and a demand for the welfare state its unending clamour for economic emancipation; and why a people – so moral in other areas – has no sense of moral obligation in its relation to the state.

[8]This doctrine was given its classic expression and official sanction in Mr. Duplessis's speeches to the electors of Verchères during the 1952 elections, and to those of Shawinigan during the 1956 elections.

general election[9] but also because such illustrations would not, *per se*, prove my point that French Canadians as a people do not believe in democracy, for other people who do profess to believe in democracy have none the less succumbed to corrupt electoral practices, the system of spoils, and so on. I prefer to quote some recent[10] and typical instances which exemplify not corruption, but the complete lack of a democratic frame of reference for French-Canadian political thinking.[11]

On the morning of the last provincial general election (June 20, 1956), the following was read over radio station CBF during the program called 'Prières du matin: Elévations matutinales':

> Sovereign authority, by whatever government it is exercised, is derived solely from God, the supreme and eternal principle of all power. . . . It is therefore an absolute error to believe that authority comes from the multitudes, from the masses, from the people, to pretend that authority does not properly belong to those who exercise it, but that they have only a simple mandate revocable at any time by the people. This error, which dates from the Reformation, rests on the false principle that man has no other master than his own reason. . . . All this explanation about the origin, the basis, and the composition of this alleged [!] sovereignty of the people is purely arbitrary. Moreover, if it is admitted, it will have as a consequence the weakening of authority, making it a myth, giving it an unstable and

[9]See André Laurendeau's series 'La Politique provinciale', *Le Devoir*, July and August 1956, during the course of which appeared the devastating denunciation written by the abbés Dion and O'Neil. See also Pierre Laporte's lengthy investigation 'Les Elections ne se font pas avec des prières', *Le Devoir*, October and November 1956. For material on the 1952 provincial elections see *Cité Libre*, December 1952.

[10]The present paper was first drafted in August 1956. As time went by I began to add references to current events, but soon discontinued this practice as it added more to the length than to the strength of my demonstration. Consequently my *recent* and *typical* instances are more typical than recent.

My original draft was written when the national Liberal Party was at the height of its glory. The accusations I shall level at it later on in this paper remain historically valid; but I must recognize that I felt less cruel in writing them a few years ago than I do in publishing them now. If it be a sop to anybody, I sadly add that the campaign waged by the Conservative henchmen in Quebec for the election of March 1958 has hardly given me reason to hope that by the sole grace of the new régime there will be a rebirth of democracy in 'la belle province'.

[11]For less recent examples of that authoritarian frame of mind, see the author's chapter in *La Grève de l'amiante*, pp. 22–7.

changeable basis, stimulating popular passions and encouraging sedition.[12]

Think *that* over before you cast your vote!

French-Canadian lack of concern for the liberties and traditions of Parliament was admirably brought out during the pipeline debate of 1956. The Toronto *Star*, the *Telegram*, the *Globe and Mail*, the Ottawa *Journal*, the *Citizen*, the Montreal *Gazette*, and many other English-language papers were all pressing for Mr. Speaker's resignation, but *L'Action catholique*, *Le Droit*, and *Le Devoir* looked with disdain on such childishness. Mr. Lorenzo Paré, a parliamentary correspondent of some repute in French-Canadian circles, wrote: 'There is no reason to stir up a great parliamentary crisis over such a trifling matter. . . . The most surprising thing is that it has been prolonged for so long and that during all these weeks the Commons has

[12]This program apparently is under the guidance of the Comité interdiocésain d'Action radiophonique. To sociologists, it is no doubt an interesting example of the intermeshing of two institutions as different as the Church and the Canadian Broadcasting Corporation. I need hardly add that Catholicism is not *per se* incompatible with democracy; as a matter of fact, many a Catholic would claim that democracy follows naturally from the Christian belief that all men are brothers and fundamentally equal. But the historical fact remains that the clergy in Quebec made no such deductions. On the contrary, the foregoing quotation shows a remarkable continuity of thought with the anti-democratic theories which Mgr. Plessis imparted to Quebec Catholics 150 years earlier. F. Ouellet has written with considerable insight on 'Mgr. Plessis et la naissance d'une bourgeoisie canadienne' in a paper presented to the Congrès de la Société canadienne de l'Histoire de l'Eglise catholique at Chicoutimi in August 1956. The following opinions of Mgr. Plessis are quoted from that paper. In 1799 the Bishop warned the faithful that if they were not protected against the influences of revolutionary France, 'the fatal tree of liberty will be planted in the middle of your town, the rights of man will be proclaimed; . . . you will be free, but it will be an oppressive freedom that will give you for masters the dregs of humanity and grind into the dust the respectable leaders who now possess your affection and your confidence.' In 1810 he denounced 'the system of the sovereignty of the people' as 'the most false and most absurd' of sophisms, and told his flock that 'J.C., in giving you a religion designed to lead you to heaven, has not asked you to control and supervise the sovereigns under whom you live.' In 1815 and 1823 he was still writing against the constitution of 1791, 'a constitution ill-suited to the genius of Canadians and which has had no other real effect than to render the governed insolent toward the governors. The spirit of democracy and of independence has won the people, has passed from them to the clergy, and you see the fruits of it.'

displayed a spectacle of surprising childishness.' *Le Devoir's* two parliamentary *courriéristes* had the same reaction. Mr. P. Laporte wrote: 'To aggravate matters the English press and the opposition have succeeded in making the real fundamentals of the problem disappear from sight. . . . Mr. St. Laurent has put things back into focus. He has practically said that it amounted to a tempest in a teapot.' And Mr. P. Vigeant:

> It is a situation that has been explained quite badly to French Canadians. One must have been brought up from childhood in the cult of parliamentary institutions in order to react vigorously to incidents that seem, at least to us, to be quite secondary. Respect for the Speaker of the House . . . is something surprising to us. . . . These incidents illustrate quite well the difficulties that face our representatives at Ottawa in adapting to English parliamentary institutions whose functioning . . . has so little in common with our French genius.[13]

Indeed, had the crisis over the Speaker's office aroused any considerable excitement at all in Quebec, it most surely would have been interpreted as a racial attack on Mr. Louis-René Beaudoin!

An unusual approach to civil liberties might also be considered as typical of French Canada. At the time of the decision on the Jehovah's Witness case, enforcing freedom of religion, public opinion in Quebec was quick to point out that the judges of the Supreme Court had been somewhat divided along racial and religious lines. The judgment of the Supreme Court on the Padlock Law drew the same kind of reaction. For instance, *Montréal-Matin* emphasized Judge Taschereau's dissent, and spoke of a Communist victory, good news for all revolutionaries in Quebec; Mr. P. Sauriol of *Le Devoir* (March 19, 1957) questioned whether 'the Supreme Court would be as careful in an opposite case when it would be a question of protecting provincial jurisdiction from a federal intrusion' and underlined 'one of the most profound differences that exist between us and English Canadians. . . . It is a question of knowing whether the defence of freedom must go as far as defending and respecting an alleged right to propagate error.'

Writing about the debate on the subservience of the C.B.C. to the party in power, and the whole issue of freedom of opinion, Mr. Gérard Filion of *Le Devoir* (April 10, 1957) remarked that if opposition parties were looking for an electoral issue,

[13]These quotations are from *Le Devoir*, July 3, 4, 10, 12, 1956.

SOME OBSTACLES TO DEMOCRACY IN QUEBEC / 113

they have probably taken the wrong road as far as French
Canada is concerned. Public opinion among us is not usually
aroused by this kind of dispute. This is probably wrong, but that
is how it is. On the other hand, the general feeling in French
Canada is that Mr. St. Laurent was right to [protest to Mr.
Dunton in order to] put in his place this young greenhorn who,
though only recently come to our country, wants to give us a
lesson on our duties toward the Empire.

If I have quoted heavily from *Le Devoir*, the reason is that it
is generally recognized even in English Canada as a truly independent daily of exceptionally high intellectual standards. But
it should go without saying that in the lesser French-Canadian
press, democracy, if it is known at all, is known as an evil. Mr.
Duplessis's paper, *Le Temps* (Quebec, September 24, 1956),
in condemning the Rassemblement, accused it of the greatest
of all sins: leading the people 'vers la laïcisation et la démo-
cratisation'. Another weekly refers to citizens as 'subjects' and
preaches realism:

> The true masters of a province or of a country are and will
> remain the money powers. . . . It is no longer necessary to be
> deeply scandalized about the favouritism that grows with
> political partisanship. Whether in a democracy or in a mon-
> archy . . . there normally develops between him [the head of
> the government] and his subordinates a camaraderie, some-
> times even a sincere friendship, that leads to compromise and
> favouritism at the expense of others, and in the end at the
> expense of the people. This is not an ideal situation, but it is a
> very human one, and it would be unrealistic to dream of a
> government that could maintain itself in power for any length
> of time without some sort of favouritism.[14]

Mr. Léopold Richer, long-time parliamentary reporter, and
now director of *Notre Temps*, a self-styled 'hebdomadaire social
et culturel' with (until recently) a wide support among the
clergy, is prone to mock 'the new religion of democracy', and
uphold authority everywhere. The following case is interesting
because Mr. Richer was indignant at the 'libertarianism' of what
many a democrat might feel to be a rather authoritarian conception of civil government. Mr. G. Filion had written in *Le
Devoir*: 'Freedom is not a gift but something that must be won.
The only freedom is that which has been torn from authority.'
At which Mr. Richer fumes: 'Have you read this? Did you

[14]Quoted by André Laurendeau in a scathing editorial, *Le Devoir*, July
20, 1956.

understand it? . . . It is defiance of established authority, whether religious or civil. It is sedition. It is revolt. Gérard Filion has been reduced to preaching revolution openly. Either he does not understand the true meaning of his words . . . or else one must regard him as an extremely dangerous journalist.' And so on.[15]

If I were to quote all the material proving that French Canadians fundamentally do not believe in democracy, and that on the whole neither the pulpit, nor the Legislative Assembly, nor the radio, nor the press is doing much to instil such a belief, I would 'exhaust time and encroach upon eternity'. In 1958, French Canadians must begin to learn democracy from scratch. For such is the legacy of a history during which – as a minority – they hammered the process of parliamentary government into a defensive weapon of racial warfare, and – as Catholics – they believed that authority might well be left to descend from God in God's good time and in God's good way.

II

Parliamentary democracy I take to be a method of governing free men which operates roughly as follows: organized parties that wish to pursue – by different means – a common end, agree to be bound by certain rules according to which the party with the most support governs on condition that leadership will revert to some other party whenever the latter's means become acceptable to the greater part of the electorate. The common end – the general welfare – which is the aim of all parties may be more or less inclusive, and may be defined in different ways by different men. Yet it must in some way include equality of opportunity for everyone in all important fields of endeavour; otherwise 'agreement on fundamentals' would never obtain. For instance, democracy cannot be made to work in a country where a large part of the citizens are by status condemned to a perpetual state of domination, economic or otherwise.[16] Essentially, a true democracy must permit the periodic transformation of political minorities into majorities.

[15]*Notre Temps* (Montreal), October 27, 1956.
[16]With others, Elton Mayo, *The Social Problems of an Industrial Civilization* (London, 1949), p. xiii, has observed that 'representative government does not work satisfactorily for the general good in a society that exhibits extreme differences in the material standards of living of its various social groups. . . . [Nor can] representative government be effectively exercised by a society internally divided by group hostilities and hatreds.'

In Canada the above conditions have never obtained. As to ends, the French Canadians would never settle for anything less than absolute equality of political rights with the English Canadians, a demand which, as I shall show below, was never seriously considered by the Colonial Office before the advent of responsible government, nor by the English-speaking majority since then. In brief, one-third of the nation disagreed with the common good as defined by the other two-thirds. Consequently parliamentary government was unworkable, for, given this situation, there arose a fundamental cleavage between a majority and a minority which could therefore not alternate in power.

It may be that after 1760 the French were just as unrealistic in their demands as the English were uncomprising in their attitude. The point remains that the English-speaking Canadians, rightly considering that self-government is the noblest way of regulating social relations among free men, proceeded to claim its benefits for Canada, but only after serving standing notice on the French that such benefits were not for members of a subject race.

It is a matter of record that the purpose of the Royal Proclamation of 1763 was complete assimilation of the French Canadians; yet it was through that instrument that the French Canadians first became acquainted with representative government. 'The proclamation tacitly assumed such an influx [of English settlers] by providing for the establishment of English law and by promising an assembly.'[17] And when Governor Murray tried to protect the *habitant* against the voracious English merchants, the latter 'demanded the immediate calling of an assembly for whose candidates the French might be allowed to vote, but of which only Protestants were to be members'.[18] Of such an assembly, Maseres, the incumbent Attorney General, was to write in 1766: 'An assembly so constituted [because of the laws against popery] might pretend to be a representative of the people there, but it would be a representative of only the 600 new English settlers, and an instrument in their hands of dominating over the 90,000 French.'[19] Instead of an assembly the Quebec Act of 1774 was

[17]E. McInnis, *Canada: A Political and Social History* (New York, 1947), p. 130.
[18]*Ibid.*, p. 138.
[19]Quoted by Wade, *The French Canadians*, p. 60.

brought down, welcomed by the Canadiens, but attacked by the English colonists for being undemocratic and establishing popery. Such attacks could only impart a peculiar understanding of democracy to a people who through the act had only received what they considered their birthright: freedom of faith and of language.

When at last French Canadians were initiated into the sanctuary of representative government, by the Constitutional Act of 1791, they discovered that it did not mean majority rule through an elected assembly, but rule by the representatives of the conquering minority, nominated to the Executive and Legislative Councils. Moreover, at its very first meeting, the elected Assembly itself split along ethnic lines over the language qualifications of the Speaker. The history of democracy in Lower Canada from 1793 to 1840 was that of one long process of warping. As Mason Wade puts it, the English colonists 'were badly scared men'. In 1793, Richardson, the able leader of the Opposition, was to explain: 'Nothing can be so irksome as the situation of the English members – without numbers to do any good – doomed to the necessity of combating the absurdities of the majority, without a hope of success.' In 1806, the English merchants raised the cry of 'French domination' because of a tax they disliked, and during the fray the Montreal *Gazette* and the Quebec *Mercury* were summoned to the bar of the Assembly for contempt of that body. In 1810, Chief Justice Sewell proposed the establishment of high property restrictions upon the franchise, to prevent French dominance in the Assembly; the union of Upper and Lower Canada for more prompt and certain anglicization. Governor Craig also regretted the presence of a French majority in the Assembly, proposed various schemes for reducing it, and advocated the playing of one ethnic group against the other.[20]

As is well known, the situation deteriorated steadily until it led to the rebellion of 1837-8. When the smoke of battle had cleared, Lord Durham observed that

> the most just and sensible of the English . . . seem to have joined in the determination never again to submit to a French majority. . . . The English complained that they, a minority, suffered under the oppressive use to which power was turned by the

[20]*Ibid.*, pp. 93, 97, 102, 108, 110, 112, 202.

French majority. . . . They assert that Lower Canada must be *English*, at the expense, if necessary, of not being *British*. . . . Nor have the English inhabitants forgotten in their triumph the terror with which they suddenly saw themselves surrounded by an insurgent majority. . . . Their only hope of safety is supposed to rest on systematically terrifying and disabling the French, and in preventing a majority of that race from ever again being predominant in any portion of the legislature of the Province.[21]

That latter design was finally[22] realized through the Act of Union in 1840. A single Legislative Council was appointed and a single Assembly was elected, with equal representation for Upper and Lower Canada, in spite of the fact that the latter province had 650,000 inhabitants against the former's 450,000. Moreover, English was to be the sole official language.

The final irrational upsurge of the frightened minority occurred in 1849, when the passing of the Rebellion Losses Bill unleashed the English-Canadian riots which led to the pelting of Governor Elgin, the burning of the Parliament buildings, and the Annexation Manifesto. But a year or so later, demographic change had at last made English-speaking Canadians the more numerous ethnic group; and forever after they were able to preach the grandeur of true democracy and to back up their preachings by their own virtuous submission to majority rule. Unfortunately, it was then too late for French Canadians to unlearn their first seventy-five years of schooling, during which time the notion of representative government had been identified with domination by an English-speaking minority. And they could hardly be expected to greet as the millennium the advent of representation by population in 1867, which could only mean continued domination, but this time by an English-speaking majority.

Future events confirmed French-Canadian scepticism with reasonable regularity: the wanton use of majorities to do away with a bilingual legislature in Manitoba, and with *droits acquis* over separate schools in various provinces; the formation of a Union Government in 1917 to ride roughshod over the whole of French Canada; the use of the plebiscite in 1942, by which

[21]*The Durham Report*, pp. 18, 35, 43.
[22]It had been advocated many times before: by Sewell and by Craig (1810), by the Duke of Richmond (1819), by Lord Dalhousie (1820). And it had almost succeeded in 1822, when a petition was signed by some fourteen hundred English-speaking Montrealers.

English Canada pretended to absolve the Liberals from their twenty years of solemn (if unwise) pledges to the French Canadians; the long-standing practice of favouring immigration from the British Isles as opposed to that from France.[23] Such examples of the use of majorities as a bludgeon to 'convince' minorities should remind us that if French Canadians made the mistake of using democracy as a tool of ethnic warfare, the English Canadians offered them the wherewithal to learn. In all cases where fundamental oppositions arose on racial lines, the French felt that a stronger force (first an army and later a majority of citizens) could always be mustered against them. Of course it would be wrong to conclude that cultural relations between the two groups in political matters were a complete failure. The converse is happily the case. But sadly enough, even in cases where complete co-operation has seemed to exist between the French minority and the English-speaking majority, within the framework of the national parties for instance,[24] democracy appears to have been thwarted.

Towards the end of the nineteenth century a well-known combination of factors brought French Canadians *en masse* into the fold of the Liberal Party. The choice of Laurier as leader and the way the Conservatives handled the Riel Rebellion convinced the French-Canadian voters that their ethnic survival could be better guaranteed by the Liberals than by the Conservatives. And so, in every federal election from 1891 to 1958 Quebec returned a majority of Liberals to Ottawa, nearly always an overwhelming majority.[25]

I shall not belittle the amazing astuteness, foresight, and (in the very early days) courage that made such a performance

[23]As early as 1763 the implicit assumption of British policy was that the French group was to be swamped by immigration (see McInnis, *Canada*, p. 130). Durham recommended that policy in his famous report (p. 180). And the laws of Canada favoured it until after the Second World War, when P.C. 4849 was amended by P.C. 4186 (September 16, 1948) and by P.C. 5593 (December 10, 1948). In fairness, it must be added that the French on either side of the Atlantic were not militant advocates of migration to Canada; but the fact of inequality under the law is not changed for all that.

[24]The following remarks apply mainly to the Liberal Party, since for nearly seventy years French-Canadian representation in the others was not numerically significant. At the present time, it is too soon to generalize about the Conservative Party.

[25]Provincially the Liberal grip on power was only broken in 1936, when an even more 'nationalist' party was born.

possible. No doubt the Liberals received great help at various times from their bungling Conservative and socialist opponents; but they still deserve credit for preventing the growth in Quebec of a federal nationalist party, even at the height of Mercier's and later of Bourassa's influence, and even when the Bloc Populaire was in full sway. For they learned to cater to French Canada's intuition that its destinies would be better protected at Ottawa by a more or less independent bloc within the party in power than by a nationalist party, bound, because of its ethnic basis, to remain forever seated on Opposition benches.

But power entails responsibilities; and there is no doubt that the Liberals tragically failed to shoulder theirs. A party cannot have the approval of a majority of the electorate for well over half a century without accepting much of the blame for that electorate's political immaturity. If French Canadians even today have learnt so little about democracy, if they twist its rules so shockingly, if they are constantly tempted by authoritarianism, it is to a large degree because the Liberal Party has been miserably remiss in its simple political duty. Instead of educating the French-speaking electorate to believe in democracy, the Liberals seemed content to cultivate the ignorance and prejudice of that electorate.[26]

I should not like to apportion blame between French- and English-speaking Liberals in this regard. The gravest faults no doubt fall squarely on the former. It is they who have failed to inject valid democratic concepts into the innumerable campaigns waged during the present century. On the contrary, forgetful of the common weal, they have always encouraged Quebeckers to continue using their voting bloc as an instrument of racial defence, or of personal gain. Their only slogans have been racial slogans. Until 1917 their cry was: Vote for a party led by a French Canadian. After 1917 it was: Vote against Borden's party. This cry was still used in recent years, though between 1947 and 1957 more sophisticated politicians were

---

[26]There were some rare exceptions. For instance, a short but meritorious effort was made during the Second World War by groups that founded the Institut démocratique, but it was soon to perish. Today, a minority within a splinter group is trying to build a democratic Fédération Libérale provinciale with the help of a weekly, *La Réforme*; both are still very far from the electorate. Whether the Liberal débâcle at Ottawa will strengthen the provincial reformers remains an open question.

able to revert to the French-Canadian leadership slogan, as well as to attack the Conservatives for being 'anti-French Canadian Protestants and imperialists' and the C.C.F. for being 'anti-French Canadian atheists and centralizers'. And it was largely on the strength of such slogans that they were elected.

But the fact remains that throughout most of its existence the federal Liberal Party was overwhelmingly an English-speaking party. And that majority in my view should bear the blame for serious faults of omission with respect to the backwardness of democracy in Quebec. They might, *à la rigueur*, be excused for not having liked to poke into the hornet's nest of their French-Canadian bloc. But the pity is that they seemed to encourage such a state of affairs. The shameful incompetence of the average Liberal M.P. from Quebec was a welcome asset to a government that needed little more than a herd of *ânes savants* to file in when the division bell rang. The party strategists had but to find an acceptable stable master – Laurier, Lapointe, St. Laurent – and the trained donkeys sitting in the back benches could be trusted to behave. Even the choice of front-benchers very often smacked of shysterism. Excepting the French-Canadian leader, who was usually a man of quality, many ministers of that ethnic group were chosen not so much for their ability to serve democracy as for their ability to make democracy serve the party; their main qualification was familiarity with machine politicians and schemers, and until lately they were traditionally put at the head of patronage departments such as the Post Office and Public Works. To sum up, English-speaking Canadians have long behaved in national politics as though they believed that democracy was not for French Canadians.

That this is so is forcefully confirmed by English-Canadian behaviour in local politics in Quebec. In precisely that province where the people had been historically conditioned to believe that government is a function of wealth and power, rather than of the will of the majority, it so happened that the English-speaking Canadians had wealth and power but not numbers. In such circumstances, it was perhaps inevitable that the English-speaking element should choose to govern with what means they had, rather than be thankless apostles of democracy, preaching in the wilderness that they had partly created. None the less, the net result is that incredible amounts are spent in

Quebec at every election, many times more per capita than in other provinces.[27] Now it is all very well to denounce the dishonesty of voters who accept refrigerators and television sets in exchange for their votes, but it must be recognized that the offering of bribes is just as detrimental to democracy as the taking of them. So the question remains: Who makes those bribes possible?

As the President of Quebec Beauharnois stated, after his company had contributed three-quarters of a million dollars to various campaign funds: 'Gratefulness was always regarded as an important factor in dealing with democratic governments.'[28] Of course, to some extent party funds come from French-Canadian business men and seekers after petty favours. But the *real* money comes from huge corporations and wealthy enterprises that give willingly to parties which, apart from being an insurance against socialism, promise (and deliver) favourable labour laws, exemptions from property taxes, special franchises, valuable contracts without tender, mining or hydro rights of inestimable value in exchange for a row of pins – to say nothing of openly tolerating profitable infringements of the law (as in the case of timber-cutting regulations). Those powerful financial interests are not to any extent directed or owned by French Canadians. Thus it is somewhat paradoxical to observe that wealthy, upper-class, English-speaking Quebeckers may sometimes return an Opposition member in their riding, thereby rejecting as individuals the undemocratic practices of the Duplessis government; but as directors and managers of wealthy concerns what a part they must play in making his elections a success!

Perhaps the prize example of such political schizophrenia is found in the Montreal *Star* and the Montreal *Gazette*. Unparliamentary procedure at Ottawa or undemocratic practices by national politicians are denounced with the vigilance which befits truly democratic organs. But these papers never have

[27]This is common knowledge among professional politicians. Attempted estimates for the 1952 provincial elections can be found in G. Pelletier and P. E. Trudeau, *Cité Libre* (December 1952), pp. 35 and 61. Guesses at amounts spent in the 1956 elections have ranged from $15 million to $25 million, though this seems hard to believe. (See *Le Devoir*'s articles referred to in n. 9.)

[28]Quoted by R. MacGregor Dawson, *The Government of Canada* (Toronto, 1949), p. 573.

editorials on, indeed often neglect to report, the innumerable cases of violation of parliamentary and democratic rights which are standard procedure for the Government they support in Quebec. It is safe to assume that a person whose reading of politics was limited to the *Star* and *Gazette* would never realize that the Premier constantly shouts orders to the Speaker of the Lower House, and has even participated in a loud voice in the conduct of the Upper House; that he vociferously commands the Speaker to expel members from the House on the flimsiest of pretexts; that several times during debate he has accused an honourable member of ingratitude for sitting on the Opposition benches after having, as a student, received assistance from the Government side; that he has introduced retroactive and vindictive legislation, sometimes bearing on individual adversaries (for example the Guindon bill, and the Picard bill in 1954; and since then the concerted legislative warfare against elected municipal representatives belonging to the Civic Action League); that he frankly tells the electorate that they will not get roads or bridges in their riding if they return a member of the Opposition; or that during the last provincial campaign his party repeatedly branded the Liberals as Communists because 'their friends in Ottawa' had given money to the Colombo Plan instead of to the farmers of Nicolet.[29]

Indeed it is hard to escape the conclusion that if in the past English Canadians went far to instil a distrust of representative government in French-Canadian minds, in the present they are doing precious little to eradicate that distrust and to spread the gospel of honest parliamentarianism in Quebec.

III

In the two foregoing sections I will perhaps have managed to displease all Canadians. Both French and English may claim

[29]These are miscellaneous examples of fairly recent occurrences. Concerning the 'discretion' of the English press in relation to more distant instances, see a pamphlet by F. R. Scott, *The Montreal Star and the C.C.F.* (Montreal, 1944). See also G. Pelletier, 'La Grève et la presse' in *La Grève de l'amiante*. As of late, this topic has drawn more and more attention. For instance, see the indignant editorials by P. Vigeant and G. Filion, *Le Devoir*, February 21, December 7, 1957; and André Laurendeau's editorials on 'La Théorie du roi nègre'. Also, probably for the first time in English, the subject was dealt with in a very remarkable editorial, 'The Shame of English Canada', which appeared in the *McGill Daily*, February 26, 1958.

that I put too much blame on their particular ethnic group. But that would be silly, for under the democratic form of government all citizens are jointly and severally responsible for the procedures by which they choose their leaders; all men are to blame who fail in their duty of denouncing undemocratic practices and shady politicians.

Democracy is not easy, even under the best of circumstances. But it is no consolation to know that under other climes other pitfalls beset democratic ways. It is important for Canadians to realize what particular pitfalls beset *them*. And there is no doubt that the unpleasant facts I have evoked play an important part in conditioning Canadian political behaviour on both sides of the ethnic barrier. I have tried to pry those facts away from the back of the collective minds of French and English Canada, and fit them into an explanatory hypothesis, for I believe that such exercises are necessary if Canadians are to know how to provide the whole of Canada with a common and enduring democratic faith.

If my hypothesis is right, the current vogue for preaching political morality in Quebec will by itself be of little avail. For so long as people do not believe in democracy there is no reason why they should accept its ethics. Political behaviour in Quebec can be described as immoral, objectively speaking; but subjectively the people are not conscious of wrongdoing, and consequently they see no reason to change that behaviour.

But this essay has run its course; further thoughts would lead me towards ground where men of action take over. And this book is no place to publish a tract for the times.

This article was first published, with slight variations, in the *Canadian Journal of Economics and Political Science*, Vol. XXIV, No. 3 (August 1958), and later as a chapter in Mason Wade (ed.), *Canadian Dualism* (Toronto: University of Toronto Press, 1960).

The Practice and
Theory of Federalism

*A great democracy must either
sacrifice self-government to unity,
or preserve it by federalism.*

LORD ACTON

GOALS have no more reality than the means that are devised to reach them. As every reformer discovers sooner or later to his chagrin, it is not sufficient to conceive ideals lofty enough, and to desire them strongly enough, for them to be automatically attained through some due process of history. And there exists no 'Operation Boot-straps' whereby dedicated parties can lift themselves by sheer force of will into the realm of justice triumphant.

Therefore inevitably, the electoral failings of democratic socialism in most industrial societies have led the partisans of social democracy in recent years to reappraise their ends and their means in the light of changing social and economic reality. For example, the nationalization of the instruments of production is now being considered less as an end than as a means, and one that might in many cases be replaced by more flexible processes of economic control and redistribution.

In Canada, the Regina Manifesto of 1933 was replaced in 1956 by the Winnipeg statement of principles which purported to fit more adequately the social and economic temper of the times. Socialist strategy likewise has been radically altered, as is shown by the recent resolutions of the C.C.F. and of the Canadian Labour Congress to launch a new party. But unfortunately socialists in Canada have seldom been guided in their doctrine and their strategy by a whole-hearted acceptance of the basic political fact of federalism.

Left-wing thinkers have too often assumed that fundamental

reform is impossible without a vast increase, in law or in fact, of the national government's areas of jurisdiction; C.C.F. parliamentarians have repeatedly identified themselves with centralism, albeit within the framework of a federal constitution; party strategists have planned accordingly; and the general public can rarely praise or damn Canadian socialism without referring to its centralizing tendencies.

In the present chapter, I will state my belief that the foregoing assumptions and inclinations have considerably harmed the cause of reform. Section I will show that, other things being equal, radicalism can more easily be introduced in a federal society than in a unitary one. Section II will claim that the dynamics of history are not urging the Canadian nation towards centralization any more than they are towards decentralization. Section III will argue that the theory of democratic socialism can make no unassailable case for centralization.

In consequence, it should follow that Canadian socialists must consider federalism as a positive asset, rather than as an inevitable handicap. However, that is not to say – and I hope the point will remain present in the reader's mind throughout – that this chapter pleads *for* provincial autonomy and *against* centralization in absolute terms. My plea is merely for greater realism and greater flexibility in the socialist approach to problems of federalism: I should like to see socialists feeling free to espouse whatever political trends or to use whatever constitutional tools happen to fit each particular problem at each particular time; and if my argument is taken to mean that the present socialist preconception in favour of centralism should permanently be replaced by a preconception in favour of provincial autonomy, I shall have completely failed to make my point.

On Strategy and Tactics

The revolutionary bases, in spite of their insignificant size, are a great political force and strongly oppose the power of the Kuomintang, which spreads over vast regions. . . .
Revolution and revolutionary wars proceed from birth to development, from small to large, from lack of power to seizure of power. . . .
MAO TSE-TUNG

If the whole of the Canadian electorate could miraculously be converted to socialist ideals at one fell swoop, there would be no reason to discuss strategy in the present context. Socialism would be achieved with or without federalism, and socialist administrations would be installed at every level of governmental affairs, no matter what the form of the constitution.

But such is not the case. In a non-revolutionary society and in non-revolutionary times, no manner of reform can be implanted with sudden universality. Democratic reformers must proceed step by step, convincing little bands of intellectuals here, rallying sections of the working class there, and appealing to the underprivileged in the next place. The drive towards power must begin with the establishment of bridgeheads, since at the outset it is obviously easier to convert specific groups or localities than to win over an absolute majority of the whole nation.

Under a system of proportional representation the argument might run differently, and indeed that is why so many reformers have stood for P.R. But it is obviously unrealistic to suppose that the governing parties will introduce electoral régimes that would hasten the accession to power of the oppositions. Consequently, radical strategy must be designed to operate under the present electoral system of one-man constituencies.

In the absence of P.R. it seems obvious that the multi-state system of a federal constitution is the next best thing. (Indeed the experience of that superb strategist Mao Tse-tung might lead us to conclude that in a vast and heterogeneous country, the possibility of establishing socialist strongholds in certain regions is the very best thing.) It is strange that on the one hand C.C.F. tacticians often argue that the road to power at the national level might have to pass through the election of socialist administrations at the municipal level, but that on the other hand, by casting themselves as very unenthusiastic supporters of provincial autonomy, they make it difficult for themselves to follow the provincial highroads towards national power. Such subservience of the tacticians to the postulates of the 'theory class' is amazing, in face of the fact that the C.C.F. has become the Government or the official Opposition in several provinces, whereas it has never come within sight of such successes in the national Parliament.

True, the successes of socialism at the provincial level,

especially around the middle 1940s, did stimulate somewhat more interest in the provincial cause. But, for all that, a change of attitude to federalism still seems to be required within the ranks of Canadian socialism. No longer must our federal constitution be regarded as something to be undone, the result of a costly historical error which is only retained at all because of the 'backward areas' of Canada. Federalism must not only be accepted as a datum with which Canada is stuck, as is many another country of semi-continental size. Federalism must be welcomed as a valuable tool which permits dynamic parties to plant socialist governments in certain provinces, from which the seed of radicalism can slowly spread.

Economists readily accept the fact that different areas have reached different stages of economic growth, and consequently that theories cannot be implemented everywhere in identical fashion.[1] Sociologists accept similar facts with similar consequences. It is urgent that socialist politicians give wider recognition to the fact that different regions or ethnic groups in Canada are at vastly different stages of their political development,[2] and that it is folly to endorse strategies that are devised to swing the whole country at the same time and in the same way into the path of socialism.

I have heard socialist leaders in Canada state with indignation that they would never 'water down' their doctrines to make them more palatable to this or that part of Canada. Such an approach, I must admit, always puzzles me; for socialism, like every other political theory, has been diluted at different times and in different places to a great variety of strengths. And in terms of political tactics, the only real question democratic socialists must answer is: 'Just how much reform can the majority of the people be brought to desire at the present time?'

The main distinction between the conservative and the progressive mind is that, in seeking the solution to the foregoing problem, the progressive will tend to overestimate the people's desire for justice, freedom, and change, whereas the conserva-

[1]See Scott Gordon's chapter in M. Oliver (ed.), *Social Purpose for Canada* (Toronto, 1961), wherein he accepts the possibility that the wage rate in the Maritimes will be lower than the Canadian average, provided the rate of growth is not. See also W. W. Rostow, *Stages of Economic Growth* (Cambridge, 1960), *passim*.

[2]The author attempted to show this in his article 'Some Obstacles to Democracy in Quebec' (p. 103 ff. of this volume).

tive will tend to err on the side of order, authority, and continuity. The true tactical position of the *democratic* socialist is on the left, *but no further*.

Such a line of thought leads to the conclusion – unpleasant only for the doctrinaires – that socialists must stand for different things in different parts of Canada. Of course there is a need for doctrinaires of a sort; or at any rate for theoreticians who will constantly expound what they think to be the nearest thing to 'pure' socialism. For, as it has been often observed, the dreamers of today frequently become the realists of tomorrow; and the educational value of painting utopias has repeatedly been established by the eventual realization of such goals through the democratic process.

Yet, so long as socialism is to seek fulfilment through parliamentary democracy, with its paraphernalia of parties and elections, there will be a constant need for the tactician as well as the theorist. And both will have to be reconciled by the strategist.

Now it should be obvious to all these groups that no national party can keep its integrity while preaching a gospel which varies as it moves *a mari usque ad mare*; neither can it keep its status as a national party if it seeks support only in narrow regionalism. Yet, on the other hand, if the party preaches the same gospel everywhere, its partisans in some areas will desert it as being too reactionary, whereas in other areas the party will fail to find adherents because it appears too revolutionary.

That dilemma can easily be solved by making full use of our federative form of government. Socialists *can* stand for varying degrees of socialism in the various provinces of Canada by standing in autonomous provincial parties. Indeed, since the strength of a national party is largely determined by the strength of its component parts, sufficient priority must be given to the building of such parts. In other words, in building a national party of the left, consideration must be given to what is provincially possible as well as to what is nationally desirable. The policy of the national party will thus be the result of a compromise between the most and the least advanced socialist thinking in various parts of Canada.

It is perhaps no coincidence that during the twentieth century – that is to say, during the period when Canada has effectively developed into a vast and heterogeneous nation spreading from

THE PRACTICE AND THEORY OF FEDERALISM / 129

coast to coast – the one national party that has been strongest and governed longest is the party that has traditionally stood for provincial rights and embraced in its ranks such provincial free-stylers as Taschereau, Hepburn, Angus Macdonald, and Smallwood. For even while the Liberals at Ottawa were riding the wave of centralism, Liberal leaders in provincial capitals were stoutly defending the cause of autonomy.

By contrast, the C.C.F. has reaped little electoral reward for its studied application in speaking with one voice and acting with one purpose in all parts of Canada. In Quebec alone, where the socialist vote has usually hovered around 1 per cent of the total, a book could be filled with the frustrations of former members of the C.C.F. who felt or imagined that provincial affairs must always be subordinate to the *raison d'état* of the national party.

In the post-war era the Quebec organization squandered its efforts and made itself ridiculous by running spurious candidates in two or three dozen ridings at each federal election, partly in order to obtain free time on the air-waves, but mainly in order that the electorate of the rest of Canada might be momentarily fooled into believing that the party was strong in Quebec. Then in 1956 and 1957, when efforts were being made to enlarge the left in Quebec by grouping all liberal-minded people in the *Rassemblement*, members of the C.C.F. – on the grounds that the C.C.F. was here to stay – refused to envisage any orientation that might lead to the setting up of a left-wing political group, newer and stronger than the C.C.F. Finally, in 1958 and 1959, when the C.C.F. had decided it was no longer here to stay but here to merge into a new party, the Quebec branch of the C.C.F. – on the grounds that it had to wait for the new party – rejected the *Union des forces démocratiques*, with the consequence, in June 1960, that the *Union nationale* party was defeated by the Liberals alone rather than by a coalition of the left and of liberal-minded people.

The historical events briefly recited in the foregoing paragraph were the result of discussion and decision by honest men. If I refer to them in the present context it cannot be with the intention of displaying hindsight; for who knows what good or evil would have followed from the contrary decisions? But such references are necessary to illustrate what great pains were taken by the C.C.F. in Quebec in order to avoid 'nationalist deviationism'. In view of Quebec's past, such a course was not without some justification, but it obviously went too far when it precluded the Quebec left from exploiting the same type of elementary opportunity as that which permitted the launching by Mr. Ed Finn of *a* new party in Newfoundland, even though *the* new party had not yet fired the starting gun.

In short, the C.C.F. in and out of Quebec always seemed to take the position that once it had become a powerful party at the national level it would easily find support in each province. Such an approach smacks of paternalism, if each province is taken singly; and it obviously begs the principle, if the situation is considered as a whole.

A greater amount of freedom for the left appears to be necessary at the provincial level. Just as each province must evolve towards political and economic maturity in its own good time, likewise radicalism in different parts of Canada must be implanted in different fashions. For a time, parties with the same name may find themselves preaching policies differing in scope from one province to the other. Perhaps even parties with different names may preach the same ideology in different provinces. And for a time, the situation of the left in Canada will not be cut and dried. It will be confused and challenging; and its diversity from province to province will stimulate competition and perhaps even establish a system of checks and balances, while at the national level the left will adopt strategies and tactics based on possibilities rather than on mere desirabilities.

The socialist mind is a planning one, so in all likelihood it will not respond enthusiastically to the pragmatic approach to strategy which is suggested here. Consequently, it may be well to point out that the present argument does not do away with the possibility of, or with the need for, planning at every level of politics; but it does lend emphasis to the importance of the plan at the provincial level, and hence it makes planning more effective.

Obviously, a strategy limited to Saskatchewan (or Quebec, or British Columbia) will be less exciting than one covering the whole of Canada. But it will also be less exciting than a plan applicable to the Socialist International. And much more telling than either!

It is sometimes argued by Canadian socialists that their opposition to the United States is not based on narrow nationalism, but on the fact that complete American domination would tend to prevent Canada as a community from realizing values good for human beings. In other words they believe that socialism can more easily be established in Canada, as a smaller unit, than on the whole North American continent. Surely, then, they should not underestimate the importance of trying to realize socialism in the even smaller units of the provinces, which have, within the limits of the constitution and particularly of Section 92, many of the prerogatives of sovereign states.

On History, Past and Future

*In so far as matters requiring concerted action
can be dealt with by co-operation among the
provinces, or between the Dominion and
the provinces, the case for additional
centralization to promote efficiency or
uniformity will not arise.*

THE ROWELL-SIROIS REPORT

Of the countries of the world, Canada has the eighth oldest written constitution, the second oldest one of a federal nature, and the oldest which combines federalism with the principles of responsible government.

Yet some of our fellow Canadians have an even more illustrious record as pioneers in constitution-making: the Confederation of Six Iroquois Nations was founded in 1570, or thereabouts, and is still in existence today. Anthropologists and sociologists have marvelled at the keen political sense of Canada's earlier inhabitants. And the question arises whether historians will have the same opinion of the subsequent settlers!

If it be true that the first hundred years are the hardest, I see no cause to despair of the future of Canadian federalism. True, its erratic advance has caused many misgivings. There has been endless discussion as to the nature of the British North America Act, whether it be of the essence of a law or of a contract; and we have heard much argument from the lawyers and the senators, deploring the provincial bias given to the constitution by the Privy Council.

In reference to practical politics, such discussions can become tedious. It should be a sufficiently workable proposition to hold that the Act of 1867 was a law of the Imperial Parliament, but a law based on an agreement between federating parties, and consequently a law which can best be understood and interpreted (and eventually amended) by referring to the spirit of that agreement.

As to the criticism of the Privy Council's interpretation of the B.N.A. Act, it is basically in the same category as the criticism of the Supreme Court interpretations by a late premier of Quebec. In the final analysis, the ultimate decisions of the courts in matters of public concern always affect someone's politics adversely and will always be attacked on that basis.

Such criticism of the Privy Council by socialists is of course a political right. But I wonder how useful it is to the cause of socialism when it can be fairly construed as an opposition to provincial autonomy. For, as I shall argue later on, in section III of this chapter, socialists do not stand to gain very much in theoretical terms from vastly increased centralization. And in practical terms, I have tried to show in section I above that they stand to lose a great deal. In point of fact, had the C.C.F. been less identified with centralization I doubt whether it would have been weaker as a national party. On the contrary, its national strength might have benefited from the improved fortunes of the provincial parties. And I do not see how democratic socialism could have been adulterated in the process.

True, in present-day politics, there exist a number of built-in centralizing forces. The combination of external pressure and of improved internal communication may tend to unify large countries to a greater extent than in the past. Legislation may tend to become as broad as the problem with which it is meant to deal, and a federal constitution may not appear to be the best instrument for dealing with a non-federal economic society. The countervailing power to a corporate élite which is nation-wide in strength may have to be a government which is nation-wide in jurisdiction. And for all these reasons, the socialist will be tempted to enhance the power of the central government at the expense of the provinces.

But the true socialist will also be a humanist and a democrat and he will be quick to realize that Canada is very much a federal society from the sociological point of view; people from various parts of Canada *do* hang together on a regional basis which very often supersedes the class basis. And the understanding of Canadian political history would be very incomplete indeed if it ignored the existence, for instance, of the Maritimer, the Quebecker, or the Westerner. In the first part of this chapter I have argued that the existence of such regional fidelities provided a tactical asset to the spread of radicalism. But I add here that they may eventually, in times when cybernetic planning is becoming a possibility, prove to be the main bulwark of democracy against a central government's *New Despotism*, its *Law and Orders* or its 'parliamentary bureaucracy'.

For there are physical limits to the control which may be exercised over the central bureaucracy by the people's representatives and by the judiciary. The executive power may tend to increase its control by increasing the number of ministers; but the cabinet will quickly reach that size beyond which deliberation becomes useless and decision impossible. (Thus, in the United Kingdom, out of some five dozen ministers, perhaps only half of them will be of cabinet rank and only twenty-odd will actually sit in the cabinet proper.) The legislative power can increase its control over the bureaucracy by increasing the length of the parliamentary session, but there again British experience shows that the entire year eventually proves too short; besides, in as large a country as Canada, Members of Parliament would lose all contact with the electorate if they had to sojourn in the federal capital indefinitely.

As regards the judiciary, its terms of reference are limited by the statutes themselves, which are generally prepared by the bureaucracy before being adopted by Parliament; the judiciary is powerless to exercise an over-all control of the bureaucracy as long as our system of administrative law remains in its present embryonic state.

In time, it is hoped that administrative law will be expanded and perfected, that Parliament will learn to use the committee system with greater effectiveness, and that other devices will be developed to protect democracy against bureaucracy. But in the meanwhile, and even after, it would be folly to disregard the device of federalism which we already have in our possession and which may be the most effective of all, since it reduces the magnitude of the task allotted to one central government.

Furthermore, in the age of the mass society, it is no small advantage to foster the creation of quasi-sovereign communities at the provincial level, where power is that much less remote from the people and where political education (and general creativeness) is related to more homogeneous and manageable groups of citizens.

Finally, it might be added that at a time when the uncontrolled production of thermo-nuclear weapons has made total war a gruesome possibility, the case for decentralization in terms of defence extends far beyond the mere scattering of industries.

Caught between centripetal and centrifugal forces, Canada's future, like its past, may continue to oscillate between times of federal and times of provincial predominance, depending upon the immediate needs of the people and the temper of their various politicians. (For it must not be forgotten that these latter have a vested interest in strengthening *that* level of government at which *they* operate.) Or – more likely – the political future of Canada will lie in the direction of greater centralization in some areas and greater decentralization in others. But at all times, co-operation and interchange between the two levels of government will be, as they have been, an absolute necessity. In that sense, I doubt whether federalism in the classical sense has ever existed, that is to say a federation which would have divided the totality of its sovereign powers between regional and central governments with such sharpness and adequacy that those governments would have been able to carry on their affairs in complete independence of one another.

Applied to Canada, the foregoing statement is easily proved. The constitutional provisions of the B.N.A. Act established intergovernmental relationship as indispensable from the outset, between the executive, the legislative, and the judicial organs.

Concerning the executive, the office of Lieutenant-Governor was designed to ensure a permanent bond between the federal and the provincial governments: the Lieutenant-Governor was definitely a federal official, appointed, paid, and in some cases dismissed by the Ottawa government. The powers of reservation and disallowance also provided a link between the two levels of government. Finally the financing of the respective administrations was established as an area of indispensable co-operation: by Confederation the provinces gave up the bulk of their sources of revenue, retaining only direct taxes and various fees; in exchange the central government pledged itself to make the four different types of payment referred to in sections 111, 118, and 119 of the B.N.A. Act.

As regards the legislative function, relations were inevitable in the areas of subordinate jurisdiction and in those of divided jurisdiction. Under the first heading fall sections 93, 94, and 95 of the B.N.A. Act, relating to education, uniform legislation, agriculture, and immigration; in that area we might also add cases of conditional legislation or of legislation by reference (but not of legislation by delegation, which is deemed unconstitutional). Under the second heading (jurisdiction divided between the federal and the provincial legislative powers) fall four types of laws: first, laws concerning matters which can be regulated either by criminal or by civil law, such as the Sunday Observance Acts; second, laws concerning matters which fall partly under the federal residual clause ('peace, order and good government') and partly under the provincial residual clause ('all matters of merely local or private nature'), such as Temperance Acts; third, laws concerning matters which, according to their extension, are either 'regulation of trade and commerce' or 'property and civil rights', such as company laws, marketing laws, and industrial legislation; fourth, laws concerning matters allocated (without subordination) to both federal and provincial jurisdiction, either by the letter of the B.N.A. Act, such as direct taxation, or by judicial interpretation, such as fisheries.

Finally, in judicial matters, co-operation was of vital importance. By Section 92, paragraph 14, the provinces were given exclusive jurisdiction over the administration of justice; by 96 the Governor General appoints 'the Judges of the Superior, District and County Courts in each Province'; and by 101 the central government may establish a general court of appeals and any additional courts. If these sections in their application had not been reasonably well integrated, the judiciary would have ceased to function: rival tribunals would have been set up, *res judicata* would have had no meaning, and clash between executive powers would have been inevitable.

From the foregoing analysis of the B.N.A. Act it is obvious that inter-governmental co-operation is not only possible but that it is in many ways constitutionally indispensable. It is not surprising therefore that the federal and provincial governments have developed many instruments for dealing with subjects of joint concern.

First in order of importance are the meetings of governments at ministerial level: the federal-provincial conferences of 1906,

1910, 1915, 1918, 1927, 1931, 1932, 1933, 1934, 1935, 1941, 1945–6, 1950, 1960 (not to be confused with the inter-provincial conferences of 1887, 1902, 1910, 1913, 1926, 1960).

Second come the meetings of departments at ministerial level. This category includes, for example, the agricultural conferences, the Ministers of Mines Committee, the tourist conferences, all of which are generally annual meetings of the appropriate ministers and other personnel. Also included in this group are the Old Age Pension Interprovincial Board, the conferences set up for the exchange of statistical material, and those convened to discuss the Trans-Canada Highway.

Third, at the purely administrative level, there exists a great variety of agreements and continuing organizations to deal co-operatively with specific matters of common concern. Typical examples include the Canadian Association of Administrators of Labour Legislation, the Conference of Commissioners on Uniformity of Legislation, the Committee on Security Frauds Prevention Law, the Committee on Uniform Company Law, the Fisheries Development Committee, the Fur Advisory Committee, the Provincial Boundary Commission, the Canadian Council on Nutrition, the Canadian Wild Life Conference, the Vocational Training Committee. Other examples might include the recently established 'Resources for Tomorrow' Conference; co-operation in the fields of agricultural and forestry research and control; arrangements concerning citizenship training classes; co-ordination of health programs; agreements whereby provincial officers administer the federal Migratory Birds Convention Act or some of the fisheries regulations enacted by the Government of Canada; agreements whereby certain provinces delegate the policing of certain towns and rural districts to the R.C.M.P.[3]

Finally, and in a category apart, one must consider the various types of financial arrangements between the federal government and the provinces. As was stated above, the B.N.A. Act made provision for certain types of federal payments. But government finance remained ever a problem: the subsidy basis

[3]The foregoing enumeration is apt to appear long and tedious to the layman. But in order that he truly grasp the tremendous scope of federal-provincial relationships, I will add that in 1950, at the request of the Privy Council Office, I made a summary of existing federal-provincial co-operative arrangements which covered more than fifty pages.

was thoroughly altered by constitutional amendment in 1907, and in various ways since then. Federal grants-in-aid to help the provinces with specific tasks were also resorted to, though rather sparingly at first, since it was generally felt that the spending of funds should not be divorced from the perception thereof. This category also includes the tax rental agreements, first begun during the Second World War, and periodically renewed, with varying degrees of provincial acceptance, the history of which is fairly well known.

The purpose of the foregoing paragraphs is to show that the story of Canadian federalism is one of constant intergovernmental exchange and co-operation. It is also in part a story of sometimes subtle, sometimes brazen, and usually tolerated encroachments by one government upon the jurisdiction of the other. For instance, the federal government (which has always shirked using the jurisdiction over education it held under Section 93, paragraph 4, of the B.N.A. Act) has used grants-in-aid to enter resolutely into the areas of technical and university education. Indeed the federal 'spending power' or so-called 'power of the purse' is at present being construed as a federal right to decide (at the taxpayers' expense!) whether provincial governments are properly exercising any and every right they hold under the constitution.[4]

On the other hand, examples can be given of provincial encroachments upon federal jurisdiction. The invasion, supported by legal fiction, into the field of indirect taxation might be one case. Another example is the appointment of judges of provincial courts whose jurisdiction far exceeds the limits beyond which only that of federal judges was supposed to go, under Section 96 of the constitution.[5]

---

[4]In a brilliant chapter published in A. R. M. Lower, F. R. Scott, *et al.*, *Evolving Canadian Federalism* (Durham, N.C., 1958), Professor Corry finds it 'extraordinary that no one has challenged the constitutionality of the assumed spending power before the Supreme Court' (p. 119). I share his wonderment; but I find it even more extraordinary that political scientists fail to see the eroding effect that the 'power of the purse' will have on Canadian democracy if the present construction continues to prevail, and in particular what chaos will result if provincial governments borrow federal logic and begin using their own 'power of the purse' to meddle in federal affairs. (For a discussion of these points, see 'Federal Grants to Universities' (p. 79 ff. of this volume).)

[5]I first heard this point raised by Mr. Benno Cohen of the Montreal Bar.

In short, it almost seems as though whenever an important segment of the Canadian population needs something badly enough, it is eventually given to them by one level of government or the other, regardless of the constitution. The main drawback to such an approach is that it tends to develop paternalistic instincts in more enterprising governments, at the expense of democratic maturation in others. In areas where there exists a clear division of responsibilities between the federal and provincial levels, there is no doubt that the only proper censor of a government which incompetently discharges its obligations is the electorate of *that* government, and not some other government responsible to some other (level of) electorate.[6] And if, for example, federal politicians are convinced that by their very nature the totality of the provincial governments *cannot* discharge their duties in some area, surely the proper procedure is for those politicians to seek the overt transfer of such areas into federal jurisdiction, either by way of constitutional amendment (as in the case of unemployment insurance), or by invoking federal powers under Section 92, paragraph 10(c).[7]

It might be wise to labour this point further, since it will illustrate how certain policies, though conceived in terms of the general welfare and applied in a spirit of co-operation, can in reality be paternalism in disguise.

Thus far in this chapter I have studiously avoided making a special case for French Canada. But at this time it is necessary to discuss the special case English-Canadian writers sometimes make on its behalf.

It has been very ably argued that 'the initial survival of French culture in Canada did not depend upon provincial

[6]I will consider the case of disallowance and of reservation later on. But it might avoid considerable misunderstanding if I state immediately and unequivocally that I hold equalization grants (enabling poorer provinces to keep pace with the richer ones) and counter-cyclical fiscal policies to be within the jurisdiction of the federal government.

[7]In this respect it might be remarked that if these latter means are infrequently used, it is partly because central governments, who occasionally like to meddle in provincial affairs, do not necessarily relish the prospect of being saddled with some new responsibility for ever. It is interesting to note that while it took over sole responsibility for unemployment *insurance*, the federal government has always scrupulously avoided the claim that unemployment *in general* was a matter within the jurisdiction of the federal government.

autonomy'; and further that 'the possession of provincial autonomy was a relatively minor factor in the growth of French
culture and influence during the first half century after 1867.'[8]
Both facts are quite true; but not true is the inference that many
people draw from them, to wit, that the survival and growth of
French-Canadian culture do not (at the present time) depend
upon the existence of provincial autonomy. Such an inference
might only be true if culture were defined to exclude the art of
self-government. As a matter of fact, if the ability to govern
themselves is such a minor facet of the French Canadians'
cultural make-up today, it is precisely because in the past French
Canadians never learned to make proper use of their elective
governments as servants of the whole community.[9]

Typically, Quebec's two most recent champions of provincial
autonomy, Premiers Taschereau and Duplessis, were socially
and economically conservatives. They barely exercised many of
the powers given to them by the autonomy they so loudly
affirmed and, as a result, social and cultural legislation was the
product of the central government over which the French-
Canadian electorate had no absolute control.

Now there is no need to remind me that the central government is not foreign, but is the government of all Canadians.
And I do not find good legislation distasteful merely because it
originates in Ottawa as opposed to Quebec.[10] The real question
lies elsewhere: can a cultural group, which by virtue of the Act
of 1867 received the right to govern itself in many areas of
jurisdiction, ever mature democratically if it persistently neg-
lects or refuses to exercise its right? And are not such omissions
or refusals inevitable if the lacunae they create are constantly
and adequately filled up by a central government which is
largely representative of another cultural group? To give but
one example: from the Quebec point of view, the most serious
objection to federal grants to universities was obviously not that
the universities had enough money or that federal money had a
peculiar odour; it was that once the universities had their bellies

---

[8]F. R. Scott, 'French-Canada and Canadian Federalism' in Lower, Scott,
et al., Evolving Canadian Federalism, pp. 57 and 59.

[9]I have tried to explain the reasons for this in the article quoted in n. 2.

[10]As a matter of fact I might be prepared to argue that some day, if and
when inter alia the political maturity of all Canadians had reached a
very high level, a more centralized state would be acceptable for
Canada.

filled with federal grants they would see no reason to oppose that provincial government which had persistently failed in its constitutional duties by leaving education in such an impoverished state; and Quebeckers would chalk up another failure in their struggle to master the art of self-government.

At this point, a comment may well be forthcoming: should the universities of the poorer provinces be faced with starvation simply because Quebec is showing signs of embarking upon the slow process of political maturation? The objection is typical of all those which keep Quebec nationalism alive. For it is basically emotional and misses the point that the university grants were not equalization grants since they were handed to all provinces, rich and poor, on the same basis. Nor, for that matter, were they anti-cyclical in nature since they were initiated and continued in times of inflation, when the central government should have been trying to reduce its spending. To the average Quebecker, therefore, the university grants appeared to be an invasion pure and simple of provincial rights.[11]

Most English Canadians fail to realize that it is their attitude (as in the above example) which exactly determines the extent and force of Quebec nationalism. Central government encroachments, which are accepted in other provinces as matters of expediency, cannot be so viewed in Quebec. For French Cana-

[11]There is here neither time nor place to deal at length with the subject of federal grants to universities. However, I wish to make it quite clear that the Quebec argument is based on the explicit position of the federal authorities that they have no jurisdiction whatsoever over education. (*Cf.* St. Laurent's speech at Sherbrooke in October 1956, and one on November 12 of that year.) Since the grants cannot be justified on grounds of federal jurisdiction over education, nor in terms of macro-economic stabilization, nor for reasons of equalization policy, there only remains the argument of 'the power of the purse'. That prerogative is interpreted to mean that any government can raise money by taxation for purposes outside of its jurisdiction, provided it gives the money without any attempt to legislate. In my view such an interpretation is not only wrong but dangerous: for it would, for instance, authorize the provinces to tax in order to pay a large bonus to any federal civil servants or military personnel who could prove their mastery of the French language; or to any federal judge whose philosophy was 'sound'. And so on. (For lengthy argument on these and other points, see the article referred to in n. 4. This business of referring to my own writings is not particularly pleasant; but in some places I feel I am writing against the grain of certain readers and I find it only fair to refer them to the places where my arguments are substantiated at some length.)

dians are not in any important sense represented in the Canadian power élite, whether governmental or financial,[12] and any attempt at unilateral transference of power from the Quebec élite to the Canadian one will naturally set the corresponding defence mechanisms in motion. On the contrary, a scrupulous respect of the postulates of federalism – by rendering such mechanisms obsolete – will lend greater force to the efforts of those Quebeckers who are trying to turn their province into an open society. And perhaps more important still, it will create a climate where the debate between autonomy and centralization can be solved through rational rather than emotional discussion.

The upshot of my entire argument in this section is that socialists, rather than water down (to use a previous expression) their socialism, must constantly seek ways of adapting it to a bicultural society governed under a federal constitution. And since the future of Canadian federalism lies clearly in the direction of co-operation, the wise socialist will turn his thoughts in that direction, keeping in mind the importance of establishing buffer zones of joint sovereignty and co-operative zones of joint administration between the two levels of government.

The establishment of such areas of confidence is very important; for when parties stand as equals at negotiations, the results are invariably better and fairer. That perhaps is why there has been a great deal of effective co-operation between federal and provincial departmental officials; each feels that he is answerable only to his own 'sovereign' government. Might not machinery be established to extend this feeling to meetings at the highest levels with similar beneficial result?

There have been many proposals for setting up machinery to ensure better co-operation between the federal and the provincial governments. The most frequent concern the desirability of having periodic federal-provincial conferences with a permanent secretariat to ensure their successful functioning. A less frequent proposal advocates the establishment of a secretary of state for the provinces at Ottawa, and a department of federal relations in each province. It has also been suggested that if

[12]See John Porter's work on economic and bureaucratic élites, *Canadian Journal of Economics and Political Science*, August 1957, p. 386, and November 1958, p. 491. For other references, see P. E. Trudeau (ed.), *La Grève de l'amiante* (Montreal, 1956), p. 77.

governments were constitutionally permitted to delegate legislative powers to one another there would be much greater co-operation between them.

Of course there exist many more devices for promoting co-operative federalism.[13] And others still await discovery. By way of example I might single out a rather neglected piece of co-operative machinery: royal commissions of inquiry could become a very important medium of co-operation between governments in Canada, rather than the causes of friction they sometimes are now. Reliable information upon matters of joint concern is essential to the pursuance of harmonious federal-provincial relations; it is therefore surprising that in such matters royal commissions tend[14] to be the exclusive creation of the executive branch of *one* government, which in effect exercises inquisitorial activities over acts within the jurisdiction of other governments. Surely, in such cases, some method should be devised for the setting up of joint commissions of inquiry, appointed by the several governments and reporting back to them.

But unfortunately there is here neither time nor place to discuss these matters further. It would be regrettable, however, if Canadian socialists found too little time to discuss them. For if it be true that Canada's future lies in the direction of co-operative federalism, it will be guided there by those parties and politicians who will have proven themselves most realistic and far-seeing in that regard.

[13]Thus in Australia co-operative action has been greatly facilitated by such institutions as the Premiers' Conferences and the Loan Council. The United States, which, it might be argued, is more centrally controlled than Canada, has also experimented with many devices of inter-state co-operation: the Governors' Conferences, the Regional Conferences of Governors, the Council of State Governments, the American Legislators' Association, the different national associations of Secretaries of State, of Supervisors of State Banks, etc.

[14]Quasi-exceptions – too rare to create a contrary trend – have existed. For instance, Mr. Mackenzie King in 1909 obtained the approval of all provinces before proceeding with the appointment of a Commission on Industrial Training and Technical Education. In 1948 the Fraser Valley Commission included commissioners nominated by federal and provincial governments, and was asked to report to both.

On Theory

*To seek to unify the state excessively is not
beneficial. . . . The state, as its unification . . .
will be a worse state, just as if one turned a
harmony into unison or rhythm into a single
foot.*

ARISTOTLE

It would seem at first glance that many of the more important economic policies of socialism can only be applied with thoroughness under a unitary form of government. Economic planning and control have little meaning unless they are part of a unified, well-integrated process. Therefore, the argument goes, a socialist must, in essence, be a centralizer.

Fiscal and monetary policies, for instance, are bound to have little beneficial effect if various central and regional governments are at liberty to cancel out each other's actions by contradictory policies. Thus a deficitary federal budget would have but slight effect upon national deflationary trends if provincial surpluses added up to an amount equal to the federal deficit.

However, it must be pointed out that from that point of view socialists are no worse off than neo-capitalists or Keynesian liberals. The stabilization policies of these latter groups might also be easier to apply in a unitary state; but in its absence, those groups do not throw up their hands in despair, nor do they cast political caution to the winds by becoming crusaders against provincial rights. They merely set out to find ways of adapting their economic theories to the political realities.

In Canada, there exists no constitutional problem as regards monetary policy, since money, banking, and the interest rate all fall under the single jurisdiction of the central government. However, regarding fiscal policy the difficulties are great, since provincial governments have autonomous budgets and consequent taxing, borrowing, and spending powers. And, for instance, Canadian post-war inflation was no doubt aggravated to the extent that certain provincial deficits operated against federal surpluses.

It is to the credit of the Liberals that they devised and implemented tax rental agreements between the central and regional governments which curtailed the degree to which the fiscal practices of the various governments might operate at cross-purposes. But as time went by it became obvious that Liberal logic, as expressed during the 1945 Conference (and in the Green Book), was in reality a vicious circle: the federal government – because it had greater financial resources – argued that it should bear greater social responsibility and therefore that its financial powers should be correspondingly increased.

It is to the credit of the reactionaries (I am referring to Mr. Duplessis and his Union Nationale)[15] that they refused to be deceived by a system whereby the federal government could, in lieu of the provincial government, tax the citizen in all the provinces in order to spend money (on a scale far in excess of that which might have been required for stabilization or equalization policies) for purposes within provincial jurisdiction. But it is not to the credit of the socialists that they should have been little more than bystanders, goading the Liberals on, during this whole episode.[16]

At the present time, when Canadian public opinion, led by the Liberal Premier of Quebec and the Conservative Premier of Ontario, apparently unopposed by the socialist Premier of Saskatchewan, seems to be running amok in favour of extreme provincialism, as witnessed by the federal-provincial conference held in the summer of 1960, there is a greater need than ever for an enlightened socialist approach to the fiscal problems of a federal form of government. If the swing towards centralism, which began with the Depression, is not now to be countered by a long swing towards excessive regionalism, there will be an urgent need for solutions based on co-operation.

It is quite conceivable that Canadian fiscal policy could be considered from month to month and year to year by a joint continuing committee of federal and provincial officials and experts. Confronted with comprehensive sets of statistical ma-

[15]See 'De libro, tributo . . . et quibusdam aliis' (p. 63 ff. in this volume).

[16]Exception should be made for the group which headed the Quebec Federation of Industrial Unions (C.C.L.). Their *Mémoire à la Commission royale d'enquête sur les problèmes constitutionnels* (Montreal, 1954) was the first document or statement I know of which reconciled the rationale of provincial tax deductibility with that of equalization grants and macro-economic stabilization. And the preface to the second edition showed that the formulae which had just been worked out by the St. Laurent and the Duplessis governments were wrong, in that they were based on unilateral action and in that they betrayed the very principles of anti-cyclical budgeting.

terial and forecasting data, such a committee – if it were immunized against all forms of political interference – could make policy recommendations as well as any body of purely central officials; and perhaps even better, since they would take greater cognizance of such problems as regional bottle-necks, local unemployment, and immobility of labour, and since the hitherto purely federal control over money and banking would be examined in the light of provincial budgetary needs.

Of course, it would be up to the several provincial and central governments to decide what they would do with the policy recommendations. And this is where co-operation at the executive levels would appear to be of extreme importance and would have to be recognized as such. But one could count, in the first place, on some degree of moral suasion to which the governments might find themselves subjected. And in the second, the various electorates – when the time came to judge the financial policies of their respective governments – would be less inclined than now to condone incompetence or ignorance.

For there is no escape from politics, nor should there be. There is always one point where the most expert economic advice must be submitted for implementation to the political representatives of the people. 'I know no safe depository of the ultimate powers of society but the people themselves; and if we think them not enlightened enough to exercise this control with a wholesome discretion, the remedy is not to take it from them, but to inform their discretion by education' (Thomas Jefferson). And as I have shown in sections I and II of this chapter, the people can 'exercise their control' just as well under a federal state as under a unitary one, and perhaps even better.

Consequently, the economic aspects of socialist theory might be a guide towards a more efficient distribution of powers under the constitution; but they need never be considered as an invitation to turn Canada, any more than all of North America or the whole world itself, into a unitary state. Planning is a possibility at any and every level of government. It may be more costly (in economic terms of outlay, leakage, multiplier effect, and so on) at one level of government than at another.[17]

---

[17]Even in strictly economic terms, however, it is too readily assumed that planning should necessarily be a centralized function. Recent studies of planning in the Soviet Union underline 'les nécessités de la décentralisation' and the importance of 'des centres de décisions autonomes' (Cahiers de l'I.S.E.A., No. 86 (Paris, 1959)). And in this con-

But the incidence of political cost (in terms of freedom, self-government, local pride, and ingenuity) might be completely the reverse.[18] The true planner is the one who tries to minimize cost and maximize satisfaction, in every way and not only in dollars and cents.

The foregoing argumentation can be applied to every aspect of economic theory. Investment planning and resource development, for instance, both become in the last analysis matters for political decision. In economic terms it may be possible to compare the costs of building and operating a zinc mine at Hay River, a railway in Labrador, a steel mill near Verchères, and a university in Prince Rupert, and the marginal productivity of each. But the social value of such enterprises can only be appreciated with reference to political realities. And the final choice will have to be a political one.

Consequently, in such matters, there is no reason to presume that the federal government will be more enlightened than the sum of the provincial governments, or even than one provincial government acting alone. Since ultimately the decisions are political rather than economic, it follows that they can be taken by provinces as well as by the central government. And a (socialist) province with a planning board might be more likely to plan wisely than a (reactionary) central government with no such board.

In other words, economic planning must eventually be reduced to political planning. And the economic theory of socialism cannot be divorced from its political theory, which is largely bound to strategy and tactics.

Thus we revert to the first section of this chapter, which recommended pragmatism, condemned paternalism, and paid

---

nection I am grateful to my friend Mr. Fernand Cadieux for having pointed out to me certain recent trends in the study of social institutions: in their book *Organizations* (New York, 1958), March and Simon invoke 'the principle of bounded rationality as an important force making for decentralization' as opposed to central planning; in other words, 'given realistic limits on human planning capacity, the decentralized system will work better than the centralized' (pp. 203–9).

[18]'The first effect of centralization is to make every sort of indigenous characteristic disappear in the different parts of a country; while it may be thought that this is the way to exalt political life in the country as a whole, it is really destroying it in its constituent parts and even in its **elements.**' Proudhon.

great heed to the different stages of political maturity. Since regionalisms do exist in Canada, such feelings should be exploited to further the cause of democracy: each community might enter into a state of healthy competition with the others in order to have better 'self-government'; and thus the whole Canadian system of government would be improved by creative tensions between the central, the provincial, and even the municipal administrations.

Regarding such tensions and competition, it is not for the socialist to cast his lot irrevocably with one level of government as opposed to another. (It is not, for instance, because the reactionaries have in the main opposed centralization that socialists should necessarily favour it!) Since the sum total of governments has the sum total of powers, the first task of the socialist is to educate all of the people to demand maximum service from all of their governments. And his second task is to show how any unhealthy tensions can be resolved through co-operation.

Since every Canadian has a right to the good life, whatever the province or community he lives in, the socialist should define the minimum conditions required for that life, and make them a part of the socialist program. But such goals must first be stated without any preconception as to whether they should be realized at the federal or at the provincial level. It is often said that the concept of provincial autonomy is favourable to corporate wealth, since it weakens the power of the (central) state. But it can just as easily be shown that it favours socialism, as in the case of Saskatchewan.[19] And, as was pointed out earlier, there is certainly no reason to believe that socialism in Canada is nearer to realization at the federal than at the provincial level.

Federalism then must be regarded as a *chose donnée* of Canadian politics; and in the debate which opposes centralization to autonomy, socialists should be as detached and pragmatic as they hope to become in the debate over public versus

[19]The riots that occurred in Belgium during the first days of 1961 underline the importance of a decentralized state to the cause of socialism. According to Jean Lambion, an outstanding socialist trade-union official, 'federation [instead of a unitary state] would give us Walloons a socialist government to carry out long overdue social and economic reforms we desperately require. There is no other way we can get those things.' (Montreal *Star*, January 7, 1961)

private ownership; those are all means, and not ends, and they must be chosen according to their usefulness in each specific case.

Of course, it should not be adduced from the foregoing paragraph that the division of sovereign powers under a federal constitution is held to be purely a matter of arbitrariness and indifference. Obviously some laws and some areas of administration should, by their very nature, come under one level of government rather than under the other. And there is surely some good in trying to improve upon, or modernize, the rational but perhaps ageing division of powers adopted by the Fathers of Confederation. I am inclined to believe, however, that Canadian socialists have exaggerated the urgency of rewriting or reinterpreting the B.N.A. Act.

Personally, I cannot share the views of those people who seem to feel that, had the trend of Privy Council decisions favouring provincial autonomy been different, the fate of the Canadian people would have been immeasurably improved in the past. Neither can I agree with those who, having read long-run centralizing trends into our political future, predict the virtual withering away of Canadian federalism and oblige the political party to which they belong to stand or fall on the fulfilment of such prophecies.

As I have shown above, most of the reforms that could come about through greater centralization could also follow from patient and painstaking co-operation between federal and provincial governments. And the remaining balance of economic advantage that might arise from forcefully transferring more power to the central government is easily offset by the political disadvantages of living under a paternalistic or bullying government.

Granted the foregoing statement, it is difficult to see why socialists devote such energy to constitutional might-have-been's or ought-to-be's, instead of generally accepting the constitution as a datum. From the point of view of 'making available to all what we desire for ourselves', it is not of such momentous consequence that the subject matter of some particular law falls within the jurisdiction of the federal as opposed to the provincial governments, since in either case the governments are responsible to one electorate or another. In other words, laws – whether they issue from one central government or from ten provincial governments – benefit the same sets of citizens. The only important thing, then, is that these latter clearly know which level of government is responsible for what area of legislation, so that they may be aroused to demand good laws from *all* their governments.

A sound rule for Canadian socialists would be to insist that, if need be, they are prepared to carry out their ideals under the present constitution. Thus, they would be encouraged to educate and organize at *all* levels of the electorate. And the various federal or provincial socialist parties and programs would tend to concentrate on that part of the socialist ideals that can be implemented at *their* level of government.

This would not prevent socialist parties from stating in certain limited cases that reforms might be carried out more efficiently if the constitution were amended. But in such cases, amendments would be clearly mentioned, and not sly encroachments which inevitably result in confusing the electorate as to which level of government is responsible for what. Nor would the proposed amendments all, and as a matter of course, tend to be in the direction of centralization.

For instance, provincial socialist parties should stand for provincial labour codes, and for co-operation between the various governments under the constitution to establish minimum labour standards from coast to coast. But that would not necessarily prevent the same men, as members of the socialist party at the national level, from standing for a constitutional amendment permitting Parliament to legislate upon a national labour code if and when the provinces should fail to arrive at one through co-operative action. There are even some cases where socialists at all levels could unite in advocating *joint* federal-provincial legislation.[20]

For example again, when socialists advocate a constitutional amendment enacting a bill of rights for all Canadians and all governments in Canada, they might simultaneously advocate the abolition of the federal right to disallow and to reserve provincial laws, since such safeguards would then be obsolete.[21] For example also, socialists might well prove their lack of bias

[20]This is spelt out in some detail on pp. 23–4 of the *Mémoire* cited in n. 16.

[21]Personally I would be prepared to argue that they are obsolete in any case.

between central and regional governments by proposing that the Supreme Court be really established as an impartial arbitrator in constitutional cases. This could be done by making the Court independent of the federal and the provincial governments, just as the Privy Council used to be. Thus the Supreme Court Act would cease to be a federal statute, and could be entrenched in the constitution. And the judges might be chosen alternately from panels submitted by the federal and the provincial governments.

To sum up and conclude this chapter, it might well be said that the basis of a socialist ideology is to work out a certain set of human values, for the fostering of which society is held collectively responsible.

The basis of a socialist program is to state what minimum standards of the good life must ensue from that set of values, and to demand that those standards be made available to all, given the federal data that some like to live by the sea, some in the plains, and that some prefer to speak French.

The basis of a socialist critique is to state clearly what the provincial governments can do and fail to do, and what the federal government can do and does not do, each within its respective jurisdiction.

Finally, the basis of socialist action is to define the various ways of striving towards socialist goals under a federal constitution, and to lead each community towards such goals as it can hope to attain.

To many an idealist, it may appear that socialism within a federal structure of government is not as pure, as exciting, and as efficient as socialism in a unitary state. That may be so, just as democratic socialism may be less efficient and far-reaching than the totalitarian brand. But just as democracy is a value in itself, which cannot be sacrificed to considerations of expediency, likewise at certain times and in certain places federalism may be held to be a fundamental value, and the penalty for disregarding it may be the complete collapse of socialism itself.

This article originally appeared in Michael Oliver (ed.), *Social Purpose for Canada* (Toronto: University of Toronto Press, 1961).

New Treason of the Intellectuals

The men whose function it is to defend
all eternal and impartial values, like
justice and reason, and whom I call the
intellectuals (les clercs), have betrayed
this function in the interests of
expediency. . . . It has been above all for
the benefit of the nation that the
intellectuals have perpetrated this betrayal.
                                    JULIEN BENDA[1]

The Geographic Approach

It is not the concept of *nation* that is retrograde; it is the idea that the nation must necessarily be sovereign.

To which the champions of independence for Quebec retort that there is nothing at all retrograde about a concept that has brought independence to India, Cuba, and a multitude of African states.

This argument postulates the equation: independence equals progress. Independence, they insist, is good in itself. And to confound the enemy they fire back the aphorism 'Good government is no substitute for self-government.'

Their frequent recourse to this battle-cry (which is invariably misquoted – but do we all have to speak English?) indicates the extent of the Separatists' muddled thinking. Self-government does not mean national self-determination. (This is not a matter of showing off one's linguistic brilliance; we have to know what we are talking about when we raise the cry for Quebec's independence.) Let us not confuse these two ideas.

That self-government is a good thing – or, more precisely, that a trend toward so-called 'responsible' government is in general a trend toward progress – I want to concede at the

[1]Julien Benda, *La trahison des clercs* (Paris, 1927 and 1946).

outset of this article. I have too often denounced Union Nationale autocracy in Quebec and Liberal and Socialist paternalism in Ottawa to be suspect on that score. I have always
maintained that the people of Quebec would never approach
political maturity and mastery of their future so long as they
failed to learn by experience the mechanisms of really responsible government. To this end they must thrust aside both the
ideologies that preach blind submission to 'the authority delegated by God' and those that have us running to Ottawa every
time there is a difficult problem to solve.

But what I was calling for then was 'liberty *in* the city',
observes G.C.[2] What we must have today, he says, is 'liberty *of*
the city', that is to say the absolute independence of the French-
Canadian nation, full and complete sovereignty for *la Laurentie*.
In short, national self-determination. Marcel Chaput writes:

> Since the end of the Second World War, more than thirty
> countries, formerly colonies, have been freed of foreign tutelage
> and have attained national and international sovereignty. In
> 1960 alone seventeen African colonies, fourteen of them
> French-speaking, have obtained their independence. And now
> today it is the people of French Canada who are beginning to
> rouse, and they, too, will claim their place among free nations.[3]

Indeed, Mr. Chaput hastens to admit that French Canada
enjoys rights these people never did. But it does not have
complete independence, and, according to him, 'its destiny
rests, in very large measure, in the hands of a nation foreign
to it.'

The confusion is utter and complete.

Practically all these 'thirty countries, formerly colonies' are
states in the same way that Canada is a state. They have acceded
to full sovereignty just as Canada did in 1931. In no way are
they nations in the sense that French Canada might be a nation.
Consequently, putting the independence of Quebec into this
particular historical context is pure sophistry.

The State of India is a sovereign republic. But there are no
less than four languages officially recognized there (which
include neither English nor Chinese nor Tibetan nor the innumerable dialects). There are eight principal religions, several
of which are mutually and implacably opposed. Which nation

[2]'Lettre d'un nationaliste', *Cité Libre* (Montreal, March 1961), p. 6.
[3]M. Chaput, *Pourquoi je suis séparatiste* (Montreal, 1961), p. 18.

are we talking about? And just what independence should we take as an example?

The State of Ceylon embraces three ethnic groups and four religions. In the Malay Federation there are three more ethnic groups. The Burmese Union arrays half a dozen nationalities one against the other. The Indonesian Republic comprises at least twelve national groups, and twenty-five principal languages are spoken there. In Viet Nam, besides the Tonkinese, the Annamese, and the Cochinchinese there are eight important tribes.

In Africa the polyethnic nature of the new states is even more striking. The frontiers of these countries simply retrace lines marked out years ago by the colonialists, according to the fortunes of conquest, exploration, and administrative whimsy. Consequently, members of one tribe, speaking the same language and sharing the same traditions, have become citizens of different states, and these states are barely more than conglomerations of distinct and rival groups. A sample of what this can lead to can be seen in the former Belgian Congo. But if we examine Ghana, the Sudan, Nigeria, or almost any other ex-colony, there, too, we find the same kind of ethnic complexity. In French West Africa, for example, the population consisted of ten scattered tribes; nevertheless, France found it convenient to divide them up into eight territories. And the course of history is at present transforming these territories into sovereign states. In vain may we look there for nation-states – that is to say, states whose delineations correspond with ethnic and linguistic entities.[4]

As for Algeria, which our *Indépendantistes* are always holding up as an example, there is no doubt what kind of state she is seeking to become. Besides inhabitants of French, Spanish, Italian, Jewish, Greek, and Levantine origin, in this particular country we must count Berbers, Kabyles, Arabs, Moors, Negroes, Tuaregs, Mazabites,[5] and a number of Cheshire cats. Of the disputes, notably between Kabyles and Arabs, we are far from having heard the end.

Finally, as far as concerns Cuba, endlessly discussed by the Separatists as a pattern to be followed, it's all obviously pure

[4] Most of these facts may be found in *The Statesman's Yearbook* (London).
[5] *Encyclopaedia Britannica.*

cock-and-bull. This country was sovereign under Batista and
it is sovereign under Castro. It was economically dependent
before and it still is. Democratic self-government was non-
existent there yesterday and it is still non-existent there today.
So what does that prove? That Castro is not Batista? To be
sure; but Hydro-Quebec under René Lévesque is not Hydro
under Daniel Johnson. A lot of good that argument does for
the Separatists.

What emerges from all this is that promoting independence
as an end good in itself, a matter of dignity for all self-respecting
peoples, amounts to embroiling the world in a pretty pickle
indeed. It has been held that every sincere anti-colonialist who
wants to see independence for Algeria ought also to want it for
Quebec. This argument assumes that Quebec is a political
dependant, which shows very poor knowledge of constitutional
history; but even if it were, logically speaking one would then
have to say that every Quebec Separatist should advocate
independence for the Kabyles, or, to give an even better example, independence for twenty-five million Bengalis included
in the State of India. Should the Separatists try to take the wind
out of my sails by saying that they would indeed like to see this
independence for Bengal, I would ask why they would stop
there in the good work; in Bengal ninety different languages are
spoken; and then there are still more Bengalis in Pakistan –
What a lovely lot of separations that would be!

To finish this particular discussion with the aphorism we
started with, I am, in the light of all this, tempted to conclude
that 'good government is a damned good substitute for national self-determination', if one means by this last term the
right of ethnic and linguistic groups to their own absolute
sovereignty. It would seem, in fact, a matter of considerable
urgency for world peace and the success of the new states that
the form of good government known as democratic federalism
should be perfected and promoted, in the hope of solving to
some extent the world-wide problems of ethnic pluralism. To
this end, as I will show later, Canada could be called upon to
serve as mentor, provided she has sense enough to conceive her
own future on a grand scale. John Conway wrote, of true
federalism, 'Its successful adoption in Europe would go a long
way towards ensuring the survival of traditional western civilization. It would be a pity, if, in Canada, so young, so rich and

vigorous and plagued with so few really serious problems, the attempt should fail.'[6]

Further on the subject of federalism, it would seem well understood that President Wilson, that great champion of the 'principle of nationality', in no way intended to invite nationalist secessions, but sought rather to ensure the right of nationalities to a certain amount of local autonomy within existing states.[7]

Moreover, it is quite wrong to insist, as our advocates of independence often do, that the principle of nationality is an internationally recognized right, and sanctioned by the United Nations. Rather than adopting Wilson's equivocal pronouncements, and finding themselves faced with a new wave of plebiscites and secessions echoing the post-World-War-I period, the U.N. has preferred to talk – citing Article I of the Charter – of the right of 'peoples' to self-determination. The term 'peoples', however, is far from being identical with 'ethnic groups'.[8]

The Historical Approach

If the idea of the nation-state is hard to justify in terms of the evolution of anti-colonialism in recent years, how does it look in the light of history as a whole?[9]

---

[6]In the *Catholic Historical Review* (July 1961).

[7]S. Wambaugh, 'National Self-Determination', *Encyclopedia of the Social Sciences* (New York, 1950).

[8]It is obvious that the language of politics is riddled with pitfalls. The word 'nation', or 'nationality', from the Latin 'nasci' (to be born), denotes most often an ethnic community sharing a common language and customs. The Japanese nation. It is in this sense that we speak of the 'principle of nationality' leading to the 'national state' or 'nation-state'. But sometimes the reverse is the case, where the state, originally made up of a number of ethnic communities, comes to think of itself as a nation; then the word is understood to mean a political society occupying a territory and sharing customs in common over a considerable period of time. The Swiss nation. In Canada, as I will explain later, there is, or will be, a Canadian nation in so far as the ethnic communities succeed in exorcizing their own respective nationalisms. If, then, a Canadian nationalism does take form, it will have to be exorcized in its turn, and the Canadian nation will be asked to yield a part of its sovereignty to a higher authority, just as is asked, today, of the French-Canadian and English-Canadian nations. (For a discussion of the vocabulary of this subject, see p. 4 of a remarkable essay by E. H. Carr in Carr *et al.*, *Nations ou Fédéralisme* (Paris, 1946), p. 4.)

[9]See, among others, M. H. Boehm and C. Hayes, 'Nationalism', from *Encyclopedia of the Social Sciences*.

At the threshold of time there was man, and also, no doubt, in keeping with man's very nature, that other undeniable fact called the family. Then, very soon, the tribe appeared, a sort of primitive community founded on common customs and speech.

Now the history of civilization is a chronicle of the subordination of tribal 'nationalism' to wider interests. No doubt there were always clan loyalties and regional cohesions. But thought developed, knowledge spread, inventions came to light, and humanity progressed wherever there was intermingling of tribes and exchange between them, gathering impetus through commerce and the division of labour, the heavy hand of conquests (from Egypt and China down to the Holy Roman Empire), and the drive of the militant religions (from Buddhism on through Christianity to Islam).

Finally, after more than sixty-five centuries of history, with the breaking down of the rigid social structure of the Middle Ages, the decline of Latin as the mark of the learned man, and the birth of the cult of individualism, the modern idea of 'nation' began to develop in Europe. The displacement of the Church by national Churches, the rise of the *bourgeoisie*, mercantilism for the protection of territorial economies, outrages committed against certain ethnic groups such as the Poles, the Jacobin Revolution, the relentless fervour of Mazzini, the domination of poor nations by industrialized ones like England: so many factors helped fan the flame of nationalist aspirations, leading to the setting up of one national state after another. The countries of Latin America revolted against Spain. Italy and Germany fought their wars of unification. The Greeks and the Slavs rebelled against the Ottoman Empire. Ireland rose against Great Britain. In short, all of Europe and a great deal of the New World took fire. The era of wars of nationalism, starting in Napoleon's day, reached its peak with the two world wars. And so it is that we have entered a new age, the nations now indulging their vanity in the possession and use of nuclear arms.

Some seven thousand years of history in three paragraphs is, of course, a little short. I will have more to say on the subject later, but for the time being it will suffice to keep three things in mind.

The first is that the nation is not a biological reality – that is, a community that springs from the very nature of man. Except for a very small fraction of his history, man has done very well without nations (this for the benefit of our young bloods, who see the slightest dent in the nation's sovereignty as an earth-shaking catastrophe).

The second is that the tiny portion of history marked by the emergence of the nation-states is also the scene of the most devastating wars, the worst atrocities, and the most degrading collective hatred the world has ever seen. Up until the end of the eighteenth century it was generally the sovereigns, not the nations, who made war; and while their sovereigns made war the civilian populations continued to visit each other: merchants crossed borders, scholars and philosophers went freely from one court to another, and conquering generals would take under their personal protection the learned men of vanquished cities. War killed soldiers, but left the various civilizations unhindered. In our day, however, we have seen nations refusing to listen to Beethoven because they are at war with Germany, others boycotting the Peking Opera because they refuse to recognize China, and still others refusing visas or passports to scholars wishing to attend some scientific or humanitarian congress in a country of differing ideology. Pasternak was not even allowed to go to Stockholm to accept his Nobel Prize. A concept of nation that pays so little honour to science and culture obviously can find no room above itself in its scale of values for truth, liberty, and life itself. It is a concept that corrupts all: in peace time the intellectuals become propagandists for the nation and the propaganda is a lie; in war time the democracies slither toward dictatorship and the dictatorships herd us into concentration camps; and finally after the massacres of Ethiopia come those of London and Hamburg, then of Hiroshima and Nagasaki, and perhaps more and more until the final massacre. I know very well that the nation-state idea is not the sole cause of all the evils born of war; modern technology has a good deal to answer for on that score! But the important thing is that the nation-state idea has caused wars to become more and more total over the last two centuries; and that is the idea I take issue with so vehemently. Besides, each time a state has taken an exclusive and intolerant idea as its cornerstone (religion, nationhood, ideology), this idea has been the very mainspring of war. In days gone by religion had to be displaced as the basis of the state before the frightful religious wars came to an end. And there will be no end to wars between nations until in some similar fashion the nation ceases to be the basis of the state.[10] As for inter-state wars, they will end only if the states give up that obsession whose very essence makes them exclusive and intolerant: sovereignty. Now – to get back to the subject – what worries me about the fact that five million Canadians of French origin cannot manage to share their national sovereignty with seven million Canadians of British origin, beside whom they live and who they know, in general, have no fleas, is that this leaves me precious little hope that several thousand million Americans, Russians, and Chinese, who have never met and none of whom are sure the others are not flea-ridden, will ever agree to abdicate a piece of their sovereignty in the realm of nuclear arms.

The third observation I would draw from the course of history is that the very idea of the nation-state is absurd. To insist that a particular nationality must have complete sovereign power is to pursue a self-destructive end. Because every national minority will find, at the very moment of liberation, a new minority within its bosom which in turn must be allowed the right to demand its freedom. And on and on would stretch the train of revolutions, until the last-born of nation-states turned to violence to put an end to the very principle that gave it birth. That is why the principle of nationality has brought to the world two centuries of war, and *not one single* final solution. France has always had its Bretons and Alsatians, Britain its Scots and its Welsh, Spain its Catalans and Basques, Yugoslavia its Croats and Macedonians, Finland its Swedes and Lapps, and so on, for Belgium, Hungary, Czechoslovakia, Poland, the Soviet Union, China, the United States, all the Latin American countries, and who knows how many others. As far as the more homogeneous countries are concerned, those that have no problems of secession find themselves problems of accession. Ireland lays claim to the six counties of Ulster; Indonesia wants New Guinea. Mussolini's nationalist Italy, when it was done with the *irredentas,* turned to dreams of reconquering the Roman Empire. Hitler would have been satis-

[10]See Emory Reeves, *A Democratic Manifesto* (London, 1943), p. 43, and also, by the same author, *The Anatomy of Peace* (New York, 1945).

fied with nothing less than the conquest of the entire non-Aryan world. Now there is something for Quebec's Separatists to sink their teeth into: if there is any validity to their principles they should carry them to the point of claiming part of Ontario, New Brunswick, Labrador, and New England; on the other hand, though, they would have to relinquish certain border regions around Pontiac and Temiskaming and turn Westmount into the Danzig of the New World.

So the concept of the nation-state, which has managed to cripple the advance of civilization, has managed to solve none of the political problems it has raised, unless by virtue of its sheer absurdity. And, where civilization has pushed ahead in spite of all, it is where the intellectuals have found the strength within themselves to put their faith in mankind before any national prejudice: Pasternak, Oppenheimer, Joliot-Curie, Russell, Einstein, Freud, Casals, and many others who have replied: *E pur si muove* to the *raison d'état*.

'Man', said Renan, 'is bound neither to his language nor to his race; he is bound only to himself because he is a free agent, or in other words a moral being.'[11]

Listen, too, to what Father Delos has to say:

> What we must know is whether Man is intended to fill a predetermined role in history, whether history encompasses Man, or whether Man possesses innate powers which transcend all historical forms of culture and civilization; the question is whether it is not a denial of Man's dignity to reduce him to mere identification with any particular mass of humanity.[12]

The Origin of Nationalism

Absurd in principle and outdated in practice as it may be, the idea of the nation-state has enjoyed extraordinary favour, and still does. How can it be? That is what I would like to explore next.

The birth of the modern state can be fixed near the end of the fourteenth century. Until then the feudal system was sufficient to maintain order in Europe, where the means of com-

[11]Cited by Benda, *op. cit.*, p. 143.
[12]J. T. Delos, *La Nation* (Montreal, 1944), Vol. I, p. 196. See also an excellent article by Professor Maurice Tremblay of Laval, 'Réflexions sur le nationalisme', from *Les Ecrits du Canada français*, Vol. V (Montreal, 1959).

munication were limited, economy and trade were essentially local, and where, consequently, political administration could remain very much uncentralized. But as trade spread and diversified, as each political-economic unit demanded a broader base and better protection, and as kings found the means of giving free rein to their ambitions, the *bourgeois* classes allied themselves with their reigning monarchs to supplant the powers of feudal lords and of free cities by strong and unified states. In 1576 Jean Bodin ascertained that the new and essential characteristic of these states was 'sovereignty', which he described as the *suprema potestas* over its citizens and subjects, unlimited under the law.

For a few centuries absolute monarchy remained master of these sovereign states. But they were not yet nation-states, because their frontiers remained a family matter, in the sense that their locations were shifted according to the fortunes of marriage and of war between the various reigning families. Nationalities were taken so little into account that Louis XIV, for example, after having annexed Alsace, made no attempt to forbid the continued use of German there, and schools for the teaching of French were introduced only twenty years later.[13]

Individualism, scepticism, rationalism, however, continued to undermine the traditional powers. And the day came when absolute monarchy, in its turn, was obliged to step aside to make way for the *bourgeoisie*, its ally of earlier days. But as the dynasties disappeared, there was already a new cohesive agent at work to fill the vacuum and head off a weakening of the state: popular sovereignty, or democratic power.

Democracy indeed opened the way, first to the *bourgeoisie* and much later to all classes, by which all could participate in the exercise of political power. The state then appeared to be the instrument by which eventually all classes – that is to say, the entire nation – could assure peace and prosperity for themselves. And quite naturally all wished to make that instrument as strong as possible in relation to other states. Thus nationalism was born, the child of liberal democracy and the mystique of equality.

Alas, this nationalism, by a singular paradox, was soon to depart from the ideas that presided at its birth. Because the moment the sovereign state was put at the service of the nation

[13]Benda, *op. cit.*, p. 268, citing Vidal de la Blache, *La France de l'Est.*

it was the nation that became sovereign – that is to say, beyond the law. It mattered little then that the prosperity of some meant the ruin of others. Nations historically strong, those that were industrialized first, those that had inherited strategic or institutional advantages, soon came to see the advantages of their situation. Here rulers closed ranks with the ruled, the haves with the have-nots, and they set out together as a body, in the name of the nationalism that bound them together, to line their pockets and feed their vanity at the expense of weaker nations.

Expansionist nationalism then began to bestow fancy titles upon itself: political Darwinism, Nietzschean mysticism, the white man's burden, civilizing mission, pan-Slavism, Magyarization, and all the other rubbish by which the strong justify their oppression of the weak.

In all these cases the result was the same. Nations that were dominated, dismembered, exploited, and humiliated conceived an unbounded hatred for their oppressors; and united by this hatred they erected against aggressive nationalism a defensive nationalism. And so a chain of wars was ignited that keeps bursting into flame all over the planet.

It is into the depths of this world-wide nationalist phenomenon that we must delve in examining the sub-sub-species Quebec of the sub-species Canada. The Seven Years' War saw the five great powers of Europe deployed against each other in accordance with a complicated system of alliances and compacts. France and Russia fought on the side of Austria, while England aligned herself with Prussia. But while Louis XV lent support to Marie Thérèse with his armies and his money, in the hope of broadening French influence in Europe, Pitt sent to Frederick II plenty of money and a small number of soldiers. These he sent off with English fleets to vanquish France in India and America, and to lay the foundations of the most formidable empire the world has ever known. We know the rest: by the Treaty of Paris, Canada, among others, became English.[14]

At this period the English were already the most nationalist of nationalists. The whole country, proud of its political and economic superiority, unanimously favoured the planting of the flag in the most far-flung lands. This nationalism was necessarily cultural, too; to English eyes they bestowed a priceless

[14]I recommend a fascinating chapter in J. Dalberg-Acton, *Lectures on Modern History* (London, 1906), p. 274.

favour on the undeserving countries they colonized: the right to share the Anglo-Saxon language and customs. And then, despite having so effectively and admirably built up the cult of civil liberties at home in England, they gave not the slightest thought to the protection of minority rights for others.[15]

From the moment of delivery of the Royal Proclamation of 1763, the intention was obvious: the French Canadian was to be completely assimilated. In 1840 Durham, while 'far from wishing to encourage indiscriminately [these] pretentions to superiority on the part of any particular race', none the less considered that assimilation was simply 'a question of time and mode'.[16]

Throughout this period, Canadians of British origin would have considered it an indignity to be in any inferior position. So they invented all kinds of stratagems by which democracy was made to mean government by the minority.[17]

Generations passed. Hopes of assimilating the French Canadians dimmed to a flicker (although right up to 1948, immigration laws continued to favour immigrants from the British Isles over those from France). But English-speaking Canadians have never given up their condescending attitude to their French-speaking fellows, even to this day.

At Ottawa and in provinces other than ours, this nationalism could wear the pious mask of democracy. Because, as English-speaking Canadians became proportionately more numerous, they took to hiding their intolerance behind acts of majority rule; that was how they quashed bilingualism in the Manitoba legislature, violated rights acquired by separate schools in various provinces, savagely imposed conscription in 1917, and broke a solemn promise in 1942.[18]

In Quebec, 'where they had the money if not the numbers,

15By 1759, 'English public law had not worked out any theory of minority rights guaranteed by law', writes F. R. Scott in Mason Wade (ed.), *Canadian Dualism* (Toronto, 1960), p. 100.
16*The Durham Report* (Coupland ed., Oxford, 1945), p. 153. See also p. 179.
17I recounted this story in 'Some Obstacles to Democracy in Quebec' (p. 103 ff. of this volume).
18André Laurendeau has just written with great clarity an account of how, with the plebiscite of 1942, the state became the tool of Anglo-Canadian nationalism, and of how that state took advantage of French-Canadian numerical weakness to divest itself of pledges it had made (*La Crise de la conscription*, Montreal, 1962). A tale even more shameful could be told of how, during the same war and with

our Anglo-Canadian fellow-citizens have often yielded to the temptation of using without restraint the means at their command'.[19] This was how, in politics, Anglo-Canadian nationalism took on the form of what André Laurendeau has so admirably named the 'cannibal-king theory' (théorie du roi-nègre). Economically, this nationalism has been expressed essentially in treating the French Canadian as *un cochon de payant*. Sometimes, magnanimously, they would go as far as putting a few straw men on boards of directors. These men invariably had two things in common: first, they were never bright enough or strong enough to rise to the top, and second, they were always sufficiently 'representative' to grovel for the cannibal-king's favours and flatter the vanity of their fellow-tribesmen. Finally, in social and cultural matters, Anglo-Canadian nationalism has expressed itself quite simply by disdain. Generation after generation of Anglo-Saxons have lived in Quebec without getting around to learning three sentences of French. When these insular people insist, with much gravity, that their jaws and ears aren't made for it and can't adapt themselves to French, what they really want to get across to you is that they will not sully these organs, and their small minds, by submitting them to a barbarous idiom.

Anglo-Canadian nationalism produced, inevitably, French-Canadian nationalism. As I have said before, speaking of the roots of our nationalism and the futility of its tendencies:

> Defeated, occupied, leaderless, banished from commercial enterprise, poked away outside the cities, little by little reduced to a minority and left with very little influence in a country which, after all, he discovered, explored and colonized, the French Canadian had little alternative for the frame of mind he would have to assume in order to preserve what remained of his own. So he set up a system of defense-mechanisms which soon assumed such overgrown proportions that he came to regard as priceless anything which distinguished him from other people; and any change whatever (be it for the better or not) he would regard with hostility if it originated from outside.[20]

'Alas,' I added, 'the nationalists' idealism itself has been their downfall. "They loved not wisely but too well." '

---

similar inspiration, the vengeful powers of the state were turned against the Japanese-Canadian minority.

[19] P. E. Trudeau, 'Réflexions sur la politique au Canada français', *Cité Libre* (Montreal, December 1952), p. 61.
[20] P. E. Trudeau (ed.), *La Grève de l'amiante* (Montreal, 1956), p. 11.

The Conflict of Nationalisms in Canada

We must accept the facts of history as they are. However outworn and absurd it may be, the nation-state image spurred the political thinking of the British, and subsequently of Canadians of British descent in the 'Dominion of Canada'. Broadly speaking, this meant identifying the Canadian state with themselves to the greatest degree possible.

Since the French Canadians had the bad grace to decline assimilation, such an identification was beyond being completely realizable. So the Anglo-Canadians built themselves an illusion of it by fencing off the French Canadians in their Quebec ghetto and then nibbling at its constitutional powers and carrying them off bit by bit to Ottawa. Outside Quebec they fought, with staggering ferocity, against anything that might intrude upon that illusion: the use of French on stamps, money, cheques, in the civil service, the railroads, and the whole works.

In the face of such aggressive nationalism, what choice lay before the French Canadians over, say, the last century? On the one hand they could respond to the vision of an overbearing Anglo-Canadian nation-state with a rival vision of a French-Canadian nation-state; on the other hand they could scrap the very idea of nation-state once and for all and lead the way toward making Canada a multi-national state.

The first choice was, and is, that of the Separatists or advocates of independence; an emotional and prejudiced choice essentially – which goes for their antagonists too, for that matter – and I could never see any sense in it. Because either it is destined to succeed by achieving independence, which would prove that the nationalism of Anglo-Canadians is neither intransigent, nor armed to the teeth, nor so very dangerous for us; and in that case I wonder why we are so afraid to face these people in the bosom of a pluralistic state and why we are prepared to renounce our right to consider Canada our home *a mari usque ad mare*. Or else the attempt at independence is doomed to failure and the plight of the French Canadians will be worse than ever; not because a victorious and vindictive enemy will deport part of the population and leave the rest with dwindled rights and a ruined heritage – this eventuality seems most unlikely; but because once again French Canadians will have poured all their vital energies into a (hypothetically) fruitless struggle, energies that should have been used to match in excellence, efficacy, and persistence a (hypothetically) fearsome enemy.

The second choice, for the multi-national state, was, and is, that of the Constitutionalists. It would reject the bellicose and self-destructive idea of nation-state in favour of the more civilized goal of polyethnic pluralism. I grant that in certain countries and at certain periods of history this may have been impossible, notably where aggressive nationalism has enjoyed a crushing predominance and refused all compromise with national minorities. Was this the case in the time of Papineau and the *patriotes*? I doubt it; but the fact remains that the upshot of this 'separatist' uprising was an Act of Union which marked a step backward for minority rights from the Constitutional Act of 1791.

As a matter of fact, this second choice was, and is, possible for French Canadians. In a sense the multi-national state was dreamed about by Lafontaine, realized under Cartier, perfected by Laurier, and humanized with Bourassa. Anglo-Canadian nationalism has never enjoyed a crushing predominance and has never been in a position to refuse all compromise with the country's principal national minority; consequently, it has been unable to follow the policy perhaps most gratifying to its arrogance, and has had to resign itself to the situation as imposed by the course of events.

The first of such events was the Quebec Act, passed under the shadow of the American Revolution. Then there were the terrible dark days – three-quarters of a century of them – when Canadians of British origin knew there were fewer of them than of French Canadians. As Mason Wade says of the Loyalists: 'They were badly scared men, who had lived through one revolution in America and dreaded another in Canada.'[21] Eventually, it was the constant threat of American domination that – like it or not – obliged Anglo-Canadian nationalism to take cognizance of the French-Canadian nation; it would have been virtually impossible otherwise to reunite the remaining colonies of British North America.

In actual fact, Anglo-Canadian nationalism has never had much of an edge. Those among French Canadians who have

[21]Mason Wade, *The French Canadians 1760–1967* (Toronto, 1968), p. 93.

had the acumen to realize it – the Constitutionalists, as I call them – have naturally wagered on the multi-national State, and have exhorted their compatriots to work for it boldly and eagerly. But those who could not see it have never ceased in their fear of a largely imaginary adversary. Among these are, first, the assimilated converts and boot-lickers who have given in to the idea that French Canada is already dead, and that the Anglo-Canadian nation-state is rising triumphant over its remains; these, though, are insignificant in number and even more so in influence, so I am writing them off as a force to be reckoned with. Secondly, there are Separatists and nationalists of all shapes and sizes baying after independence, who devote all their courage and capabilities to stirring up French-Canadian nationalism in defiance of the Anglo-Canadian variety. These are incessantly promoting what Gérard Pelletier has very aptly called 'the state-of-siege mentality'. Now, recalling something I once wrote, 'the siege was lifted long ago and humanity has marched ever onward, while we remain stewing steadily in our own juice without daring even once to peek over the edge of the pot.'[22]

If Canada as a state has had so little room for French Canadians it is above all because we have failed to make ourselves indispensable to its future. Today, for example, it would seem that a Sévigny or a Dorion could perfectly well leave the federal cabinet, as a Courtemanche did, without causing irreparable damage to the machinery of government or the prestige of the country. And, with the sole exception of Laurier, I fail to see a single French Canadian in more than three-quarters of a century whose presence in the federal cabinet might be considered indispensable to the history of Canada as written – except at election time, of course, when the tribe always invokes the aid of its witch-doctors. Similarly, in the ranks of senior civil servants, there is probably not one who could be said to have decisively and beneficially influenced the development of our administration as has, for example, an O. D. Skelton, a Graham Towers, or a Norman Robertson.

Consequently, an examination of the few nationalist 'victories' carried off at Ottawa after years of wrangling in high places will reveal probably none that could not have been won in the course of a single cabinet meeting by a French Canadian

[22]In *Notre Temps* (Montreal), November 15, 1947.

of the calibre of C. D. Howe. All our cabinet ministers put together would scarcely match the weight of a bilingual cheque or the name of a hotel.

To sum up, the Anglo-Canadians have been strong by virtue only of our weakness. This is true not only at Ottawa, but even at Quebec, a veritable charnel-house where half our rights have been wasted by decay and decrepitude and the rest devoured by the maggots of political cynicism and the pestilence of corruption. Under the circumstances, can there be any wonder that Anglo-Canadians have not wanted the face of this country to bear any French features? And why would they want to learn a language that we have been at such pains to reduce to mediocrity at all levels of our educational system?

No doubt, had English-speaking Canadians applied themselves to learning French with a quarter the diligence they have shown in refusing to do so, Canada would have been effectively bilingual long ago. For here is demonstrated one of the laws of nationalism, whereby more energy is consumed in combating disagreeable but irrevocable realities than in contriving some satisfactory compromise. It stands to reason that this law works to greatest ill effect in respect to minority nationalisms: namely, us.

Let me explain.

The Sorry Tale of French-Canadian Nationalism

We have expended a great deal of time and energy proclaiming the rights due our nationality, invoking our divine mission, trumpeting our virtues, bewailing our misfortunes, denouncing our enemies, and avowing our independence; and for all that not one of our workmen is the more skilled, nor a civil servant the more efficient, a financier the richer, a doctor the more advanced, a bishop the more learned, nor a single solitary politician the less ignorant. Now, except for a few stubborn eccentrics, there is probably not one French-Canadian intellectual who has not spent at least four hours a week over the last year discussing separatism. That makes how many thousand times two hundred hours spent just flapping our arms? And can any one of them honestly say he has heard a single argument not already expounded *ad nauseam* twenty, forty, and even sixty years ago? I am not even sure we have exorcized any of our original bogey men in sixty years. The Separatists of 1962 that I have met really are, in general, genuinely earnest and nice people; but the few times I have had the opportunity of talking with them at any length, I have almost always been astounded by the totalitarian outlook of some, the anti-Semitism of others, and the complete ignorance of basic economics of all of them.

This is what I call *la nouvelle trahison des clercs*: this self-deluding passion of a large segment of our thinking population for throwing themselves headlong – intellectually and spiritually – into purely escapist pursuits.

Several years ago I tried to show that the devotees of the nationalist school of thought among French Canadians, despite their good intentions and courage, were for all practical purposes trying to swim upstream against the course of progress. Over more than half a century 'they have laid down a pattern of social thinking impossible to realize and which, from all practical points of view, has left the people without any effective intellectual direction.'[23]

I have discovered that several people who thought as I did at that time are today talking separatism. Because their social thinking is to the left, because they are campaigning for secular schools, because they may be active in trade union movements, because they are open-minded culturally, they think that their nationalism is the path to progress. What they fail to see is that they have become reactionary *politically*.

Reactionary, in the first place, by reason of circumstances. A count, even a rough one, of institutions, organizations, and individuals dedicated to nationalism, from the village notary to the Ordre de Jacques Cartier, from the small businessman to the Ligues du Sacré-Cœur, would show beyond question that an alliance between nationalists of the right and of the left would work in favour of the former, by sheer weight of numbers. And when the leftists say they will not make such an alliance until it is they who are in the majority, I venture to suggest once again[24] that they will never be so as long as they continue to waste their meagre resources as they do now. Any effort aimed at strengthening the nation must avoid dividing it; otherwise such an effort loses all effectiveness so far as social

[23]*La Grève de l'amiante*, p. 14.
[24]I have already tried to point out the strategic inanity of the nationalists of the left, in *Cité Libre*, March 1961, p. 4.

reform is concerned, and for that matter can only lead to con-
solidation of the *status quo*. In this sense the alliance is already
working against the left, even before being concluded.

In the second place, the nationalists – even those of the left –
are politically reactionary because, in attaching such importance
to the idea of nation, they are surely led to a definition of the
common good as a function of an ethnic group, rather than of
all the people, regardless of characteristics. This is why a nationalistic government is by nature intolerant, discriminatory,
and, when all is said and done, totalitarian.[25] A truly democratic government cannot be 'nationalist', because it must pursue the good of all its citizens, without prejudice to ethnic
origin. The democratic government, then, stands for and en-
courages good citizenship, never nationalism. Certainly, such
a government will make laws by which ethnic groups will benefit, and the majority group will benefit proportionately to its
number; but that follows naturally from the principle of equality
for all, not from any right due the strongest. In this sense one
may well say that educational policy in Quebec has always been
democratic rather than nationalistic; I would not say the same
for all the other provinces. If, on the other hand, Hydro-Quebec
were to expropriate the province's hydro-electric industries for
nationalistic rather than economic reasons, we would already
be on the road to fascism. The right can nationalize; it is the
left that socializes and controls for the common good.

In the third place, any thinking that calls for full sovereign
powers for the nation is politically reactionary because it would
put complete and perfect power in the hands of a community
which is incapable of realizing a complete and perfect society.
In 1962 it is unlikely that any nation-state – or for that matter
any multi-national state either – however strong, could realize
a complete and perfect society;[26] economic, military, and cul-

---

[25]As early as 1862, Lord Acton was already writing thus: 'The nation is
here an ideal unit founded on the race. . . . It overrules the rights and
wishes of the inhabitants, absorbing their divergent interests in a ficti-
tious unity; sacrifices their several inclinations and duties to the higher
claim of nationality, and crushes all natural rights and all established
liberties for the purpose of vindicating itself. Whenever a single
definite object is made the supreme end of the State – the State becomes for the time being inevitably absolute.' John Dalberg-Acton,
Essays on Freedom and Power (Glencoe, 1948), p. 184.

[26]See Jacques Maritain, *Man and the State* (Chicago, 1951), p. 210.

tural interdependence is a *sine qua non* for states of the twentieth century, to the extent that none is really self-sufficient. Treaties, trade alliances, common markets, free trade areas, cultural and scientific agreements, all these are as indispensable for the world's states as is interchange between citizens within them; and just as each citizen must recognize the submission of his own sovereignty to the laws of the state – by which, for example, he must fulfil the contracts he makes – so the states will know no real peace and prosperity until they accept the submission of their relations with each other to a higher order. In truth, the very concept of sovereignty must be surmounted, and those who proclaim it for the nation of French Canada are not only reactionary, they are preposterous. French Canadians could no more constitute a perfect society than could the five million Sikhs of the Punjab. We are not well enough educated, nor rich enough, nor, above all, numerous enough, to man and finance a government possessing all the necessary means for both war and peace. The fixed per-capita cost would ruin us. But I shall not try to explain all this to people who feel something other than dismay at seeing *la Laurentie* already opening embassies in various parts of the world, 'for the diffusion of our culture abroad'. Particularly when these same people, a year ago, seemed to be arguing that we were too poor to finance a second university – a Jesuit one – in Montreal.

To this third contention, that sovereignty is unworkable and contradictory, the Separatists will sometimes argue that, once independent, Quebec could very well afford to give up part of her sovereignty on, for instance, re-entering a Canadian Confederation, because then her choice would be her own, a free one. That abstraction covers a multitude of sins! It is a serious thing to ask French Canadians to embark on several decades of privation and sacrifice, just so that they can indulge themselves in the luxury of choosing 'freely' a destiny more or less identical to the one they have rejected. But the ultimate tragedy would be in not realizing that French Canada is too culturally anaemic, too economically destitute, too intellectually retarded, too spiritually paralysed, to be able to survive more than a couple of decades of stagnation, emptying herself of all her vitality into nothing but a cesspit, the mirror of her nationalistic vanity and 'dignity'.

NEW TREASON OF THE INTELLECTUALS / 171

The Younger Generation

What French Canadians now in their twenties will find hard to forgive in people of my generation a few years from now is the complacency with which we have watched the rebirth of separatism and nationalism. Because by then they will have realized how appallingly backward French Canada is in all fields of endeavour. What! they will say to the intellectuals, you did so little writing and so little thinking and yet you had time to ruminate over separatism? What! they will say to the sociologists and political scientists, in the very year that men were first put into orbit you were replying gravely to inquiries on separatism that in your opinion, perhaps, yes, one day, no doubt, possibly. . . . What! they will say to the economists, with the western world in its age of mass production striving, by all kinds of economic unions, to reproduce market conditions already enjoyed within such large political unions as the United States and the Soviet Union, how could you, in Quebec, have looked on with satisfaction at a movement whose aims would have reduced to nil any common market for Quebec industry? What! they will say to the engineers, you could not even manage to build a highway that would survive two Canadian winters and you were pipe-dreaming of a Great Wall all the way around Quebec? What! they will say to the judges and lawyers, civil liberties having survived in the province of Quebec thanks only to the Communists, the trade unions, and the Jehovah's Witnesses, and to English and Jewish lawyers and the judges of the Supreme Court in Ottawa,[27] and you had nothing better to do than cheer on the coming of a sovereign state for French Canadians? Finally they will come to the party politicians. What! they will say, you, the Liberals, spent twenty-five years growing fat on sovereignty filched from the provinces; you, the Conservatives, alias Union Nationale, subjected Quebec to two de-

[27]Seven times in the last decade alone, beginning in 1951, the Supreme Court in Ottawa has reversed the decisions of the Court of Appeal of the Province of Quebec, decisions which would have spelled disaster for civil liberties: the Boucher case (seditious libel); the Alliance case (loss of union certification); the Saumur case (distribution of pamphlets); the Chaput case (religious assembly); the Birks case (compulsory religious holidays); the Switzman case (padlock law); the Roncarelli case (administrative discretion). At the moment of going to press we learn that yet an eighth case can now be added to this list: the case of *Lady Chatterly's Lover*.

cades of retroactive, vindictive, discriminatory, and stultifying laws; and you, of the Social-Democratic-cum-New-Democratic Party, in the name of some obscure sort of federal *raison d'état*, had sabotaged the *Union des forces démocratiques* and thereby snuffed out any glimmer of hope for Quebec's radicals; and you all discovered, all of a sudden, that Quebec must have more independence, some of you to the point of becoming avowed Separatists?

I venture to predict that among these young people of such acid criticism there will be one called Luc Racine, who will be a little sorry that he once wrote as follows in *Cité Libre*: 'If today's youth has turned to separatism, it is not from indifference to the great problems facing humanity, but from the desire to concentrate its efforts on conditions that are within its power to change.'[28] Because by then he will understand that a given people, at a given moment in their history, possess only a given amount of intellectual energy; and that if a whole generation devotes the greater part of that energy to imbecilities, that generation, for all practical purposes, will indeed have shown its 'indifference to the great problems facing humanity'. (I would lend a word of advice to Racine, however: that in 1972 he not take it into his head to talk about nationalism as a form of alienation, because my friend André Laurendeau will once again feel compelled to fly to the defence of his forebears, protesting that in 1922 the Abbé Groulx deserved our complete respect.)[29]

So much for that. But how does it happen that separatism enjoys such a following *today* among the younger generation? How is it, for example, that so many young people, responding to *Cité Libre*'s editorial 'Un certain silence', have declared themselves for separatism?

Pelletier has pointed out that, having preached – through

[28]February 1962, p. 24.

[29]An emotional allusion to an emotional rejoinder by Laurendeau, *Le Devoir*, March 3, 1961. This soul of refinement, one of the fairest-minded men I know, who shares with Bourassa the privilege of being the favourite target of the Separatists (who, logically enough, will not allow that nationalism could be anything but separatist), rarely speaks of nationalism without betraying, in some little detail, a blind spot. Thus it was that in an otherwise excellent editorial (*Le Devoir*, January 30, 1962), he put forth the ridiculous idea of a 'moral conscription of French Canadians'. What! Mr. Laurendeau? Conscription!?

Cité Libre – systematic scepticism in the face of established dogmatism, and having practised it as regards most of our traditional institutions, we should hardly be surprised if a new generation should turn it against one of the establishments we ourselves have spared: the Canadian state.

This has some validity at the psychological level; but it fails to explain the reactionary direction of their dissension.

For my part, I would think there would be some analogy to be found in the democratic impetus that gave birth to the various nationalisms in Europe a century or two ago. The death of Duplessis marked the end of a dynasty and of the oligarchy it had fostered. The advent of liberal democracy to the province bore promise of power for all classes henceforth. But in practice the newly self-conscious classes have found most roads to a better life blocked: the clergy clings to its grip on education, the English continue to dominate our finances, and the Americans intrude upon our culture. Only Quebec as a state would appear to belong unquestionably to French Canadians; and the fullest power for that state is therefore highly desirable. Democracy having declared all men equal within the nation, so all nations should enjoy equality one to another, meaning in particular that ours should be sovereign and independent. It is predicted that the realization of our nation-state will release a thousand unsuspected energies, and that, thus endowed, French Canadians will at last take possession of their rightful heritage. In other words, there is supposed to be some sort of creative energy that will bestow genius on people who have none and give courage and learning to a lazy and ignorant nation.

This is the faith that takes the place of reason for those who are unable to find a basis for their convictions in history, or economics, or the constitution, or sociology. 'Independence', writes Chaput, 'is much more a matter of disposition than of logic. . . . More than reason, we must have pride.'[30] That is the way all those dear little girls and young ladies feel, who like to put it in a nutshell thus: 'Independence is a matter of dignity. You don't argue about it; you feel it.' Isn't that the sort of thing that many poets and artists say? Jean-Guy Pilon writes:

> When the day comes that this cultural minority, hitherto only tolerated in this country, becomes a nation unto itself within its own borders, our literature will take a tremendous leap

[30]*Op. cit.*, p. 10.

ahead. Because the writer, like everyone else in this society, will feel free. And a free man can do great things.[31]

Now it would seem that Chaput is an excellent chemist. What I would like to know, though, is how the energies set in motion by independence are going to make him a better one; he need show us nothing else in order to woo us into separatism. As for his book, it bears the mark of an honest and dedicated man, but it destroys itself with one of its own sentences: 'To hope that one day, by some sort of magic, the French-Canadian people will suddenly reform and become as one body respectful of the law, correct in its speech, devoted to culture and high achievement, without first becoming imbued with some inspiring ideal: this is a dangerous aberration.'[32] So Chaput rejects magic, but counts on an inspiring ideal as the way of salvation for our people. As if reform, correctness of speech, culture, and high achievement – *all of which are already accessible to us under the existing Canadian constitution* – were not in themselves inspiring ideals! And in what way is the other ideal he proposes – the nation-state – any more than a kind of magic called forth to fill in for our lack of discipline in pursuing the true ideals?

It would seem, too, that Pilon is a good poet. I would like him to tell me – in prose, if he likes – how national sovereignty is going to make him 'a free man' and 'capable of doing great things'. If he fails to find within himself, in the world about him and in the stars above, the dignity, pride and other well-springs of poetry, I wonder why and how he will find them in a 'free' Quebec.

No doubt bilingualism is attainable only with some difficulty. But I will not admit that this should be any insurmountable hurdle to men who call themselves intellectuals, particularly when the language they carp over is one of the principal vehicles of twentieth-century civilization. The day of language barriers is finished, at least as far as science and culture are concerned; and if Quebec's intellectuals refuse to master another language than their own, if they will recognize no loyalty but to their nation, then they may be renouncing forever their place among the world's intellectual élite.

For men of intellect the talk about energy set in motion by

[31]*Le Quartier Latin* (Montreal), February 27, 1962.
[32]*Op. cit.*, p. 144.

national independence means nothing. Their function, particularly if they come from a milieu where sentiment takes the place of reason and prejudice the place of understanding, is to think, and then think some more. If their intellectual pursuits have led to a dead end, there is only one thing to do: turn around and go back. Any attempt at escaping through intellectual hocus-pocus is contemptible; as Arthur Miller has said in *l'Express*, 'The task of the real intellectual consists of analyzing illusions in order to discover their causes.'

True enough, but for people in general it is another matter. Nationalism, as an emotional stimulus directed at an entire community, can indeed let loose unforeseen powers. History is full of this, called variously chauvinism, racism, jingoism, and all manner of crusades, where right reasoning and thought are reduced to rudimentary proportions. It could be that in certain historical situations, where oppression was intolerable, misery unspeakable, and all alternative escape routes blocked, it was nationalism that sparked the subsequent break for freedom. But the arousing of such a passion as a last resort has always had its drawbacks, and the bad has invariably gone hand in hand with the good. This bad has almost always included a certain amount of despotism, because people who win their freedom with passion rather than with reason are generally disappointed to find themselves just as poor and deprived as ever; and strong governments are necessary to put an end to their unrest.

I was in Ghana during the first months of her independence. The poets were no better, the chemists no more numerous, and, on a more tangible level, salaries were no higher. Since the intellectuals were unable to explain to the people why this should be, they distracted their attention to some obscure island in the Gulf of Guinea which needed to be 'reconquered'. To this end a large slice of this economically destitute state's budget was earmarked for the army – which ultimately served to put the parliamentary opposition in jail.

A similar thing has happened in Indonesia. This former-colony-turned-state, which is only barely succeeding in governing itself and has yet to achieve prosperity, has called its people to arms to liberate its territories in New Guinea. Now these territories do not belong to it for any reason whatever, neither of race, nor language, nor geography. Nevertheless, I have met, in Quebec, men of radical convictions who – through inability to reason in any terms other than of national sovereignty – consider the operation justified. The State of Quebec can count on these men one day, when, unable to improve social conditions for her people, she sends them off to win 'her islands' in Hudson Bay. Already the Honourable Mr. Arsenault is preparing us for this glorious epic. And Lesage stands ready with his applause.[33]

Most fortunately, the backbone of our people entertain fewer illusions on such subjects, and show more common sense, than do our intellectuals and *bourgeoisie*. The province's large trade unions have pronounced themselves categorically against separatism. They are well aware of the powers latent in mob passion; but, rightly, they shrink from setting in motion a vehicle with faulty steering and unsound brakes.

In short, those who expect to 'release energies' by independence (or the feeling of independence) are playing the sorcerer's apprentice. They are resolving not one single problem by the exercise of reason; and in stirring up collective passions they are engaging an unpredictable, uncontrollable, and ineffective mechanism. (It will be noted that I am talking here primarily of energies supposedly to be released *by* independence; about the energies behind the *origins* of today's separatism, I had something to say in *Cité Libre* of March 1961, p. 5. But on that, Messrs. Albert and Raymond Breton offer in the present issue by far the most serious study ever made on the subject.)

As a final argument, certain young people justify their flirtation with separatism as a matter of tactics: 'If the English get scared enough we'll get what we want without going as far as independence.' This tactic has already provoked concessions of purely symbolic value for French Canadians: one slogan ('The French Canadians deserve a New Deal'), two flags (Pearson-Pickersgill), a few new names for old companies (e.g. La Compagnie d'électricité Shawinigan), several appointments to boards of directors, and a multitude of bilingual cheques (Diefenbaker). *De minimis non curat praetor*, but all the same I must confess that the flap among English-speaking politicians and businessmen is funny to see. It bears witness certainly to a guilty conscience for their own nationalistic sins. But that could have its repercussions, too. There is nothing

[33]*Le Devoir*, January 29 and 31, 1962.

meaner than the coward recovered from his fright. And I would like to think that then French Canada would be bolstered by a younger generation endowed with richer assets than their nationalistic passion.

The Future

If, in my opinion, the nation were of purely negative value, I would not be at such pains to discredit a movement that promises to lead the French-Canadian nation to its ruin.

The nation is, in fact, the guardian of certain very positive qualities: a cultural heritage, common traditions, a community awareness, historical continuity, a set of mores; all of which, at this juncture in history, go to make a man what he is. Certainly, these qualities are more private than public,[34] more introverted than extroverted,[35] more instinctive and primitive than intelligent and civilized,[36] more self-centred and impulsive than generous and reasonable. They belong to a transitional period in world history. But they are a reality of our time, probably useful, and in any event considered indispensable by all national communities.

Except to pinpoint ourselves in the right historical perspective, then, there is not much to be gained in brushing them aside on the ground that the nation of French Canadians will some day fade from view and that Canada itself will undoubtedly not exist forever. Benda points out that it is to the lasting greatness of Thucydides that he was able to visualize a world in which Athens would be no more.[37]

But the future with which we should concern ourselves here is the one we are building from day to day. The problem we must face squarely is this: without backsliding to the ridiculous and reactionary idea of national sovereignty, how can we protect our French-Canadian national qualities?

As I have already said earlier in this article, we must separate once and for all the concepts of state and of nation, and make Canada a truly pluralistic and polyethnic society. Now in order

[34]Delos, op. cit., p. 179.

[35]Maritain, op. cit., p. 5.

[36]Acton, op. cit., p. 188. See also p. 186: 'In the ancient world idolatry and nationality went together, and the same term is applied in Scripture to both.'

[37]Op. cit., p. 141.

for this to come about, the different regions within the country must be assured of a wide range of local autonomy, such that each national group, with an increasing background of experience in self-government, may be able to develop the body of laws and institutions essential to the fullest expression and development of their national characteristics. At the same time, the English Canadians, with their own nationalism, will have to retire gracefully to their proper place, consenting to modify their own precious image of what Canada ought to be. If they care to protect and realize their own special ethnic qualities, they should do it within this framework of regional and local autonomy rather than a pan-Canadian one.

For the incorporation of these diverse aspirations the Canadian constitution is an admirable vehicle. Under the British North America Act, the jurisdiction of the federal State of Canada concerns itself with all the things that have no specific ethnic implications, but that have to do with the welfare of the entire Canadian society: foreign affairs, the broader aspects of economic stability, foreign trade, navigation, postal services, money and banking, and so on. The provinces, on the other hand, have jurisdiction over matters of a purely local and private nature and those that affect ethnic peculiarities: education, municipal and parochial affairs, the administration of justice, the celebration of marriage, property and civil rights, and so forth. Nevertheless, in keeping with the fact that none of the provincial borders coincide perfectly with ethnic or linguistic delineations, no provincial government is encouraged to legislate exclusively for the benefit of a particular ethnic group in such a way as to foster a nation-state mentality at the provincial level. On this point the record of Quebec's treatment of its minorities can well stand as an example to other provinces with large French, German, Ukrainian, and other minorities.

I have no intention of closing my eyes to how much Canadians of British origin have to do – or rather, undo – before a pluralist state can become a reality in Canada. But I am inclined to add that that is *their* problem. The die is cast in Canada: there are two main ethnic and linguistic groups; each is too strong and too deeply rooted in the past, too firmly bound to a mother-culture, to be able to engulf the other. But if the two will collaborate at the hub of a truly pluralistic state, Canada could become the envied seat of a form of federalism that belongs to tomorrow's world. Better than the American melting-pot, Canada could offer an example to all those new Asian and African states already discussed at the beginning of this article, who must discover how to govern their polyethnic populations with proper regard for justice and liberty. What better reason for cold-shouldering the lure of annexation to the United States? Canadian federalism is an experiment of major proportions; it could become a brilliant prototype for the moulding of tomorrow's civilization.

If English Canadians cannot see it, again I say so much the worse for them; they will be subsiding into a backward, short-sighted, and despotic nationalism. Lord Acton, one of the great thinkers of the nineteenth century, described, with extraordinarily prophetic insight, the error of the various nationalisms and the future they were preparing. Exactly a century ago he wrote:

> A great democracy must either sacrifice self-government to unity or preserve it by federalism. . . . The co-existence of several nations under the same State is a test, as well as the best security of its freedom. It is also one of the chief instruments of civilization. . . . The combination of different nations in one State is as necessary a condition of civilized life as the combination of men in society. . . . Where political and national boundaries coincide, society ceases to advance, and nations relapse into a condition corresponding to that of men who renounce intercourse with their fellow-men. . . . A State which is incompetent to satisfy different races condemns itself; a State which labours to neutralize, to absorb, or to expel them is destitute of the chief basis of self-government. The theory of nationality, then, is a retrograde step in history.[88]

It goes without saying that if, in the face of Anglo-Canadian nationalism, French Canadians retreat into their own nationalistic shell, they will condemn themselves to the same stagnation. And Canada will become a sterile soil for the minds of her people, a barren waste prey to every wandering host and conquering horde.

I will say it once again: the die is cast in Canada. Neither of our two language groups can force assimilation on the other. But one or the other, or even both, could lose by default, destroying itself from within, and dying of suffocation. And accordingly, by the same law of retribution and in just reward

[88]*Op. cit., passim.*

for faith in humanity, victory is promised to the nation that rejects its nationalistic obsessions and, with the full support of its members, applies all the powers at its command to the pursuit of the most far-reaching and human ideal.

By the terms of the existing Canadian constitution, that of 1867,[39] French Canadians have all the powers they need to make Quebec a political society affording due respect for nationalist aspirations and at the same time giving unprecedented scope for human potential in the broadest sense. (On pages 98–9 of his book, Mr. Chaput proposes sixteen items of economic reform which could be undertaken by an independent Quebec. Except for the first, which would abolish taxes levied by Ottawa, all these reforms could be undertaken under the present constitution! On pages 123–4, Mr. Chaput outlines, in seven items, the measures by which an independent Quebec could ensure the protection of French-Canadian minorities outside Quebec. None of these, except the declaration of sovereignty itself, would be any more accessible to an independent Quebec than they are to present-day Quebec.)

If Quebec became such a shining example, if to live there were to partake of freedom and progress, if culture enjoyed a place of honour there, if the universities commanded respect and renown from afar, if the administration of public affairs were the best in the land (and none of this presupposes any declaration of independence!) French Canadians would no longer need to do battle for bilingualism; the ability to speak French would become a status symbol, even an open sesame in business and public life. Even in Ottawa, superior competence on the part of our politicians and civil servants would bring spectacular changes.

Such an undertaking, though immensely difficult, would be possible; it would take more guts than jaw. And therein, it would seem to me, is an 'ideal' not a whit less 'inspiring' than that other one that has been in vogue for a couple of years in our little part of the world.

For those who would put their shoulders to the wheel, who would pin their hopes for the future on the fully-developed man

[39]This was what I had in mind when I wrote – referring to the younger Separatists – something that annoyed a great many people: 'They . . . are tilting headlong at problems which already had their solution a century ago.' (*Cité Libre*, December 1961, p. 3.)

of intellect, and who would refuse to be party to *la nouvelle trahison des clercs*, I close with a final word from the great Lord Acton:

> Nationalism does not aim either at liberty or prosperity, both of which it sacrifices to the imperative necessity of making the nation the mould and measure of the State. Its course will be marked with material as well as moral ruin, in order that a new invention may prevail over the works of God and the interests of of mankind.[40]

[40]*Op. cit.*, p. 194.

Cité Libre, April 1962. Translated from the French by Patricia Claxton.

Federalism, Nationalism, and Reason *

State and Nation

The concept of federalism with which I will deal in this paper is that of a particular system of government applicable within a sovereign state; it flows from my understanding of state and nation. Hence I find it necessary to discuss these two notions in part I of this paper, but I need only do so from the point of view of territory and population. Essentially, the question to which I would seek an answer is: what section of the world's population occupying what segment of the world's surface should fall under the authority of a given state?

Until the middle of the eighteenth century, the answer was largely arrived at without regard to the people themselves. Of course in much earlier times, population pressures guided by accidents of geography and climate had determined the course of the migrations which were to spill across the earth's surface. But by the end of the Middle Ages, such migrations had run their course in most of Europe. The existence of certain peoples inhabiting certain land areas, speaking certain languages or dialects, and practising certain customs, was generally taken as data – *choses données* – by the European states which arose to

*I wish to thank my friends Albert Breton, Fernand Cadieux, Pierre Carignan, Eugene Forsey, and James Mallory, who read the manuscript and helped me clarify several ideas. Since the paper was read, on June 11, 1964, other friends have been very helpful with their comments; I dare not acknowledge them by name until I have had time to work their suggestions into this paper.

establish their authority over them.

It was not the population who decided by what states they would be governed; it was the states which, by wars (but not 'people's wars'), by alliances, by dynastic arrangements, by marriages, by inheritance, and by chance, determined the area of territory over which they would govern. And for that reason they could be called territorial states. Except in the particular case of newly discovered lands, the population came with the territory; and except in the unusual case of deportations, very little was to be done about it.

Political philosophers, asking questions about the authority of the state, did not inquire why a certain population fell within the territorial jurisdiction of a certain state rather than of another; for the philosophers, too, territory and population were just data; their philosophies were mainly concerned with discovering the foundations of authority over a *given* territory and the sources of obedience of a *given* population.

In other words, the purpose of Locke and Rousseau, not unlike that of the medieval philosophers and of the ancient Stoics, was to explain the origins and justify the existence of political authority *per se*; the theories of contract which they derived from natural law or reason were meant to ensure that within a given state bad governments could readily be replaced by good ones, but not that one territorial state could be superseded by another.

Such then was the significance of social contract and popular sovereignty in the minds of the men who made the Glorious Revolution, and such it was in the minds of those who prepared the events of 1776 in America and 1789 in France. As things went, however, the two latter 'events' turned out to be momentous revolutions, and the ideas which had been put into them emerged with an immensely enhanced significance.

In America, it became necessary for the people not merely to replace a poor government by a better one, but to switch their allegiance from one territorial state to another, and in their own words, to

> declare, that these United Colonies, are, and of right ought to be, free and independent states; that they are absolved from all allegiance to the British crown, and that all political connection, between them and the state of Great Britain, is and ought to be totally dissolved; and that, as free and independent states,

they have full power to levy war, conclude peace, contract alliances, establish commerce, and to do all other acts and things which independent states may of right do.

Here then was a theory of government by consent which took on a radically new meaning. Since sovereignty belonged to the people, it appeared to follow that any given body of people could at will transfer their allegiance from one existing state to another, or indeed to a completely new state of their own creation. In other words, the consent of the population was required not merely for a social contract, which was to be the foundation of civil society, or for a choice of responsible rulers, which was the essence of self-government; consent was also required for adherence to one territorial state rather than to another, which was the beginning of national self-determination.

Why the theory of consent underwent such a transformation at this particular time is no doubt a matter for historical and philosophical conjecture. Perhaps the prerequisites had never been brought together before: a population (1) whose political traditions were sufficiently advanced to include the ideology of consent, (2) subject to a modern unitary state the centre of which was very remote, and (3) inhabiting a territory which was reasonably self-contained.

Be that as it may, it appears to be at this juncture in history that the word 'nation' became charged with a new potential. In the past, the *word* had meant many things, from Machiavelli's 'Ghibelline nation' to Montesquieu's 'pietistic nation'; its broadest meaning seems to have been reached by the *Encyclopédistes* who understood thereby 'une quantité considérable de peuple, qui habite une certaine étendue de pays, renfermée dans de certaines limites, et qui obéit au même gouvernement'. The *idea* of nation also had roots which plunged deep in history;[1] and a sentiment akin to nationalism had sometimes inspired political action, as when French rulers reacted against Italian popes. But the idea, like the word, only took on its modern meaning during the last quarter of the eighteenth century.

Consequently, it might be said that in the past the (territorial) state had defined its territorial limits which had defined the people or nation living within. But henceforth it was to be the

[1]For a history of the use and meaning of the term, see Elie Kedourie, *Nationalism* (New York, 1960), and Hans Kohn, *The Idea of Nationalism* (New York, 1944).

people who first defined themselves as a nation, who then declared which territory belonged to them as of right, and who finally proceeded to give their allegiance to a state of their own choosing or invention which would exercise authority over that nation and that territory. Hence the expression 'nation-state'. As I see it, the important transition was from the *territorial state* to the *nation-state*. But once the latter was born, the idea of the *national state* was bound to follow, it being little more than a nation-state with an ethnic flavour added. With it the idea of self-determination became the principle of nationalities.

Self-determination did not necessarily proceed from or lead to self-government. Whereas self-government was based on reason and proposed to introduce liberal forms of government into existing states, self-determination was based on will and proposed to challenge the legitimacy and the very existence of the territorial states.

Self-determination, or the principle of nationalities (I am talking of the doctrine, for the expressions became current only later) was bound to dissolve whatever order and balance existed in the society of states prevailing towards the end of the eighteenth century. But no matter; for it was surmised that a new order would arise, free from wars and inequities. As each of the peoples of the world became conscious of its identity as a collectivity bound together by natural affinities, it would define itself as a nation and govern itself as a state. An international order of nation-states, since it would be founded on the free will of free people, would necessarily be more lasting and just than one which rested on a hodge-podge of despotic empires, dynastic kingdoms, and aristocratic republics. In May 1790, the Constituent Assembly had proclaimed: 'La nation française renonce à entreprendre aucune guerre dans un but de conquête et n'emploiera jamais de forces contre la liberté d'aucun peuple.'

Unfortunately, things did not work out quite that way. The French Revolution, which had begun as an attempt to replace a bad government by a good one, soon overreached itself by replacing a territorial state by a nation-state, whose territory incidentally was considerably enlarged. In 1789, the *Déclaration des droits de l'homme et du citoyen* had stated: 'Le principe de toute souveraineté réside essentiellement dans la Nation. Nul corps, nul individu ne peut exercer d'autorité qui n'en émane expressément.' But who was to be included in the nation? Danton having pointed out in 1793 that the frontiers of France were designated by Nature,[2] the French nation willed itself into possession of that part of Europe which spread between the Rhine, the Pyrenees, the Atlantic Ocean, and the Alps.

France was indeed fortunate, in that her natural frontiers thus enabled her to correct the disadvantage which might have arisen in Alsace, for example, from a will based on linguistic frontiers. Fortunately for German-speaking peoples, however, Fichte was soon to discover that the natural frontiers were in reality the linguistic ones; thus the German nation could will itself towards its proper size, provided of course that the language principle be sometimes corrected by that of historical possession, in order for instance to include Bohemia. Other nations, such as Poland, enlightened their will by greater reliance on the historical principle, corrected when necessary by the linguistic one. Then finally there were nations who, spurning such frivolous guide-lines as geography, history, and language, were favoured by direct communication with the Holy Ghost; such was the privilege of the United States of America who saw the annexation of Texas, California, and eventually Canada as – in the words of O'Sullivan – 'the fulfillment of our manifest destiny to overspread the continent alloted by Providence for the free development of our yearly multiplying millions'.[3]

The political history of Europe and of the Americas in the nineteenth century and that of Asia and Africa in the twentieth are histories of nations labouring, conspiring, blackmailing, warring, revolutionizing, and generally willing their way towards statehood. It is, of course, impossible to know whether there has ensued therefrom for humanity more peace and justice than would have been the case if some other principle than self-determination had held sway. In theory, the arrangement of boundaries in such a way that no important national group be included by force in the territorial limits of a state which was mainly the expression of the will of another group, was to be conducive to peaceful international order. In practice, state boundaries continued to be established and maintained largely by the threat of or the use of force. The concept of right in international relations became, if anything, even more a function

[2]The Abbé Gregoire had spoken of the 'Archives de la nature' in 1792. See Kedourie, *Nationalism*, p. 122.

[3]Reading no. 12 in Hans Kohn, *Nationalism* (New York, 1955).

of might. And the question whether a national minority was 'important' enough to be entitled to independence remained unanswerable except in terms of the political and physical power that could be wielded in its favour. Why did Libya become a country in 1951 and not the Saar in 1935, with a population almost as great? Why should Norway be independent and not Brittany? Why Ireland and not Scotland? Why Nicaragua and not Quebec?

As we ask ourselves these questions, it becomes apparent that more than language and culture, more than history and geography, even more than force and power, the foundation of the nation is will.[4] For there is no power without will. The Rocky Mountains are higher than the Pyrenees but they are not a watershed between countries. The Irish Sea and the Straits of Florida are much narrower than the Pacific Ocean between Hawaii and California, yet they are more important factors in determining nationhood. Language or race do not provide, in Switzerland or Brazil, the divisive force they are at present providing in Belgium or the United States.

Looking at the foregoing examples, and at many others, we are bound to conclude that the frontiers of nation-states are in reality nearly as arbitrary as those of the former territorial states. For all their anthropologists, linguists, geographers, and historians, the nations of today cannot justify their frontiers with noticeably more rationality than the kings of two centuries ago; a greater reliance on general staffs than on princesses' dowries does not necessarily spell a triumph of reason. Consequently, a present-day definition of the word 'nation' in its juristic sense would fit quite readily upon the population of the territorial states which existed before the French and American revolutions. A nation (as in the expressions: the French nation, the Swiss nation, the United Nations, the President's speech to the nation) is no more and no less than the entire population of a sovereign state. (Except when otherwise obvious, I shall try to adhere to that juristic sense in the rest of this paper.) Because no country has an absolutely homogeneous population, all the so-called nation-states of today are also territorial states. And the converse is probably also true. The distinction between a nation-state, a multi-national state, and a

[4]*Cf.* A. Cobban, *Dictatorship* (New York, 1939), p. 42, and Kohn, *The Idea of Nationalism*, p 15

territorial state may well be valid in reference to historical origins; but it has very little foundation in law or fact today and is mainly indicative of political value judgments.

Of course, the word 'nation' can also be used in a sociological sense, as when we speak of the Scottish nation, or the Jewish nation. As Humpty Dumpty once told Alice, a word means just what one chooses it to mean. It would indeed be helpful if we could make up our minds. Either the juristic sense would be rejected, and the word 'people' used instead (the people of the Soviet Union, the people of the United States; but what word would replace 'national'? People's? Popular?); in that case 'nation' would be restricted to its sociological meaning, which is also closer to its etymological and historical ones. Or the latter sense would be rejected, and words like 'linguistic', 'ethnic', or 'cultural group' be used instead. But lawyers and political scientists cannot remake the language to suit their convenience; they will just have to hope that 'the context makes it tolerably clear which of the two [senses] we mean.'[5]

However, for some people one meaning is meant to flow into the other. The ambiguity is intentional and the user is conveying something which is at the back of his mind – and sometimes not very far back. In such cases the use of the word 'nation' is not only confusing, it is disruptive of political stability. Thus, when a tightly knit minority within a state begins to define itself forcefully and consistently as a nation, it is triggering a mechanism which will tend to propel it towards full statehood.[6]

That, of course, is not merely due to the magic of words, but to a much more dynamic process which I will now attempt to explain. When the erstwhile territorial state, held together by divine right, tradition, and force, gave way to the nation-state, based on the will of the people, a new glue had to be invented which would bind the nation together on a durable basis. For very few nations – if any – could rely on a cohesiveness based

[5]Eugene Forsey, 'Canada: Two Nations or One?' *Canadian Journal of Economics and Political Science*, Vol. XXVIII (November 1962), p. 488. Mr. Forsey's discussion is as usual thorough and convincing.

[6]*Cf.* Max Weber, *Essays in Sociology* (London, 1948), p. 176: 'A nation is a community of sentiment which would adequately manifest itself in a state of its own; hence, a nation is a community which normally tends to produce a state of its own.' And R. MacIver, *Society* (New York, 1937), p. 155: 'There are nations then which do not rule themselves politically, but we call them nations only if they seek for political autonomy.'

entirely on 'natural' identity, and so most of them were faced with a terrible paradox: the principle of national self-determination which had justified their birth could just as easily justify their death. Nationhood being little more than a state of mind, and every sociologically distinct group within the nation having a contingent right of secession, the will of the people was in constant danger of dividing up – unless it were transformed into a lasting consensus.

The formation of such a consensus is a mysterious process which takes in many elements, such as language, communication, association, geographical proximity, tribal origins, common interests and history, external pressures, and even foreign intervention, none of which, however, is a determinant by itself. A consensus can be said to exist when no group within the nation feels that its vital interests and particular characteristics could be better preserved by withdrawing from the nation than by remaining within.

A (modern) state needs to develop and preserve this consensus as its very life. It must continually persuade the generality of the people that it is in their best interest to continue as a state. And since it is physically and intellectually difficult to persuade continually through reason alone, the state is tempted to reach out for whatever emotional support it can find. Ever since history fell under the ideological shadow of the nation-state, the most convenient support has obviously been the idea of nationalism. It becomes morally 'right', a matter of 'dignity and honour', to preserve the integrity of the nation. Hence, from the emotional appeal called nationalism is derived a psychological inclination to obey the constitution of the state.

To say that the state uses nationalism to preserve its identity is not to say that the state is the inventor of nationalism. The feeling called nationalism is secreted by the nation (in whatever sense we use the word) in much the same way as the family engenders family ties, and the clan generates clannishness. And just like clannishness, tribalism, and even feudalism, nationalism will probably fade away by itself at whatever time in history the nation has outworn its utility: that is to say, when the particular values protected by the idea of nation are no longer counted as important, or when those values no longer need to be embodied in a nation to survive.[7]

[7]On these values see 'New Treason of the Intellectuals' (p. 151 ff. of this volume).

But that time is not yet; we have not yet emerged from the era of the nation-state when it seemed perfectly normal for the state to rely heavily, for the preservation of the national consensus, on the gum called nationalism, a natural secretion of the nation. In so doing, the state (or the political agents who desired a state) transformed the feeling into a political doctrine or principle of government. Nationalism, as defined by history, is a doctrine which claims to supply a formula for determining what section of the world's population occupying what segment of the world's surface *should* fall under the authority of a given state; briefly stated, the formula holds that the optimum size of the sovereign state (in terms of authority and territory) is derived from the size of the nation (in terms of language, history, destiny, law, and so forth).[8]

It might be remarked here that history is not always logic; and in the case of nationalism it has embarked upon a type of circular reasoning which leaves the mind uneasy. The idea of nation which is at the origin of a new type of state does not refer to a 'biological' reality (as does, for instance, the family); consequently the nation has constantly and artificially to be reborn from the very state to which it gave birth! In other words, the nation first decides what the state should be; but then the state has to decide what the nation should remain.

I should add that some people who call themselves nationalists would not accept this line of reasoning. Nationalism to them has remained a mere feeling of belonging to the nation (in a sociological or cultural sense); they liken it to a dream which inspires the individual and motivates his actions, perhaps irrationally but not necessarily negatively. I cannot, of course, quarrel with people merely because they wish to drain two centuries of history out of a definition. I can only say that it is not about *their* nationalism that I am writing in this paper; it is only fair to remind them, however, that their 'dreams' are being converted by others into a principle of government.

Let us then proceed to see what happens when the state relies on nationalism to develop and preserve the consensus on which it rests.

[8]*Cf.* Kedourie, *Nationalism*, p. 1: 'The doctrine [of nationalism] holds that . . . the only legitimate type of government is national self-government.

Nationalism and Federalism

Many of the nations which were formed into states over the past century or two included peoples who were set apart geographically (like East and West Pakistan, or Great Britain and Northern Ireland), historically (like the United States or Czechoslovakia), linguistically (like Switzerland or Belgium), racially (like the Soviet Union or Algeria). Half of the aforesaid countries undertook to form the national consensus within the framework of a unitary state; the other half found it expedient to develop a system of government called federalism. The process of consensus-formation is not the same in both cases.

It is obviously impossible, as well as undesirable, to reach unanimity on all things. Even unitary states find it wise to respect elements of diversity, for instance by administrative decentralization as in Great Britain,[9] or by language guarantees as in Belgium; but such limited securities having been given, a consensus is obtained which recognizes the state as the sole source of coercive authority within the national boundaries. The federal state proceeds differently; it deliberately reduces the national consensus to the greatest common denominator between the various groups composing the nation. Coercive authority over the entire territory remains a monopoly of the (central) state, but this authority is limited to certain subjects of jurisdiction; on other subjects, and within well-defined territorial regions, other coercive authorities exist. In other words, the exercise of sovereignty is divided between a central government and regional ones.

Federalism is by its very essence a compromise and a pact. It is a compromise in the sense that when national consensus on *all* things is not desirable or cannot readily obtain, the area of consensus is reduced in order that consensus on *some* things be reached. It is a pact or quasi-treaty in the sense that the terms of that compromise cannot be changed unilaterally. That is not to say that the terms are fixed forever; but only that in changing them, every effort must be made not to destroy the consensus on which the federated nation rests. For what Ernest Renan said

[9]Since the Government of Ireland Act, 1920, it might be more exact to think of Great Britain and Northern Ireland as forming a quasi-unitary state.

about the nation is even truer about the federated nation: 'L'existence d'une nation est . . . un plébiscite de tous les jours.'[10] This obviously did not mean that such a plebiscite could or should be held every day, the result of which could only be total anarchy; the real implication is clear: the nation is based on a social contract, the terms of which each new generation of citizens is free to accept tacitly, or to reject openly.

Federalism was an inescapable product of an age which recognized the principle of self-determination. For on the one hand, a sense of national identity and singularity was bound to be generated in a great many groups of people, who would insist on their right to distinct statehood. But on the other hand, the insuperable difficulties of living alone and the practical necessity of sharing the state with neighbouring groups were in many cases such as to make distinct statehood unattractive or unattainable. For those who recognized that the first law of politics is to start from the facts rather than from historical 'might-have-been's', the federal compromise thus became imperative.

But by a paradox I have already noted in regard to the nation-state, the principle of self-determination which makes federalism necessary makes it also rather unstable. If the heavy paste of nationalism is relied upon to keep a unitary nation-state together, much more nationalism would appear to be required in the case of a federal nation-state. Yet if nationalism is encouraged as a rightful doctrine and noble passion, what is to prevent it from being used by some group, region, or province within the nation? If 'nation algérienne' was a valid battle cry against France, how can the Algerian Arabs object to the cry of 'nation kabyle' now being used against them?

The answer, of course, is that no amount of logic can prevent such an escalation. The only way out of the dilemma is to render what is logically defensible actually undesirable. The advantages *to the minority group* of staying integrated in the whole must on balance be greater than the gain to be reaped from separating. This can easily be the case when there is no real alternative for the separatists, either because they are met with force (as in the case of the U.S. Civil War), or because they are met with laughter (as in the case of the *Bretons bretonnisants*). But when there is a real alternative, it is not so easy. And the

[10]Ernest Renan, *Discours et conférences* (Paris, 1887), p. 307 – also p. 299.

greater the advantages and possibilities of separatism, the more difficult it is to maintain an unwavering consensus within the whole state.

One way of offsetting the appeal of separatism is by investing tremendous amounts of time, energy, and money in nationalism, *at the federal level*. A national image must be created that will have such an appeal as to make any image of a separatist group unattractive. Resources must be diverted into such things as national flags, anthems, education, arts councils, broadcasting corporations, film boards; the territory must be bound together by a network of railways, highways, airlines; the national culture and the national economy must be protected by taxes and tariffs; ownership of resources and industry by nationals must be made a matter of policy. In short, the whole of the citizenry must be made to feel that it is only within the framework of the federal state that their language, culture, institutions, sacred traditions, and standard of living can be protected from external attack and internal strife.

It is, of course, obvious that a national consensus will be developed in this way only if the nationalism is emotionally acceptable to all important groups within the nation. Only blind men could expect a consensus to be lasting if the national flag or the national image is merely the reflection of one part of the nation, if the sum of values to be protected is not defined so as to include the language or the cultural heritage of some very large and tightly knit minority, if the identity to be arrived at is shattered by a colour-bar. The advantage as well as the peril of federalism is that it permits the development of a regional consensus based on regional values; so federalism is ultimately bound to fail if the nationalism it cultivates is unable to generate a national image which has immensely more appeal than the regional ones.

Moreover, this national consensus – to be lasting – must be a living thing. There is no greater pitfall for federal nations than to take the consensus for granted, as though it were reached once and for all. The compromise of federalism is generally reached under a very particular set of circumstances. As time goes by these circumstances change; the external menace recedes, the economy flourishes, mobility increases, industriali-zation and urbanization proceed; and also the federated groups grow, sometimes at uneven paces, their cultures mature, sometimes in divergent directions. To meet these changes, the terms of the federative pact must be altered, and this is done as smoothly as possible by administrative practice, by judicial decision, and by constitutional amendment, giving a little more regional autonomy here, a bit more centralization there, but at all times taking great care to preserve the delicate balance upon which the national consensus rests.

Such care must increase in direct proportion to the strength of the alternatives which present themselves to the federated groups. Thus, when a large cohesive minority believes it can transfer its allegiance to a neighbouring state, or make a go of total independence, it will be inclined to dissociate itself from a consensus the terms of which have been altered in its disfavour. On the other hand, such a minority may be tempted to use its bargaining strength to obtain advantages which are so costly to the majority as to reduce to naught the advantages to the latter of remaining federated. Thus, a critical point can be reached in either direction beyond which separatism takes place, or a civil war is fought.

When such a critical point has been reached or is in sight, no amount, however great, of nationalism can save the federation. Any expenditure of emotional appeal (flags, professions of faith, calls to dignity, expressions of brotherly love) at the national level will only serve to justify similar appeals at the regional level, where they are just as likely to be effective. Thus the great moment of truth arrives when it is realized that *in the last resort* the mainspring of federalism cannot be emotion but must be reason.

To be sure, federalism found its greatest development in the time of the nation-states, founded on the principle of self-determination, and cemented together by the emotion of nationalism. Federal states have themselves made use of this nationalism over periods long enough to make its inner contradictions go unnoticed. Thus, in a neighbouring country, Manifest Destiny, the Monroe Doctrine, the Hun, the Red Scourge, the Yellow Peril, and Senator McCarthy have all provided glue for the American Way of Life; but it is apparent that the Cuban 'menace' has not been able to prevent the American Negro from obtaining a renegotiation of the terms of the American national consensus. The Black Muslims were the answer to the argument of the Cuban menace; the only answer to both is the voice of reason.

It is now becoming obvious that federalism has all along been a product of reason in politics. It was born of a decision by pragmatic politicians to face facts as they are, particularly the fact of the heterogeneity of the world's population. It is an attempt to find a rational compromise between the divergent interest-groups which history has thrown together; but it is a compromise based on the will of the people.

Looking at events in retrospect, it would seem that the French Revolution attempted to delineate national territories according to the will of the people, without reference to rationality; the Congress of Vienna claimed to draw state boundaries according to reason, without reference to the will of the people; and federalism arose as an empirical effort to base a country's frontiers on both reason and the will of the people.

I am not heralding the impending advent of reason as the prime mover in politics, for nationalism is too cheap and too powerful a tool to be soon discarded by politicians of all countries; the rising *bourgeoisies* in particular have too large a vested interest in nationalism to let it die out unattended.[11] Nor am I arguing that as important an area of human conduct as politics could or should be governed without any reference to human emotions. But I would like to see emotionalism channelled into a less sterile direction than nationalism. And I am saying that within sufficiently advanced federal countries, the auto-destructiveness of nationalism is bound to become more and more apparent, and reason may yet reveal itself even to ambitious politicians as the more assured road to success. This may also be the trend in unitary states, since they all have to deal with some kind of regionalism or other. Simultaneously in the world of international relations, it is becoming more obvious that the Austinian concept of sovereignty could only be thoroughly applied in a world crippled by the ideology of the nation-state and sustained by the heady stimulant of nationalism. In the world of today, when whole groups of so-called sovereign states

---

[11]On the use of nationalism by the middle classes, see Cobban, *Dictatorship*, p. 140. And for a striking and original approach, see Albert Breton, 'The Economics of Nationalism', *Journal of Political Economy*, August 1964.

are experimenting with rational forms of integration, the exercise of sovereignty will not only be divided within federal states; it will have to be further divided between the states and the communities of states. If this tendency is accentuated the very idea of national sovereignty will recede and, with it, the need for an emotional justification such as nationalism. International law will no longer be explained away as so much 'positive international morality', it will be recognized as true law, a 'coercive order . . . for the promotion of peace'.[12]

Thus there is some hope that in advanced societies, the glue of nationalism will become as obsolete as the divine right of kings; the title of the state to govern and the extent of its authority will be conditional upon rational justification; a people's consensus based on reason will supply the cohesive force that societies require; and politics both within and without the state will follow a much more functional approach to the problems of government. If politicians must bring emotions into the act, let them get emotional about functionalism!

The rise of reason in politics is an advance of law; for is not law an attempt to regulate the conduct of men in society rationally rather than emotionally? It appears then that a political order based on federalism is an order based on law. And there will flow more good than evil from the present tribulations of federalism if they serve to equip lawyers, social scientists, and politicians with the tools required to build societies of men ordered by reason.

Who knows? humanity may yet be spared the ignominy of seeing its destinies guided by some new and broader emotion based, for example, on continentalism.

Canadian Federalism: The Past and the Present

Earlier in this paper, when discussing the concept of national consensus, I pointed out that it was not something to be forever taken for granted. In present-day Canada, an observation such as that need not proceed from very great insight. Still, I will start from there to examine some aspects of Canadian federalism.

Though, technically speaking, national self-determination only became a reality in Canada in 1931, it is no distortion of political reality to say that the Canadian nation dates from

[12]Hans Kelsen, *Law and Peace* (Cambridge, 1948), pp. 1 and 7.

1867, give or take a few years. The consensus of what is known today as the Canadian nation took shape in those years; and it is the will of that nation which is the foundation of the state which today exercises its jurisdiction over the whole of the Canadian territory.

Of course, the will of the Canadian nation was subjected to certain constraints, not least of which was the reality of the British Empire. But, except once again in a technical sense, this did not mean very much more than that Canada, like every other nation, was not born in a vacuum, but had to recognize the historical as well as all other data which surrounded its birth.

I suppose we can safely assume that the men who drew up the terms of the Canadian federal compromise had heard something of the ideology of nationalism which had been spreading revolutions for seventy-five years. It is likely too that they knew about the Civil War in the United States, the rebellions of 1837–8 in Canada, the Annexation Manifesto, and the unsatisfactory results of double majorities. Certainly they assessed the centrifugal forces that the constitution would have to overcome if the Canadian state was to be a durable one: first, the linguistic and other cultural differences between the two major founding groups, and secondly the attraction of regionalisms, which were not likely to decrease in a country the size of Canada.

Given these data, I am inclined to believe that the authors of the Canadian federation arrived at as wise a compromise and drew up as sensible a constitution as any group of men anywhere could have done. Reading that document today, one is struck by its absence of principles, ideals, or other frills; even the regional safeguards and minority guarantees are pragmatically presented, here and there, rather than proclaimed as a thrilling bill of rights. It has been said that the binding force of the United States of America was the idea of liberty,[13] and certainly none of the relevant constitutional documents let us forget it. By comparison, the Canadian nation seems founded on the common sense of empirical politicians who had wanted to establish some law and order over a disjointed half-continent. If reason be the governing virtue of federalism, it would seem that Canada got off to a good start.

Like everything else, the Canadian nation had to move with

[13]Kohn, *Nationalism*, p. 20.

the times. Many of the necessary adjustments were guided by rational deliberation: such was the case, for instance, with most of our constitutional amendments, and with the general direction imparted to Canadian law by the Privy Council decisions. It has long been a custom in English Canada to denounce the Privy Council for its provincial bias; but it should perhaps be considered that if the law lords had not leaned in that direction, Quebec separatism might not be a threat today: it might be an accomplished fact. From the point of view of the damage done to Quebec's understanding of the original federal compromise, there were certainly some disappointing – even if legally sound – judgments (like the New Brunswick, Manitoba, and Ontario separate school cases) and some unwise amendments (like the B.N.A. No. 2 Act, 1949); but on balance, it would seem that constitutional amendment and judicial interpretation would not by themselves have permanently damaged the fabric of the Canadian consensus if they had not been compounded with a certain type of adjustment through administrative centralization.

Faced with provinces at very different stages of economic and political development, it was natural for the central government to assume as much power as it could to make the country as a whole a going concern. Whether this centralization was always necessary, or whether it was not sometimes the product of bureaucratic and political empire-builders acting beyond the call of duty,[14] are no doubt debatable questions, but they are irrelevant to the present inquiry. The point is that over the years the central administrative functions tended to develop rather more rapidly than the provincial ones; and if the national consensus was to be preserved some new factor would have to be thrown into the balance. This was done in three ways.

First, a countervailing regionalism was allowed and even fostered in matters which were indifferent to Canada's economic growth. For instance, there was no federal action when Manitoba flouted the constitution and abolished the use of the French language in the legislature;[15] and there was no effective federal

---

[14]As an example of unjustifiable centralization, J. R. Mallory mentions the federal government's policy concerning technical schools (Montreal *Star*, February 4, 1964).

[15]The French language was also abolished in the territories. See F. R. Scott, *Civil Liberties and Canadian Federalism* (Toronto, 1959), p. 32.

intervention[16] under paragraphs 3 and 4 of Section 93 (B.N.A. Act) or under paragraphs 2 and 3 of Section 22 (Manitoba Act) when New Brunswick, Ontario, and Manitoba legislated in a way which was offensive to the linguistic or religious aspirations of their French-speaking populations.

Second, a representative bureaucracy at the central level was developed in such a way as to make the regions feel that their interests were well represented in Ottawa. A great administrative machine was created, in which 'the under-representation of Quebec can be considered an ethnic and educational factor rather than a regional one.'[17] It was this efficient bureaucracy, by the way, which was unable to convert the machinery of government to the production of bilingual cheques and letterheads during the forty years it took to debate the subject in Parliament; then suddenly the reform took place in five minutes without help even from the cabinet. But such are the miracles of automation!

Third, tremendous reserves of nationalism were expended, in order to make everyone good, clean, unhyphenated Canadians. Riel was neatly hanged, as an example to all who would exploit petty regional differences. The Boer War was fought, as proof that Canadians could overlook their narrow provincialisms when the fate of the Empire was at stake. Conscription was imposed in two world wars, to show that in the face of death all Canadians were on an equal footing. And lest nationalism be in danger of waning, during the intervals between the above events Union Jacks were waved, Royalty was shown around, and immigration laws were loaded in favour of the British Isles.

Need I point out that in those three new factors, French Canadians found little to reconcile themselves with centralization? First, regionalism as condoned by Ottawa meant that the French Canadians could feel at home in no province save Quebec. Second, representative bureaucracy for the central

[16]The operative word here is 'effective'. It will be remembered that Bowell's government in Ottawa did try to remedy the situation, first by order-in-council – the dispositions of which Manitoba refused to obey – and then by a bill in the House of Commons – which was obstructed by Laurier's Liberals, who went on to win the 1896 election.

[17]John Porter, 'Higher Public Servants and the Bureaucratic Elite in Canada', *Canadian Journal of Economics and Political Science*, Vol. XXIV (November 1958), p. 492.

government meant that regional safeguards would be entrusted to a civil service somewhat dominated by white Anglo-Saxon Protestants. And third, nationalism as conceived in Ottawa was essentially predicated on the desirability of uniting the various parts of the nation around one language (English) and one flag (the Union Jack).

I readily admit that there are elements of oversimplification in the four preceding paragraphs. But I am prepared to defend quite strenuously the implications which are contained therein: that the rational compromise upon which the nation rested in 1867 was gradually replaced by an emotional sop; and that this sop calmly assumed away the existence of one-third of the nation. In other words, the French-Canadian denizens of a Quebec ghetto, stripped of power by centralization, were expected to recognize themselves in a national image which had hardly any French traits, and were asked to have the utmost confidence in a central state where French Canada's influence was mainly measured by its not inconsiderable nuisance value.

Under such circumstances, Canadian nationalism – even after it ceased looking towards the Empire, which took quite some time – could hardly provide the basis for a lasting consensus. So time and time again, counter-nationalist movements arose in Quebec which quite logically argued that if Canada was to be the nation-state of the English-speaking Canadians, Quebec should be the nation-state of the French Canadians. But these warning signals were never taken seriously; for they were hoisted in years when Quebec had nowhere to go, and it obviously could not form an independent state of its own. But a time was bound to come – 'Je suis un chien qui ronge l'os' – when French-Canadian national self-determination could no longer be laughed out of court; a time when the frightened Quebec and Ottawa governments (albeit in obvious contempt of their respective constitutional mandates) found sense in making 'scientific' studies of separatism.[18]

In short, during several generations, the stability of the Canadian consensus was due to Quebec's inability to do anything about it. Ottawa took advantage of Quebec's backwardness to centralize; and because of its backwardness that province was unable to participate adequately in the benefits of centralization. The vicious circle could only be broken if Quebec

[18]*La Presse*, May 12, 1964. Montreal *Gazette*, May 21, 1964.

managed to become a modern society. But how could this be done? The very ideology which was marshalled to preserve Quebec's integrity, French-Canadian nationalism, was setting up defence mechanisms the effect of which was to turn Quebec resolutely inward and backwards. It befell the generation of French Canadians who came of age during the Second World War to break out of the dilemma; instead of bucking the rising tides of industrialization and modernization in a vain effort to preserve traditional values, they threw the flood-gates open to forces of change. And if ever proof be required that nationalism is a sterile force, let it be considered that fifteen years of systematic non-nationalism and sometimes ruthless anti-nationalism at a few key points of the society were enough to help Quebec to pass from a feudal into a modern era.

Technological factors could, practically alone, explain the sudden transformation of Quebec. But many agents from within were at work, eschewing nationalism and preparing their society to adapt itself to modern times. Typical amongst such agents were the three following. Laval's *Faculté des sciences sociales* began turning out graduates who were sufficiently well equipped to be respected members of the central representative bureaucracy. The *Confédération des travailleurs catholiques du Canada* came squarely to grips with economic reality and helped transform Quebec's working classes into active participants in the process of industrialization. The little magazine *Cité Libre* became a rallying point for progressive action and writing; moreover it understood that a modern Quebec would very soon call into question the imbalance towards which the original federal compromise had drifted, and it warned that English-Canadian nationalism was headed for a rude awakening; upholding provincial autonomy and proposing certain constitutional guarantees, it sought to re-establish the Canadian consensus on a rational basis.

The warnings went unheeded; Ottawa did not change.[19] But Quebec did: bossism collapsed, blind traditionalism crumbled, the Church was challenged, new forces were unleashed. When

[19]Who would have thought it possible, five years ago, that a prime minister of Canada, after giving into various provincial ultimata, would go on to say: 'I believe that the provinces and their governments will play an increasingly important role in our national development. I for one welcome that as a healthy decentralization. . . ." (Montreal *Star*, May 27, 1964.) Too much, too late. . . .

in Europe the dynasties and traditions had been toppled, the new societies quickly found a new cohesive agent in nationalism; and no sooner had privilege within the nation given way to internal equality than privilege *between* nations fell under attack; external equality was pursued by way of national self-determination. In Quebec today the same forces are at work: a new and modern society is being glued together by nationalism, it is discovering its potentialities as a nation, and is demanding equality with all other nations. This in turn is causing a backlash in other provinces, and Canada suddenly finds herself wondering whether she has a future. What is to be done?

If my premises are correct, nationalism cannot provide the answer. Even if massive investments in flags, dignity, protectionism, and Canadian content of television managed to hold the country together a few more years, separatism would remain a recurrent phenomenon, and very soon again new generations of Canadians and Quebeckers would be expected to pour their intellectual energies down the drain of emotionalism. If, for instance, it is going to remain *morally wrong* for Wall Street to assume control of Canada's economy, how will it become *morally right* for Bay Street to dominate Quebec's or – for that matter – Nova Scotia's?

It is possible that nationalism may still have a role to play in backward societies where the *status quo* is upheld by irrational and brutal forces; in such circumstances, *because there is no other way*, perhaps the nationalist passions will still be found useful to unleash revolutions, upset colonialism, and lay the foundations of welfare states; in such cases, the undesirable consequences will have to be accepted along with the good.

But in the advanced societies, where the interplay of social forces can be regulated by law, where the centres of political power can be made responsible to the people, where the economic victories are a function of education and automation, where cultural differentiation is submitted to ruthless competition, and where the road to progress lies in the direction of international integration, nationalism will have to be discarded as a rustic and clumsy tool.

No doubt, at the level of individual action, emotions and dreams will still play a part; even in modern man, superstition remains a powerful motivation. But magic, no less than totems and taboos, has long since ceased to play an important role in the normal governing of states. And likewise, nationalism will eventually have to be rejected as a principle of sound government. In the world of tomorrow, the expression 'banana republic' will not refer to independent fruit-growing nations but to countries where formal independence has been given priority over the cybernetic revolution. In such a world, the state – if it is not to be outdistanced by its rivals – will need political instruments which are sharper, stronger, and more finely controlled than anything based on mere emotionalism: such tools will be made up of advanced technology and scientific investigation, as applied to the fields of law, economics, social psychology, international affairs, and other areas of human relations; in short, if not a pure product of reason, the political tools of the future will be designed and appraised by more rational standards than anything we are currently using in Canada today.

Let me hasten to add that I am not predicting which way Canada will turn. But because it seems obvious to me that nationalism – and of course I mean the Canadian as well as the Quebec variety – has put her on a collision course, I am suggesting that cold, unemotional rationality can still save the ship. Acton's prophecy, one hundred years ago, is now in danger of being fulfilled in Canada. 'Its course', he stated of nationality, 'will be marked with material as well as moral ruin, in order that a new invention may prevail over the works of God and the interests of mankind.' This new invention may well be functionalism in politics; and perhaps it will prove to be inseparable from any workable concept of federalism.

This article was read to a joint meeting of the Canadian Political Science Association and the Association of Canadian Law Teachers in June 1964, and was subsequently published in P. A. Crepeau and C. B. Macpherson (eds.), *The Future of Canadian Federalism* (Toronto: University of Toronto Press, 1965).

Separatist Counter-Revolutionaries

*We are against the leaders who are of the left
and who hide behind Marxist-Leninist ideology
but who make it represent chauvinism. . . .
They now offer a reactionary thesis founded
on a union of peoples based on racism and
nationalism.*
N. KHRUSHCHEV, *La Presse, April 10, 1964*

The Dictators

I get fed up when I hear our nationalist brood calling itself
revolutionary. It conceives of revolution as a deep upheaval,
but forgets that this is also characteristic of counter-revolution.

Fascism and Naziism overturned quite a few things. Notably,
they replaced democratic institutions with a totalitarian system.
It is true that democracy under Victor Emmanuel III and in
the Weimar Republic was not a terrific success. Parliamentary
democracy had shallow roots in post-Versailles Italy and Germany, the idea of a liberal state being accepted only slowly by
countries of which one had long been subjected to authoritarian
Catholicism and the other had grown up under Prussian mili-
tarism. At the national level, ineffectualness and corruption
were playing havoc, and the government often seemed incapable of making the transition from deliberation to action.

But nevertheless the idea of liberty was honoured in these
democracies. A great many men still believed that a rational
political order should get its bearings from open discussion
rather than a fanatical refusal of dialogue; should be founded
on a consensus rather than on intolerance; should come to
power through elections rather than subversion and violence.

True, freedom is often less efficacious than authority as the
basis of short-term organization. And reason is often not so

strong as emotion as a public driving force. That is why the progress of democracy was slow in those countries. Then other men came along claiming exclusive possession of political truth. That, obviously, freed them from the need to seek that truth by means of the public confrontation which democracy provides. So as soon as they could they replaced the parliamentary system with so-called plebiscitary democracy; they abolished the opposition and installed the single-party system; they murdered liberty and enthroned themselves as dictators. All this was done in the name of the nation, whose rights (weren't they?) were superior to those of the individual, be he alien, Jew, or simply dissident.

These dictators were called Hitler and Mussolini. There were others called Stalin, Franco, and Salazar. It cannot be denied that they all claimed to be serving the destiny of their respective national communities; further, three of them called themselves socialists. But who would call the whole of their work revolutionary? They upset a great many institutions, they even opened the way for some material progress; but they abolished personal freedom, or at least prevented it from growing; that is why history classes them as counter-revolutionaries.

Freedom

And so I get fed up when I hear our nationalist brood calling itself revolutionary. Quebec's revolution, if it had taken place, would first have consisted in freeing man from collective coercions: freeing the citizens brutalized by reactionary and arbitrary governments; freeing consciences bullied by a clericalized and obscurantist Church; freeing workers exploited by an oligarchic capitalism; freeing men crushed by authoritarian and outdated traditions. Quebec's revolution would have consisted in the triumph of the freedoms of the human being as inalienable rights, over and above capital, the nation, tradition, the Church, and even the State.

But this revolution never took place. Certainly there have been men in Quebec to work for it and to advance freedom and democracy over the last century, but the collective power always finished by reducing them to impotence: interdicts by the Church against an Asselin or a Buies, racial proscriptions against a Rabinovitch or a Roncarelli, government arbitrariness against a Picard or a Guindon, police truncheons against the strikers of Asbestos or Louiseville.

Nevertheless, around 1960 it seemed that freedom was going to triumph in the end. From 1945 on, a series of events and movements had combined to relegate the traditional concepts of authority in Quebec to the scrap-heap; the post-war stirrings, 'Refus Global', Asbestos, the unions, the judicial victories of Frank Scott and of Jacques Perrault, *Cité Libre*, the defeat of the Union Nationale, just to give some diverse examples. So much so that the generation entering its twenties in 1960 was the first in our history to receive fairly complete freedom as its lot. The dogmatism of Church and State, of tradition, of the nation, had been defeated. Authority had returned to its proper place in a free system. A lawyer could head the Lay Movement without losing his clients. Professors could say 'no to the Jesuits' without being barred from the university. Comedians or movie producers could subscribe to Marxism without being discharged by the government corporations. Students could try to impose their views on educational institutions without being kicked out. The Family itself had lost its power over young men and young women.

In 1960, everything was becoming possible in Quebec, even revolution. In fact revolution would probably not have been necessary, so wide open was the road to power for all who had mastered the sciences and the techniques of the day: automation, cybernetics, nuclear science, economic planning, and what-not else. A whole generation was free at last to apply all its creative energies to bringing this backward province up to date. Only it required boldness, intelligence, and work. Alas, freedom proved to be too heady a drink to pour for the French-Canadian youth of 1960. Almost at the first sip it went at top speed in search of some more soothing milk, some new dogmatism. It reproached my generation with not having offered it any 'doctrine' – we who had spent the best part of our youth demolishing servile doctrinairism – and it took refuge in the bosom of its mother, the Holy Nation.

As a friend wrote me recently, for religious sectarianism was substituted national sectarianism. The separatist devout and all the other zealots in the Temple of the Nation already point their fingers at the non-worshipper. And a good many non-believers find it to their advantage to receive their nationalist sacrament, for they hope thus to attain sacerdotal and episcopal, if not pontifical, office, and to be permitted thereby to recite prayers, to circulate directives and encyclicals, to define dogma, and to pronounce excommunication, with the assurance of infallibility. Those who do not attain the priesthood can hope to become churchwardens in return for services rendered; at the very least they will not be bothered when nationalism becomes the state religion.

Neo-Clericalism

The new clerical party, which already had its popes and its nuncios, has just found a Torquemada. After all, the new separatist counter-revolution must have its little Inquisition, mustn't it? Otherwise, what use are those lists of the proscribed that have been circulating for quite a while? I was sad to learn that François Hertel had volunteered for this task. I would not have thought that this man, whom I have long respected because he used to have the rare courage to reject all forms of conformity, would wind up as a churchmouse in the separatist chapel.

So now from Paris, beyond the reach of our criminal courts but not of our contempt, he writes: 'Assassinate for me a traitor who's really one of our people. It would be a good job. For instance relieve poor Laurendeau of the existence that seems to bore him so much' . . . and so forth. To address such words to a public preparing to sacrifice all values – especially personal freedom and safety – to the idol of collectivity, and which has already begun to take terrorists for heroes and martyrs, is the act of a dangerously irresponsible man.

But the ultimate in irresponsibility is to publish these words in *Le Quartier Latin* (April 9, 1964) as 'an extraordinary document'; what's more, alongside other documents inciting to murder. Of course, I should have expected anything from a newspaper director who recognizes the single-party system as an acceptable course for the Quebec of tomorrow.

The more so because this same director, in this same student newspaper, had printed two days previously another 'document' on the subject of freedom of the press which proved precisely that he held that freedom of little account. I refer to an article headed 'Mr. Gérard Pelletier and the Freedom of the Press' in which Professor Jean Blain writes: 'In the name of the freedom of the press he [Pelletier] refuses me freedom to express myself.' That is a falsehood. As *Le Devoir* of April 8 reported, Pelletier offered to print Professor Blain's statement complete in the letters columns of *La Presse*, and it was the professor who refused. *Le Quartier Latin* could have learned this fact if it had any regard for an elementary principle of justice: 'hear the other side'. But a certain Goebbels had already proved that justice and truth count for little when it is a case of nationalist auctioneering.

As for the root of the Pelletier-Blain argument, what can I say to people who have never read John Stuart Mill, *On Liberty*? 'The beliefs which we have most warrant for have no safeguard to rest on, but a standing invitation to the whole world to prove them unfounded.' No man can demand freedom of speech if he finds it a matter of indifference that public debate and free confrontation should be brushed aside as a means of arriving at political truths; these ideas are indissolubly linked. Now *Parti Pris*, according to Professor Blain himself, is based on 'refusal of dialogue'. Indeed, Pelletier, in the last edition of *Cité Libre*, brought out the totalitarian character of *Parti Pris* thinking. And for greater certainty, in the April number of that counter-revolutionary review, on page 51, there is a confession that 'there is a necessary totalitarianism'. (This article tries to pick a quarrel with me, it seems. But not over my ideas, since the fairness of the epithet 'totalitarian' is recognized, but over my pocket-book. Really, the driving forces behind this revolt are lacking in disinterest.)

But it is not only the students, those *petits-bourgeois* of tomorrow, who embrace counter-revolutionary sectarianism. Naturally there are also the *petits-bourgeois* of today. Mr. Jean-Marc Léger, who has always had the courage and the consciousness of his nationalism – and I cannot say the same for those who looked down on him from a great height fifteen years ago but who have come today to think like him because they want to be 'liked by youth' – Mr. Léger called at the Saint-Jean-Baptiste conference for 'the creation of a climate of national fervour in the schools', and, to achieve this, 'forbidding French-speaking parents to enter their children in English-speaking establishments in Quebec' (*Le Devoir*, March 16, 1964). It goes without saying that this neo-clericalist thinking was welcomed by our newspapers, and nobody seemed to be alarmed that education in Quebec might pass from religious confessionality to compulsory linguistic confessionality.

For that matter it is remarkable that the only case in a very long time in which French-Canadian public opinion has really been aroused about the liberty of the person is the case of the Coroner's Act. This act has been in our provincial statutes for forty years or so, and must have been used to deprive innumerable poor devils of their freedom and their dignity, including, obviously, many French Canadians. But we had to wait until sons of the *petite bourgeoisie*, in the service of a *petit-bourgeois* ideology, fell victim to it before our intellectuals and our professional classes took up a hue and cry for reform.

Persecution

For humanity, progress is the slow journey towards personal freedom. Those responsible for a sudden reversal of this course can be defined as counter-revolutionaries.

Certainly there are historical cases in which personal freedom has scarcely been protected at all by established institutions; it has been possible, then, for a genuine revolutionary to stress collective freedom as a preliminary to personal freedom: Castro, Ben Bella, Lenin. . . .

But when personal freedom exists, it would be *inconceivable that a revolutionary should destroy it* in the name of some collective ideology. For the very purpose of a collective system is better to ensure personal freedom. (Or else you are fascist.)

That is why in Quebec today you have to speak of separatist counter-revolution. True, personal freedom has not always been honoured in Quebec. But, I repeat, we had pretty well reached it around 1960. Thanks to English and Jewish lawyers (ah, yes!), thanks to the Supreme Court in Ottawa, personal freedom had at last triumphed over the obscurantism of Quebec's legislators and the authoritarianism of our courts. (See *Cité Libre*, April 1962, p. 12.) Thanks also to those diverse movements and events I mentioned earlier, there was scarcely a sector of Quebec life in which personal freedom at all levels of the population was not making sure progress and in which censorship, interdiction, authoritarianism, clericalism, and dictatorship were not in clear retreat.

But now, today, scarcely a week passes without a handful of separatist students coming to tell me they are against democracy and for a single-party system; for a certain totalitarianism and against the freedom of the individual. In this they are in the pure tradition of all that our society has always produced that was most traditionalist, most clerical, most monolithic, most reactionary. They want to return our people to the mentality of a state of siege.

The fact is that at bottom the Separatists despair of ever being able to convince the public of the rightness of their ideas. That long work of education and persuasion among the masses undertaken by the unions for many decades, done by the Social Crediters themselves for thirty years – for this the Separatists have neither the courage, nor the means, nor, especially, that respect for the other man's freedom which is essential in undertaking it and leading it to success.

So they want to abolish freedom and impose a dictatorship of their minority. They are in sole possession of the truth, so others need only get into line. And when things don't go fast enough they take to illegality and violence. On top of everything, they claim to be persecuted. Imagine that, the poor little souls. There are numbers of them in the editorial rooms of our newspapers, they swarm at the C.B.C. and the National Film Board, they press with all their weight (?) on the mass media, but still they find the place given them in this society unfair.

Because a few of their people have been bothered because of their ideas (so they say), they want to be done with peaceful and constitutional methods. They proclaim to the newspapers that from now on they will go underground. These terrorized terrorists will be led by a Mr. X. And, in courageous anonymity, they will sow their ideas while waiting to set their bombs.

No kidding! In the province of Quebec the Jehovah's Witnesses and the Communists, two tiny minorities, have been mocked, persecuted, and hated by our entire society; but they have managed by legal means to fight Church, government, nation, police, and public opinion. Union men, in spite of being kicked out of their jobs for union activity, have never thought to destroy personal freedom but, on the contrary, have always made themselves its defenders, as also champions of the democratic cause.

But our nationalists – of whom the 'experts' claim there is

one dozing in the heart of every French Canadian – they despair of ever legally getting their 'message' accepted by a majority of French Canadians. They cry persecution to justify going underground as fugitives from reality.

The Wigwam Complex

The truth is that the separatist counter-revolution is the work of a powerless *petit-bourgeois* minority afraid of being left behind by the twentieth-century revolution. Rather than carving themselves out a place in it by ability, they want to make the whole tribe return to the wigwams by declaring its independence. That, of course, will not prevent the world outside from progressing by giant's strides; it will not change the rules and the facts of history, nor the real power relationship in North America.

But at least inside the tribe the counter-revolutionaries will be kings and sorcerers. They will have legal authority to declare war (making it will be a different story), to name (*bourgeois*) plenipotentiaries, to open (*bourgeois*) banks, and to impose tariffs favourable to the *petite bourgeoisie*. They will also be able to transfer the title to property and to declare that from now on foreign industries will belong to the tribal *bourgeoisie*. The tribe risks being gravely impoverished; but what matters, of course, is that the counter-revolutionaries shall not be.

Some of the counter-revolutionaries deceive themselves by dressing up in Marxist-Leninist disguise, as has already been done by those African chieftains whom, indeed, they take as models. But all this masquerade has been admirably described by Frantz Fanon in *Les damnés de la Terre*, which nevertheless our counter-revolutionaries say is the book they keep beside their beds. (This makes me think they read no more in bed than elsewhere; so I shall do them the favour of quoting at some length from this book published by Maspero in 1961 and of which they have perhaps only leafed through the chapter on violence.)

> A national *bourgeoisie* never ceases to demand nationalization of the economy and the commercial sectors. . . . For it, nationalization means very precisely the transfer to the native population of the favours inherited from the colonial period. (p. 115) . . . It uses its class aggressiveness to corner the

positions formerly held by the foreigners. . . . It will fight pitilessly against those people who 'insult the national dignity'. . . . In fact its course will become more and more coloured with racism. (p. 118) . . . Everywhere that this national *bourgeoisie* has shown itself unable to expand its view of the world sufficiently, we witness a return toward tribal positions; we witness, with rage in our hearts, the embittered triumph of ethnics. (p. 120) Internally . . . the *bourgeoisie* chooses the solution that seems easiest to it, that of the single party. . . . The single party is the modern form of dictatorship, without mask, without disguise, without scruple, cynical. (p. 124) . . . All ideological activity is limited to a succession of variations on the right of peoples to dispose of themselves. (p. 128) . . . At the institutional level it [the national *bourgeoisie*] skips the parliamentary phase and chooses a dictatorship of the national-socialist type. (p. 129) . . . This tribalization of power brings with it, naturally, regionalist thinking, separatism. (p. 137)

Separatism a revolution? My eye. A counter-revolution; the national-socialist counter-revolution.

Cité Libre, May 1964.
Translation courtesy of the Montreal *Star.*